THE JUDGE

THE JUDGE

26 Machiavellian Lessons

By Ronald K.L. Collins

AND

David M. Skover

OXFORD
UNIVERSITY PRESS

OXFORD

UNIVERSITY PRESS

Oxford University Press is a department of the University of Oxford. It furthers
the University's objective of excellence in research, scholarship, and education
by publishing worldwide. Oxford is a registered trade mark of Oxford University
Press in the UK and certain other countries.

Published in the United States of America by Oxford University Press
198 Madison Avenue, New York, NY 10016, United States of America.

Library of Congress Cataloging-in-Publication Data
To Come
ISBN 978-0-19-049014-0

1 3 5 7 9 8 6 4 2
Printed by [Insert printer details: Name and location]

We are much beholden to Machiavelli and other writers of that class, who openly and unfeignedly declare or describe what men do, and not what they ought to do.

Francis Bacon

Image 1. Portrait of Chief Justice John Marshall, circa 1831

It is emphatically the province and duty of the judicial department to say what the law is.

John Marshall

Image 2. Portrait of Niccolò Machiavelli

Since my intent is to write something useful to whoever understands it, it has appeared to be more fitting to go directly to the effectual truth of the thing than to the imagination of it.

Niccolò Machiavelli

CONTENTS

CONTENTS

PROLOGUE

HYPOCRISY. Few defend it, though many practice it. No one admits to it, not even when vowing to tell the whole truth and nothing but the truth. The hypocrite extols objectivity; he feigns detachment. In the process, something is concealed, but it must appear otherwise. If one is to master the art of hypocrisy, one must categorically repudiate it. The greatest hypocrite in the law, then, is the judge who values the appearance of virtue more than its actuality. He thus pretends to be true to the law. By that measure, hypocrisy is a word well suited to the calling of a judge[1] . . . or we should say, a special kind of Judge.

This all may sound sinister, or even evil. Hypocrisy seems especially immoral when associated with judging, which should be aligned with justice. Our aim, however, is not to praise the deeds of demons, but rather to highlight the virtues of realism – a new and vibrant realism, a modern-day legal realism fit for our times. That raw realism is acutely mindful of the *necessity of deception*[2] and how the pretense of principled objectivity bows to that necessity. After all, honesty and integrity have their costs; they can often deprive us of our desires; they may also force us to compromise when we are reluctant to do so.

In the struggle between confrontation and compromise, pretense provides a tactical alternative. Label it hypocrisy, or rationalization, or whatever, it is a lie in the service of some cause, whether praiseworthy or not. Tellingly, hypocrisy thrives in the most principled of contexts where the bar of integrity is set very high. Where it is low, as in aberrant political times, hypocrisy may yield an even greater bounty. The judge who insists on fidelity to elevated notions of law and who sanctimoniously demands it of others typically trades in hypocrisy. The same is true of the more cautious jurist who from time to time steals from the till of his or her own professed objectivity. Given that, to condemn such hypocrisy is to condemn much of modern appellate judging. Hence, we invite you to see our jurisprudential world for what it is, and then judge it for what it is. In several ways our tract is meant to help you, our readers, do just that.

How you judge our lessons – which are non-partisan and which can serve honorable purposes – will depend on how honest you are about the role of hypocrisy in our system of jurisprudence. As you will see, it has become ever more difficult in American society to tether judge-proclaimed law to its revered moorings. And when that occurs, hypocrisy hurries to the scene to demand its due, sometimes by those with the best of intentions.

Thus we begin. Hypocrisy helps one to navigate the necessities of judging, the various ones we discuss in our 26 chapters. It might be understood as a sort of virtue in the service of avarice, of that all-too-human desire to acquire power or glory or both. Such avarice, if you will, need not be viewed as either a virtue or a vice,[3] but rather as a way of how people tend to be – or at least that much is often said to be the case. If the lessons we offer are to be useful and effective, then a Justice must learn to be unjust, at least sometimes, if only because the measure of the law derives not from the ideal but from the real. Ours, after all, is not the City of God.

So step into the light of a new sun. Behold what your eyes rarely see. For you have little to lose save the lies that shackle you, the ones that have been told to you as truths. Open your minds and free yourselves from the manacles of myths. Only then should you judge *The Judge*.

Law is political.

That is the common refrain of our times. It is the calling cry of conservatives disgusted with liberal "result-oriented" judicial decision-making, and of liberals who rail against "unprincipled" conservative decision-making. Fueled by hypocrisy, the charge goes back and forth as the ideological conflicts escalate. Neither side tires in this test of wills.

No one vying for appellate judicial office dares defend the term *activist*. No, everyone is a moderate, a centrist, someone who interprets the law but never makes it. For decades, the debate over "judicial activism" has raged on. Whatever the political stripes, the charge is always the same: Judge-made law has become politicized. With relentless frequency, conservatives and liberals accuse the other of "politicizing" the courts so as to produce the results each side wants. In this ideological war zone, hackneyed phrases – "originalism," "textualism," "neutral principles," the "living Constitution," and so forth – are hurled about like rhetorical daggers. As the hostility continues, judges often remain unaffected as they invoke one or another self-serving theory to reach the results they want. The ideological war of words persists. And the key word in that war is this: *political*.

It is difficult to deny: "In many important cases, the predispositions of the judges play a significant role in determining the nature of people's legal rights."[4] The momentous constitutional cases of our times, we are told, "have to be political."[5] That charge takes on added strength with each passing year: "Judges are inevitably political actors, and hence their decisions are ultimately based on their ideological convictions. Sure, judges hide behind the law, and they purport to be speaking for it, but we shouldn't be fooled."[6] Thus, the judicial art is little more than a disguise to conceal the real nature of the enterprise.[7] Judges are like "political actors" or "politicians wearing robes."[8]

Some argue that the "Constitution has become a wholly malleable document that compels no particular result."[9] And what of objective decision-making grounded in the rule of the law as written? "This is nonsense and has always been," declares one of the most distinguished constitutional scholars of our times; the Supreme Court, he adds, consists of nine individuals "who inevitably base their decisions on their own values, views, and prejudices."[10] Others say that today's judges are unable to "articulate legal principles that clearly transcend politics."[11] Hoping to exploit that reality, more and more appellate litigators have come to appreciate that the federal "courts are a sort of untapped resource for pursuing [one side or another's political] agenda."[12]

The virtues characteristically associated with judging – impartiality, dispassion, and an abiding commitment to the letter of the law – too often yield to the vices associated with ideological impulses. An obstinate faith in one's own convictions often rules. That faith, of course, is bolstered by hypocrisy. Some judges cram their opinions with half-truths that would have made the great Greek sophists blush. Many a so-called objective theory of decision-making is little but fertile soil for the seeds of a lie striving to bloom. Indeed, those who advance such theories know this; they know the lie. That judges do not believe wholeheartedly in their constitutional creed – as evidenced by the way they can breach it with abandon – does not stop them from demanding of others that they honor that creed. Label it a noble pretext or a necessary screen, it all leads to a lesson in hypocrisy: Objectivity is a mask behind which to hide one's predilections and prejudices. Regardless of whether this is philosophically true, it is nonetheless perceived as the truth of our times.

The temptation to violate the touted virtues of jurisprudential objectivity and dispassionate impartiality is all the greater given the many opportunities for judges to become political actors. Such opportunities arise from the ever-expanding involvement of the courts in a wide swatch of issues that are fiercely political in nature. Over the years the Supreme Court has, in its own special ways, interjected itself into many controversial ideological clashes. There is scarcely a politically fraught dispute that is free of judicial oversight. In this way among others, politics has become law and law has become politicized.

Even those clad in black robes speak the words "politics" and "judging" in the same judicial breath. For example, one noted federal jurist conceded that "judging in America is unquestionably steeped in politics."[13] Making much the same point, a widely respected sitting federal appellate judge was equally blunt: "[V]iewed realistically, the Supreme Court, at least most of the time, when it is deciding constitutional cases is a political organ."[14] Echoing the same sentiment, Judge Richard Posner unabashedly declared in 2016: "the Supreme Court is not an ordinary court but a political court, or more precisely a politicized court, which is to say a court strongly influenced in making its decisions by the political beliefs of the judges."[15] The public perception of the Supreme Court is consistent with that view, or so a sitting Supreme Court Justice has declared: "More and more people think that what's important to us is *political*," and the public see the Justices as "nine junior varsity politicians. That's what they think."[16] As for the partisan character of America's high Court, an important study highlighted "the profound role of party polarization on today's Court" and concluded that it is "likely" to be "enduring."[17]

Given that, can we escape the consequential truth of our times – that law has become ever more political? The immense gap between law, as it has been traditionally portrayed, and what it truly is or has become, invites a reconsideration (or reconfiguration) of law and the necessities to which it must now yield.[18]

Supreme Court Justices are not as political as their counterparts in the other two branches of the national government. After all, they don't run for office; they are not beholden to campaign contributors and lobbyists; and they tend to speak in more measured tones (though there are exceptions) than members of Congress or Executive officials. Still, and with increasing frequency, the matter is more one of degree than of kind. For example, studies by social scientists point time and again to the partisan drift of Supreme Court decision-making.[19] Not surprisingly, the charge is that the Constitution is cleverly invoked to justify results that comport more with the partisan policy calls of lawmakers than with detached jurisprudential calls. But there is more: Even in statutory cases (especially those involving "hot-button issues"[20]), the line between judicial detachment and judicial prejudice can be easily crossed. Thus, there are similarities and differences between ordinary "politics" and "judicial politics."

In all of this, context can be determinative, changing circumstances might be dispositive, and interpersonal relations may be decisive. Hence, the 26 lessons that follow must be adjusted to the situation at hand, with due respect paid to the dictates of chance. Some of these lessons will work most of the time and others not; still others will work part of the time if tailored to meet the demands of a given case. Accordingly, a special kind of jurist is required to effectuate the lessons provided here.[21]

The modern Judge embraces the new realist modes and orders in bold ways. For that judge, law is more prerogative than principle. If that is the measure, then the goal of the judicial art is to maximize power, minimize dependence, and reduce risk.[22] This insight counsels that the realist judge need not be modest, at least not in understanding his or her calling. And it is that awareness, skillfully executed, that enables a judge to rise above the din and claim his or her due, like a fearless Cesare Borgia[23] or a foxlike Don Vito Corleone. This is a lesson, one of many, drawn from *The Prince*[24] by Niccolò Machiavelli – lessons aptly adapted, to be sure.

Those judges are greatest who understand the advantages of replacing the old virtues of judging (rooted in neutrality) with the new virtues of judging (grounded in hypocrisy). They appreciate the value of deception. They understand that the finger of the law does not always point in one direction. What the law is invariably depends on many variables susceptible to many interpretations. Therein lies a treasure trove of opportunity for the judge willing and able to seize it. To alter the metaphor, the law is there to bend to his will. Of course, hypocrisy is the handmaiden that makes this possible.

As a matter of practice and theory, what does it mean to declare that the nation's high Court is often political? The question gives rise to bold answers in *The Judge*. We propose to explain anew law and the judicial art, much as Niccolò Machiavelli explained power and the ruling art in *The Prince*.[25] Perhaps because of lack of foresight or lack of courage, no one has carefully studied a course of judicial decision-making premised on stratagems that flow from the merger of law and judicial politics. Seen in that light, the old vice of hypocrisy stands to become a central component of the new virtue of judging. In this regard, it has been said that "*The Prince* . . . can open doors that we may not have known were there."[26] It is just such doors that we have set out to open.

Anyone very familiar with the workings of the Supreme Court will recognize many of the stratagems or maxims (i.e., moves and counter moves) set forth in our 26 lessons. By no means does this book exhaust the range of possible tactics. Nevertheless, these are among the most vital strategic lessons that famous American jurists have sometimes practiced – jurists from Chief Justice John Marshall's time to Chief

Justice John Roberts' time. Mindful of these lessons, general rules of judicial behavior for certain jurists can be deduced.[27] Properly understood, those stratagems reveal how some judges maximize judicial power while minimizing risk, and how others might likewise do so in a more methodical, informed, and calculating manner. The converse is also true: Those who disregard these lessons on judicial behavior stand to find themselves on the losing side of significant cases or controversies that come before them.

He dares to do what has never been done before, and he is willing to risk infamy to do so.[28]

Power. It is that ability to make something happen. It is linked to one's will and combined with one's ability to be effective in promoting some objective. Judge or politician, priest or philosopher, all seek power of one kind or another. For those who think otherwise, consider this: "The feeling of having no power over people and events is generally unbearable to us – when we feel helpless we feel miserable."[29] Such human emotions are not foreign to the men and women who wear robes and wield power by judicial mandates. In fact, it would be strange if the will of judges cut against the grain of their all-too-human nature.

How best to amass power and to preserve and perpetuate it depends very much on the context, as Machiavelli well knew. In that world of contingencies, a judge stands to lose much unless he or she avoids falling prey to an unkind fate. Moreover, an appetite for power can never ignore the demands of prudence.[30] Such virtues, about which more will be said later, are key to a judge who aims to seize the greatest measure of power possible. Hence, the laws of power are the very ones that an extraordinary judge must honor and always uphold.

Still, power is not a word typically associated with judging and the judicial branch. Its domain is elsewhere – in the more overtly political spheres. Or so goes the traditional tale. In the tripartite American constitutional scheme of things, the judiciary is said to be the least powerful, and thus the least dangerous branch. It was said long ago by Alexander Hamilton in *Federalist* No. 78 that the judiciary "may truly be said to have neither Force nor Will, but merely judgment; and must ultimately depend upon the aid of the executive arm even for the efficacy of its judgments."[31] Clearly, there is truth there, and it is counsel of which a prudent judge should consider. That said, Hamilton's account of the constitutional order must be understood in tandem with the constitutional handiwork of his Federalist friend, John Marshall. Even in his own day, Hamilton was sympathetic to Marshall's campaign to expand the powers of Article III judges. Despite the opaqueness of the judicial powers set forth in Article III, "John Marshall remedied that deficiency, and many of the Supreme Court decisions he handed down were based on concepts articulated by Hamilton."[32] Yet even were one to remain firmly fixed on *Federalist* No. 78's depiction of the judiciary, that vision is considerably different from what today passes for the power of Supreme Court Justices – a power so great as to proclaim who shall be the President of the United States.[33] For such reasons, and others, it has rightly been observed that the "least dangerous branch of the American government is the most extraordinarily powerful court of law the world has ever known."[34]

If power is the capacity to impose one's will, then how is that capacity related to the art of judging? First and foremost, the answer has to do with what is called *judicial interpretation*. What does the law mean? The power to answer that question in an official way and have it enforced is a power of great moment. Think of it: At some point the interpretive power is the power to *make* the law.[35] The landmark ruling in *Brown v. Board of Education*[36] is but one example of that principle at work in the American judicial system, given the more than plausible claim that the Court's opinion ran contrary to many of the declared intentions of the drafters of the Fourteenth Amendment to the Constitution.[37] This interpretive power is even more spectacular when one considers that it is, in the *final* analysis, the province of the judiciary[38] and can only be politically overridden by the cumbersome process of a constitutional amendment.

A cautionary note: Just how one's will is imposed (for lack of a better word) is complex. For example, it may be through the ruling in an isolated case (e.g., a government subsidized healthcare case); or through the doctrine developed in a category of cases (e.g., racial discrimination cases); or even through a broader and immensely more difficult objective of reshaping public policy in a meaningful and enduring way (e.g., abortion cases).[39] In all of these respects, it must be remembered that politics blend differently in a judicial beaker than in an executive or legislative one. Part of the delicate mix in the context of judicial politics is knowing how best to have one's decisions honored (to the extent it is reasonably possible) by the power brokers in the other branches of government. In more Machiavellian terms, this is but another way of endeavoring to diminish "the domain of contingency"[40] and thereby render a judge less vulnerable to vagaries of chance. By exercising the virtues of calculated innovation, the modern judge better positions himself to realize his objectives.

If the judicial power is emboldened by modern judicial review, then the ability to interpret the law is itself a power base. It is from that base that a careful judge can be most effective in gradually translating his or her will into law. If judges already do that whenever they interpret laws, whether constitutional or statutory ones, then they can be said to be acting faithfully to the laws *as they understand them*, either as they are or should be. This insight energizes the power principle in the judicial context. In the various chapters that follow, we venture to explain how this is so as a jurisprudential and tactical matter.

There are, to be sure, differences between the advice given in our work and that offered by the fifteenth century Florentine philosopher in his ingenious book. For one thing, Machiavelli's world and work were more overtly political (and thus brutal) in any number of ways. His was a treacherous time dominated by corrupt papal figures, dukes, countesses, wealthy families, war lords, madmen, and foreign kings, all vying for political power. In such combative and dangerously duplicitous scenarios, physical force of the most savage kind (the "way of beasts") was sometimes required. Mindful of those considerations, Machiavelli sought to counsel one who wielded power – and in so doing, be the beneficiary of his advice. In several notable ways, he was an insider in that world. Our jurisprudential context and our mission are different – we are not insiders in the judicial world (though we both served in it for a brief time years ago as aides to a state supreme court justice, a federal appellate judge, and to the Chief

Justice of the United States). We expect no favor of any judge or justice. We seek no appointment to any office owing to what we have written.[41] And, of course, we would never counsel violent force. In these and others ways, our mission is a much more modest one, a more civil one adapted to the demands of its own particular context.

Our modesty notwithstanding, some will be quick to judge our realist tract before taking the time needed to piece together the puzzles of our thinking. Most assuredly, those who preach the lofty ideal of judicial detachment will vigorously disparage our explicit lessons. If so, their counterfeit gospels will only buttress the truth of our realist claims. After all, there is no faith in a cause that is so sound as to admit its own folly.

Let us be clear: We do not countenance reckless bravado; we condemn it. Why? Because appearances matter; because a judge must seem judicious; because to look otherwise will prove ruinous to any judge who seeks to improve his or her lot. Moreover, there are certain moves taken by judges that are so imprudent as to be beyond the effectual powers of the judicial domain. Sometimes, "passive virtues"[42] can serve one well, even if one betrays them as circumstances require. Thus understood, the reality of circumstances, and not some fixed principle, constrains or emboldens power. Precisely because of the importance of circumstances, principle will occasionally need to be cast aside in the name of perception, the kind of perception that can either ruin a judge's reputation or enhance it.

The extraordinary Judge – the one who possesses the virtues of prudence and prowess – knows all too well that the acquisition, use, and maintenance of judicial power demand time, skill, and a long view of things. That judge is cautious, not impetuous. Patience, indirection, and an appreciation of the subtle are strong suits. Like the Roman god Janus, the Judge looks back in time to learn from the lessons of the past while always looking forward to chart each move in a path to power. Yes, the Judge is his or her own ruler, but is also one who knows the limits of power well enough not to squander it when little is to be gained and much lost.

Machiavelli was among the most honest . . . of men.[43]

Why this book? And what are the lessons to be learned from it? Here are a few preliminary answers.

First, one aim of the book is to test the certainty of the convictions of those who hold that law is politics. What follows might be seen as an attempt (by way of constructive provocations) to prompt readers to consider seriously the theoretical and real-world consequences of their view of things. That is, what would it mean if the law-as-politics maxim were truly unbound?[44]

Second, *The Judge* frees the lessons of *The Prince* from the confines of other spheres and introduces them into a domain where their effectual truths may play out. It is curious that Machiavellian principles have not received much explicit and extended attention in the judicial context. Perhaps the explanation inheres in the belief that the rules of politics are inapplicable to the judicial craft. But as appellate law becomes ever more politicized, the old ideas are vulnerable to attack and susceptible to reconsideration in light of the workings of the modern realist world.[45] Such reconsideration is long overdue. Just where such new thinking will lead is yet another question *The Judge* invites its readers to ponder.

Third, our disclosure of the stratagems of judicial power may have the effect of educating judges on how best to practice their judicial art, both in defensive and offensive ways in the circumstances in which they find themselves.[46] Armed with such information, lesser judges may recognize such tactics and thereby counter them as best they can. Then again, they might attempt to employ such lessons in the service of their own power ambitions. All of this reveals one of the key issues raised in *The Judge*: how does one most effectively use information? This is what Machiavelli understood as powers "well used" or "badly used."[47]

Fourth, the revelations made in *The Judge* might also be said to democratize knowledge about judging for the benefit of the general public; the information provided might thus enable lay people to see judicial power politics in a truer light.[48] The sinister moves of the consciously deceitful should be exposed. Here too, and more importantly so, a question arises: What are the consequences, probable or conjectural, of exposing such judging for what it really is?

Fifth, while lessons of the kind set forth in this book may point to the path of cynicism, they need not necessarily do so. Once one truly understands the status quo in appellate judging and the machinations by which it often operates, one can expose it and refuse to participate in it.[49] Such an act of withdrawal would be akin to a move away from Machiavelli's realism and towards Rousseau's idealism.[50] This move, however, raises an important question related to some of those just asked: What would it mean to remove the necessity of deception from the art of appellate judging? Think about it; think hard.

Finally, should the prior answers prove unsatisfactory in whole or in part, an even bolder reply remains: Principled moderation is useless to the wise. Carefully applied, Power is the principle that ought to guide a judge of more than ordinary skill. How to win and wield that power is the more obvious subject of this discourse on modern judging. If you would have it otherwise, obey the advice of Saint Augustine – never lie.[51]

What follows is the product of decades of considerable reflection on, and research related to, law, judicial politics, and political philosophy. While Machiavelli's *Prince* provides some of the conceptual template for our project, and while an understanding of that work and its author informs parts of what we write, *The Judge* does not purport to be a commentary on or an interpretation of *The Prince*. Hence, the philosophical differences among the likes of Quentin Skinner,[52] J. G. A. Pocock,[53] Leo Strauss,[54] and Philip Bobbitt,[55] among others,[56] on Machiavelli's true intent (cynical or humanist, realist or relativist, patriotic or despotic, republican or royalist, tough-minded or diabolically-minded, etc.) need not be discussed here. Nor is it our intention to evaluate the merits of Machiavelli's mission in his own times.[57] It is suitable enough for our unorthodox tract that people understand Machiavelli's *Prince* as Francis Bacon[58] and countless others may have, namely, as a collection of cunning maxims in the service of power, loosely defined.

As you will soon discern, many of our lessons pivot on the grand achievements of great judges, informed as they might have been by lessons learned from the failings of mediocre ones. Of course, when we use this or that example of judges or cases, we do not mean to say that any intent we assign to them was actually there. It might have been, but then again, it might not. Hence, we use such examples to support our lessons. It is important to remember this as you read the many examples set out in our book.

The deck now cleared, we can proceed more directly. Be ready for what follows. For in it you will read what ought not to be written . . . or so you will be led to believe. You will read what ought not to be urged . . . or so the purveyors of judicial restraint will say. You will read what ought not to be trusted . . . or so the masters of deceit will want you to think. And you will read what ought not to be acted upon . . . or so the righteous will advise you.[59] If such warnings worry you, then spare yourself. Put down this book now. If, however, you are reluctant to surrender to the untested counsel of others, then read on. That said, proceed with this assurance: Our lessons may serve some well.

Thus it is, our prologue to the judicial principles of power. Behold the new day, and welcome it. The dawn of *The Judge* has arrived.

Chapter 1

The Confirmation Process and the Virtues of Duplicity

When a judge undertakes to speak in public about any subject that might be of more interest than the law of incorporeal hereditaments, he embarks upon a perilous enterprise.

– Robert H. Bork[1]

Robert Bork was a fool. Why? Because he was too truthful. And for his truthfulness he was denied a seat on the Supreme Court. His 1987 Senate confirmation hearings marked the last time any Court nominee spoke as forthrightly and without cowardice. No matter that he was very qualified. No matter that he had previously served as a federal appellate judge, as solicitor general, as acting attorney general, and as a distinguished professor at Yale Law School. Merit was not to be his measure. His hearings were a spectacle, a catastrophic farce, a lesson of what can go terribly wrong when a self-made man speaks too much truth to power. In the process Bork's name became a verb -- meaning to be systematically defamed.

In word, demeanor, appearance, and tactic, Robert Bork violated every rule of modernity. He did not feign meekness. He did not prevaricate. He did not fully disavow his former views. He did not kowtow to the whims of his senatorial adversaries. He did not play to the press. He remained conceited and confident throughout. And all of this in the face of a voluminous record of speeches, scholarly writings, and judicial opinions certain to invite opposition. In short, Robert Bork did not pretend to be the man he was not. The result: 58 senators voted against him and 42 for. So much for the old way, the Bork way.

Judge Bork should have been rejected, and roundly so, for one reason – his folly. He did not appreciate the necessity of deception. He did not understand the importance of perception. And he did not realize the dangers of exposition. It all brought him down like an avalanche that he set in motion against himself. The Bork confirmation hearings are thus a case study of what *not* to do if one seeks the power that comes with being confirmed. To better understand his folly, we return to those times and flag some of the ruinous mistakes he made in that politically volatile world. Having done so, we will be better positioned to turn to the virtues of being duplicitous, virtues that will continue to serve one well should he or she be able to delude the Senate and the public enough to secure a seat of trust on the Supreme Court.

⧈

Even before Judge Bork appeared before the Senate Judiciary Committee in October of 1987, controversy was in the air. First and foremost, he was being considered as the replacement for Justice Lewis Powell, a Nixon appointee who had veered beyond ideological barriers often to the great displeasure of most conservatives. Bork was President Ronald Reagan's man, a certifiedly conservative jurist. For that reason alone, he was a target with a bull's eye on his chest. Moreover, he had been too outspoken. He had been aligned too closely with an ideological camp. He had been too true to his job in the "Saturday Night Massacre" in which he fired Watergate special prosecutor Archibald Cox.[2] With that act, Robert Bork tied his tail to the plummeting kite of the ostracized Richard Nixon. And Bork's gruff manner made it easy for his adversaries to cast him as constitutionally demonic. Worse still, President Reagan would abandon him, although by artful inaction, when Bork needed him most. It was all a formula for defeat. Even so, Bork's pride pushed him ahead – right into the perfect storm.

With all his qualifications and accomplishments, one might have assumed that Judge Bork would readily receive the American Bar Association's highest rating, and by a unanimous vote. To assume so much, however, would be to ignore the political reality of the realm. It would be to expect partisans to shed their ideological stripes. By that measure, it is surprising that the fifteen-member ABA committee gave Bork its highest rating. But five of the Committee's members voted otherwise. Four went so far as to brand Bork unqualified. Amazing. Not since Clement Haynesworth was rejected as a Supreme Court nominee in the 1960s had the ABA been so split.[3] Even so, it was still highly unusual for a judge of Bork's distinction to be rebuffed. In retrospect, even Bork conceded that the "split vote . . . was extremely damaging . . . since the judgment was nominally about professionalism."[4] Indeed. It was a bad omen, one that Judge Bork nonetheless ignored as he advanced with unbridled brashness.

His White House handlers counseled Bork to prepare himself as a witness. He was, however, skeptical. Still, he yielded, and in August of 1987 participated in a three-hour mock hearing held in the Old Executive Office Building. "It was a disaster. . . [T]he questions were 'poorly prepared' [and] 'silly. Bork was not intellectually challenged.'"[5] It was all too trite, contrived, and below his intellectual pay grade. It was a waste of his time. The very idea of it all seemed preposterous to him. According to White House Counsel A.B. Culvahouse, Bork "and the White House thereafter lost touch with the hearing strategy to the extent that there was one."[6]

Meanwhile, his larger-than-life Ronald Reagan Conservative image drew more and more attention in liberal circles. Ronald Dworkin, the darling of liberal legalism, branded Bork "a constitutional radical," someone whose "views do not lie within the scope of the longstanding debate between liberals and conservatives about the proper role of the Supreme Court."[7] The idea that Bork was outside the mainstream of American law was one that needed to be countered, not by boldness but rather by nuance, by moves designed to make him look less Borkean. But that was a move that cut against his psychological grain.

The Judge was losing momentum at a time when the political whirlwind drew ever closer to him. The anti-Bork forces continued to threaten him.[8] Already, a report had been prepared and circulated to the media – a report "wholeheartedly" endorsed by such luminaries as Floyd Abrams (a noted and respected First Amendment lawyer), Clark

Clifford (former White House Counsel and Secretary of Defense), Walter Dellinger (a Duke Law professor and seasoned appellate lawyer), and Laurence Tribe (a Harvard Law professor and the leading constitutional scholar of the day). The "Biden Report" was devastating in its portrayal of Judge Bork's jurisprudence. In relevant and damning part it read: "Judge Bork's extensive record shows that he has opposed virtually every major civil rights advance on which he has taken a position . . . ."[9] Adding fuel to that fire, Senator Edward Kennedy spoke in sensational spades: "Robert Bork's America is a land in which women would be forced into back-alley abortions, blacks would sit at segregated lunch counters, rogue police could break down citizens' doors in midnight raids, and schoolchildren could not be taught about evolution."[10]

Against that backdrop and more, Robert Bork stood ready to appear before Senator Joseph Biden's Judiciary Committee. His calling card: Brave, smart, steadfast, and self-confident. Undoubtedly, he could defend himself; clearly, he could counter the charges against him; obviously, he could better his senatorial adversaries; and surely, he could reverse the tide rising against him – or so he thought.

∽

Robert Bork . . . was quite willing to answer questions about his views . . . .
-- Lee Epstein & Jeffrey Segal [11]

He had posed as supremely apolitical, as just letting the chips fall where they may.
-- Richard Posner[12]

The aesthetics of the moment escaped him. Visuals were of no consequence. All that really mattered was substance – cold, detached, dead-letter law unconcerned with the whims of a changing world. Or so it seemed to many who turned on their televisions and tuned into the spectacle known as the "Bork hearings."

A dapper looking Chairman Biden presided; next to him sat a distinguished looking Senator Kennedy. Appearing before both of these Bork foes and the Committee was a lone, burly, scraggily bearded, unruly haired nominee speaking rather sternly and looking quite uncomfortable.[13] In both style and substance, Robert Bork was largely his own man, which was just the man his adversaries hoped him to be.

When Chairman Biden pressed Bork on his views concerning a citizen's right to privacy – this in light of *Skinner v. Oklahoma*[14] (a forced sterilization case) and *Griswold v. Connecticut*[15] (a contraceptives and marital privacy case) – the Judge sounded like a tedious technician: "[W]here the Constitution does not speak, there's no provision in the Constitution that applies to the case, then a judge may not say, I place a higher value upon a marital relationship than I do upon economic freedom. If there is nothing in the Constitution, the judge is enforcing his own moral values."[16] Textually, historically, Bork was probably right. But this was not a law school classroom in which such originalist ideas might be expounded to critique the Supreme Court. This was his bid to become a member of the Court – a platform from which, like Justices Antonin Scalia and Clarence Thomas after him, he could develop just such an originalist jurisprudence. The difference between the classroom, where he was in control, and the Senate, where his opponents were in control, too often escaped Bork. Thus, he continued in his all too professorial ways.[17]

There was another surprising exchange, this one with Republican Senator Orrin Hatch, who asked: "In your lengthy constitutional studies, is there any Supreme Court decision that has stirred more controversy or criticism amongst scholars and citizens [as that of *Roe v. Wade*]?" Bork's reply lifted many an eyebrow: "I suppose the only candidate for that, Senator, would be *Brown v. Board of Education*." Realizing the need to correct the record, Hatch quickly held out a life rope: "Or possibly the *Dred Scott* case." The nominee was eager to agree. "Yes, that's right," Judge Bork interjected. As "Senator Hatch immediately grasped," wrote Linda Greenhouse, "the nominee had violated a cardinal rule of modern judicial confirmation hearings, which is that *Brown v. Board of Education* is beyond debate. . . . [T]he moral dimension seemed to elude [Judge Bork] as he tossed *Brown* into the same box with the abortion decision of which he had been so scathingly dismissive."[18]

Aided by his responses, Bork's Senate adversaries were readily able to paint him as anti-privacy, anti-woman, anti-civil rights, and anti-free speech. He was a man out of touch with his world, a man indifferent to the plight of victims of discrimination, and a man willing to turn the constitutional clock backwards to a time before 1954. Was it true? True or not, what mattered was the perception of the man. While that public perception was crafted, in large part, by liberal groups aided by an all-too-receptive media, it was enabled repeatedly by a man too proud to appreciate that he was a pawn in a game he simply could not win. And as the stakes grew higher, he upped the ante.

For all his bluntness and willingness to confront the Senate Committee, there were times when even Robert Bork realized the importance of shifting ground, though in obscure ways.[19] It made for a mishmash of answers, many bold and confrontational, others reticent and obliging. The more he spoke, the more a troubling truth became obvious: "It was the perception of his right-of-center ideology, or more precisely his ideological incompatibility with the Senate, that kept Bork from a seat on the high Court."[20]

⋘

After the Bork fiasco, his successors learned the lesson of duplicity. They realized the need to appear other than what they truly were; and they understood the value of saying much while revealing little. Incredibly, some of them were, in important respects, just as conservative or perhaps more so than Bork. They, however, had become masters of moderation, however feigned. Who could deny it?

In the years that followed Bork's failed confirmation hearings, the constitutionally mandated screening process became little more than a TV show, a sham proceeding in which, to quote then-Professor Elena Kagan, the "practice of substantive inquiry" had "suffered a precipitous fall."[21] In truth, the real problem was not so much the inquiry as it was the opaque answers designed to evade tough questions. Hence, the common refrain: Senator, I regret that I cannot answer that question, because if confirmed it may come up before me in a case. Such a response and others were non-responsive. The confirmation process had become a pageant in which the tricks of the trade were on parade. Not surprisingly, Professor Kagan was stern in her critique of the process: "When the Senate ceases to engage nominees in meaningful discussion of legal issues, the confirmation process takes on an air of vacuity and farce, and the Senate becomes incapable of either properly evaluating nominees or appropriately educating the public."[22] Sharp words. But could they stand the test of time?

In politics, as in nature, one's capacity to survive hinges on the ability to adapt to new circumstances. While Professor Kagan denied that proposition, nominee Kagan embraced it. In doing so, she joined the group of those Supreme Court nominees who refused to be forthright – that is, Bork-like.

Be scripted, evasive, polished, repetitive, polite, trite, and also be as engaging as possible – those are the skills that must be mastered in a post-Bork confirmation world. Never be forthcoming. Savor silence; let long-winded senators steal your time. Appear sophisticated yet always avoid substance, controversy, complexity, and anything that might be offensive to any group. Lies and half-truths will be countenanced provided they are delivered softly and with a honest smile. Captivating soundbites are more important than professorial gradations or professional integrity. Backpedaling is also permissible so long as it is done with enough skill to give the impression that something profound is being said. And be sure to be well-groomed, well-suited, and TV-friendly. Appearances are as important as the untruths they conceal. Or to cast it in Machiavellian vernacular: "Everyone sees what you seem to be, few know what you really are."[23]

The result: Five Senate Republicans (joined by 56 Democrats and 2 independents) supported Elena Kagan's bid for the Supreme Court. It was something of a feat in the fiercely anti-Obama environment in which her confirmation hearings occurred. Repeatedly, and buttressed by cautious brevity or apt humor, she either deflected controversial topics or replied in a conservative sounding way. It was a style she had perfected earlier when she appeared before the Senate in connection with her nomination as Solicitor General. In that confirmation context, Kagan cleverly went so far as to appear to deny her own constitutional creed: "There is no federal constitutional right to same-sex marriage," she declared in response to a written question posed by Senator John Cornyn.[24]

Robert Bork was a martyr to a lost cause, the cause of authenticity. After his defeat, and with long-suffering majesty, he proclaimed: "When the Court is perceived as a political rather than a legal institution, nominees will be treated like political candidates."[25] Remarkably, he failed to understand that realist truth, and it thus cost him dearly. When law tumbles with politics, the latter must triumph lest a nominee find himself or herself on the pointed end of a confirmation dagger. Judge Bork never fully appreciated that. Though all who came after would deny it, and rightfully so, every successful nominee since Robert Bork has practiced, albeit to different degrees, the art of duplicity.[26] As they have come to realize, it is a talent that served them well and prepared them for even greater conquests.

Chapter 2

How to Be Aggressive and Passive ... and Great

Grand strategy is the art of looking beyond the battle and calculating ahead.

It requires that you focus on your ultimate goal and plot to reach it. . . .

Let others get caught up in the twists and turns of the battle, relishing their little victories.

Grand strategy will bring you the ultimate reward.

– Robert Greene[1]

John Marshall was a genius. Why? Because he was cunning. And for his cunningness he won the most revered place in the palladium of American Law. No matter that he was unethical; Sunday-school virtue was not his measure. No matter that he skirted the law; faithful acquiescence was not his suit. No matter that he made new law without authority; formal constitutional compliance was not his aim. No matter that he went beyond the boundaries of legitimacy; fidelity to idle principle was of no moment to him. And no matter that he tweaked the ire of a President and diluted the power of Congress; he did so with enough shrewdness to prevail over the other two more powerful branches. In the process, Marshall's name became iconic – the greatest Chief Justice, the greatest defender of the rule of law.

The fourth Chief Justice's judicial genius mirrored that of the greatest military strategists. In those arts, it is well understood that losing a battle may be necessary to win a war. Similarly, the prudent jurist knows well that a sacrifice in an immediate controversy may be the price necessary to pay for a future triumph. In this way and others, Marshall knew when to be aggressive and when to be passive; when to be direct and when to be devious; and when to appear just and when to be unjust. The example of John Marshall – particularly in the celebrated case of *Marbury v. Madison* (1803)[2] – should be appreciated for what it really is, a lesson in resourceful and unorthodox strategic decisionmaking. To more fully understand Marshall's brilliance, we reconsider *Marbury* in a radical new light, one infused with Machiavellian craft. Put into bold relief, the virtues of being cunning must be revered as essential to judicial politics.

ᴓ

> *John Marshall's* Marbury v. Madison *is "a masterwork of indirection, a brilliant example of Marshall's capacity to sidestep danger while seeming to court it, to advance in one direction while his opponents were looking in another."*
>
> – *Robert McCloskey*[3]

Laudatory adjectives are seldom spared when it comes to portraying John Marshall. He has been called the "Great Chief Justice," [4] the one who "saved the nation." [5] Some hale him as "one of the towering figures in the landscape of American law."[6] Others push the superlative to name him the "single best representative of American constitutional law"[7] and "the greatest judicial figure to have ever graced the Supreme Court of the United States."[8]

No less praise has been heaped upon Marshall's opinion in *Marbury v. Madison*. It has been billed an "epic decision"[9] that is "the cornerstone of constitutional law."[10] One commentator unconditionally gushed that "*Marbury v. Madison* is our foremost symbol of judicial power."[11] And whatever the deserved critique levied against Marshall's handiwork,[12] it cannot be gainsaid at the very least that "the mythical *Marbury* is destined to carry the day."[13]

By Machiavellian measures, all the kudos directed to John Marshall and *Marbury* are warranted, but not for the reasons typically given. Conversely, the criticisms generally raised against the man and his extraordinary opinion are ill-deserved by Machiavellian norms. For that matter, Marshall's moves should be judged as virtues, and not vices, in the scheme of judicial politics.

By way of conceptual backdrop, consider the rapid swirl of political maneuvering that gave rise to the controversy in *Marbury*:

- On February 4, 1801, John Marshall assumed the office of Chief Justice of the United States, to which he was appointed by outgoing Federalist President John Adams – this while retaining his office as Adams's Secretary of State.
- On February 13, the Federalist Congress, anticipating the Republican Party's ascension to power in three weeks, passed the Circuit Courts Act empowering Adams to nominate and the Congress to confirm sixteen new circuit court judges. Ten days later, the same Congress passed a law authorizing Adams to appoint 42 Justices of the Peace for a five-year term.
- On March 3, the last day of the Federalist administration, the Senate confirmed the appointments for Justices of the Peace. Later that day, Secretary of State Marshall busily affixed the official seals to the commissions, while his brother James hurriedly attempted to deliver them. William Marbury's commission, however, was one of the documents that remained undelivered.
- The following day, Thomas Jefferson took office after being sworn in by Chief Justice Marshall. One of Jefferson's first acts was to direct his Secretary of State, James Madison, to withhold the undelivered judicial commissions.
- Almost ten months later, Marbury and three other appointees sought a writ of mandamus in the U.S. Supreme Court to compel Madison to deliver their judicial commissions. On December18, the Court ordered the Secretary of State to show cause why mandamus should not issue. Jefferson's Attorney General Levi Lincoln appeared reluctantly before the Court,

but argued that Madison was not amenable to judicial power respecting his official duties.[14]

In a 43-page opinion rendered only 13 days after the case was argued, the 47 year old Chief Justice made history . . . by his Machiavellian moves. Among those moves, four are particularly noteworthy.

First, it was elementary ethics: John Marshall should have recused himself in *Marbury*. How could he possibly claim to be objective when he was so substantially steeped in the controversy? After all, he wore two hats – one as the executor of the law and the other as the arbiter of it. Moreover, as one of the players in the case, he had an obvious conflict of interest in judging it. Despite this, the Chief Justice never opted to remove himself from the case. Such *bona fide* ethical qualms notwithstanding, had Marshall succumbed to them, his own stature and that of his seminal opinion would never have been so exalted. He was cunning enough to set aside legal ethics in the interests of judicial power.

Second, Marshall's opinion stacked the deck in his favor by cleverly prioritizing the three main issues in the case. He considered the substantive questions of Marbury's right to a judicial commission and his entitlement to a mandamus remedy *before* deciding a foundational issue – whether the Court had jurisdiction over the case to begin with. If, as it ultimately turned out, the Court lacked jurisdiction, it could never have passed on the right and remedy questions. But this the Chief Justice was loathe to do – if only because it would have deprived him of the opportunity to declare that both the President and the Congress were amenable to the rule of law as interpreted by his Court. With this procedural sleight of hand, Marshall prolonged the judicial power long enough to maximize it.

Third, the Chief Justice launched a "judicial *coup d'etat*"[15] against the President and his cabinet by subordinating their powers to the authority of his Court – on an issue that had not really been argued by the parties and that outraged the Jefferson administration. Marshall artfully distinguished between two types of Executive actions: political actions reserved by the Constitution to the President's sole discretion and mandatory ministerial duties assigned to the President by law and amenable to judicial examination. Significantly, this dichotomy itself was suspect insofar as the judicial power was textually explicit in extending "to *all* cases arising under the Constitution."[16] Nevertheless, by this ingenious move, Marshall feigned judicial restraint over other potential cases while forsaking all restraint in this case.[†] Determining that the Executive's obligation to deliver Marbury's commission fell into the category of legal questions, Marshall announced the Court's superiority over the Presidency in establishing the requisites of law and essentially denounced it for its lawlessness. In fact, Alexander Hamilton's Federalist newspaper gleefully charged as much with the headline "Constitution Violated by the President."[17] In his interpretive moment, the Chief Justice adroitly subjugated the President's authority to execute the law to the judiciary's powers to decipher the law – and this even before he had fully demonstrated how the Constitution vested the judicial review power. To that point, Marshall then turned.

For his last point, the Chief Justice turned finally to the issue of the Court's jurisdiction. He concluded that it had none by setting up a conflict –many saw it as a false conflict[18] – between a federal statute and the Constitution. Though he might have easily resolved that conflict by interpreting either law differently, it was not in his best interests to do so. On the one hand, Marshall could have interpreted the federal statute as permitting the Court to issue writs of mandamus only in appellate cases, and not in cases of original jurisdiction[††] like this one. By that argument, Marbury would have lost because his case would simply have been dismissed. On the other hand, Marshall could have construed the Constitution to empower Congress to add to the Court's authority to grant writs of mandamus in cases of original jurisdiction. By that argument, Marbury would have won because the Court would now issue the writ of mandamus he sought. Neither alternative was acceptable, since only a conflict between the laws permitted Marshall to invalidate the federal law and reject jurisdiction at one and the same time. Thus, he

---

†. Ironically, Chief Justice John Roberts billed *Marbury v. Madison* as "the epitome of restraint." Robert Barnes, "Independence, Restraint Should Guide Court," *Washington Post*, 9 May 2016, sec. A, p. 9.

†. Under the Constitution, the Supreme Court has both original and appellate jurisdiction. The former allows the Justices to act as a trial court in certain cases.

wielded power over Congress while forfeiting power in Marbury's politically controversial cause.

ॐ

There was a Janus-like quality to John Marshall's opinion in *Marbury v. Madison*. One head faced Congress and acted with daring conviction in striking down a federal law, while the other faced the Executive and acted meekly insofar as it was powerless to grant Marbury the relief he sought. Marshall's stratagem: appear aggressive in one respect, passive in the other. When done, he strengthened the hand of the Judiciary without triggering the dangerous reactions of a President eager to disobey any hostile order. And it was of little consequence that he achieved such success by facile logic and fanciful rhetoric. The force of the former more than made up for the weakness of the latter.

William Marbury had actively campaigned for John Adams in the presidential election of 1800.[19] Neither that effort nor the battle he waged in the Supreme Court proved to be of any moment, however. When it was all said and done, Mr. Marbury never became a justice of the peace. Though his name is known to generations of law students, lawyers, scholars, and judges, that of John Marshall always eclipses it. And when the name *Marbury* was invoked in cases like *Cooper v. Aaron*,[20] it was added to yield even more staying power to Marshall's momentous precedent. This points to another major insight that the Great Justice had: by bolstering the institution of judicial review, he provided future generations with a wondrous prism through which to shine their own dreams about life and law. Their aspirations thus ensured his enduring fame.

It is a truism impossible to deny: Chief Justice John Marshall was *the* master craftsman of the judicial art. In ways at once learned and cunning, he outmaneuvered the President, trumped Congress, empowered the Supreme Court, and secured a lasting legacy for himself and the cause of judicial supremacy. And unlike Chief Justice Roger Taney in *Dred Scott v. Sandford*,[21] the very next case in which a federal law was declared unconstitutional, John Marshall was too astute to sacrifice his powers on the altar of a calamitous cause.

Chapter 3

Recusal and the Vices of Impartiality

Machiavelli taught us to take a posture
of detachment in the face of vice.

-- Hadley Arkes[1]

All of us today are, in a sense, Machiavellians   .

-- Carnes Lord[2]

Yes, today we may all be Machiavellians. But that claim needs nuance. That is, while many may believe the claim, few actually practice it in an effective way. And while Machiavelli taught detachment when it comes to vice, here, too, few can turn that maxim into an advantageous course of judicial action. If legal ethics are cast in the light of the aggrandizement of power, then new opportunities will present themselves to a shrewd Judge.

The ethics of a great Judge are *counter-ethics*. They do not bow to law's old pieties, the ones grounded in the myths of justice impartially applied. This should not shock anyone,[3] for many know that the law is often tainted by the biases of judges. Still, the myth of impartiality lives on and, strangely enough, some judges (the weaker ones) actually take their decisional cues from such pious norms. In the modern world of modes and orders of judicial behavior, however, it would be foolish for a Machiavellian Judge to honor such limits on his or her power.

ᢀ

Since the seventeenth century, a fundamental axiom of Anglo-American law
  has been that "no man shall be a judge in his own case."
  In matters of judicial ethics, however, each Justice is precisely that.

  -- Lincoln Caplan[4]

They follow either no rule or their own rule.

Curious as it surely is, this is the norm when it comes to the "rules" of recusal applicable to Supreme Court Justices. As Professor David O'Brien subtly observes: "There are no *fixed* rules . . . for a Justice's recusal, nor do the Justices even have to explain to their colleagues why they think they have a potential financial or personal conflict of interest that disqualifies them from voting on a case."[5] While federal statutory law ostensibly restrains Supreme Court Justices in matters of recusal,[6] there is a rub: Chief Justice John Roberts explained that the "individual Justices decide for themselves whether recusal is warranted" under that law.[7] And while the federal Code of Judicial Conduct[8] may seem applicable to Supreme Court Justices, the Chief Justice advises us to the contrary: The code of conduct, he stressed, does not apply to the Justices because of "a fundamental difference between the Supreme Court and the other federal courts."[9]

No fixed rules means no limits; each Justice can chart his or her own ethical course. Notably, that course was craftily charted in the Founding era by our most revered Chief Justice. As we described *Marbury v. Madison* (1803)[10] in Chapter 2, Marshall did not recuse himself from the decision even though he was directly involved as Secretary of State in the very controversy. Could there be a more egregious example of bias than that? And yet, John Marshall did not let that ethical peccadillo bar his path to greatness. When one walks down the grand halls of the Supreme Court and comes upon the glorious bronzed statue of John Marshall, who remembers his grotesque breach of ethics?

Justice Hugo Black followed in John Marshall's footsteps. His recusal quandary swirled around a 1945 case, *Jewell Ridge Coal Corp. v. Local 6167, United Mine Workers*,[11] a controversy involving an interpretation of the Fair Labor Standards Act. Senator Black had conceived and sponsored that bill, the final version of which he had helped to draft.[12] During the Court's conference discussion, Justice Douglas recalled: "Black was very, very strong and vocal" on behalf of the miners.[13] When the matter was decided, the vote was 5-4 with Justice Black in the majority and Justice Jackson dissenting. Shortly thereafter, the coal company petitioned for rehearing of the case arguing that Justice Black should have recused himself. Totally apart from the jurist's integral connection to the act that the majority had just interpreted, the recusal complaint was based on the fact that the Justice's former law partner, Crampton Harris, argued the case for the union.[14] Perhaps irritated by Black's failure to disclose this conflict, Jackson vehemently insisted that his colleague disqualify himself.†‡ Justice Black refused and the Court denied the petition for rehearing. Unrelentingly, Jackson insisted on writing a separate opinion focusing on the recusal issue. He conceded that he knew of "no authority" by which "a majority of the Court" could "under any circumstances ... exclude one of its duly commissioned Justices from sitting or voting in any case." [15] The inference was, nonetheless, plain: Black should have stepped aside.[16] No matter. The 5-4 ruling stood. And Jackson left in a huff to be the chief Allied prosecutor for the war crimes trials in Nuremberg.[17]

Justice William Rehnquist followed in Hugo Black's footsteps. The case was *Laird v. Tatum*,[18] which produced a 5-4 ruling in an Army surveillance controversy involving the right of the plaintiff to challenge such practices. After the decision came down (with Rehnquist in the majority), the losing parties moved for rehearing because Rehnquist had served as head of the Office of Legal Counsel when the surveillance program was first devised and implemented. He had even defended the program in testimony before Congress.[19] The motion was denied and Rehnquist issued an in chambers opinion in which he discounted any actual bias.[20] Years later when the matter came up during Rehnquist's confirmation hearing to be Chief Justice, "some senators cited the *Laird* case in voting against the nomination."[21] The recusal brouhaha notwithstanding, William Rehnquist was confirmed to be Chief Justice by a

---

† "Jackson never mentioned his own role as a draftsman of the act who testified on its behalf before the joint congressional hearings chaired by Black." Roger K. Newman, *Hugo Black: A Biography* (New York, NY: Pantheon Books, 1994), p. 335.

65-33 vote. Beyond the ethical pale, there is this: *Laird v. Tatum* remains good law to this date.[22]

John Marshall did not waver in the face of ethical norms. Similarly, Hugo Black did not permit ethical obstacles to block his path to five votes. Likewise, William Rehnquist did not allow recusal principles to sway his opinion. Theirs was a counter-ethic – the ethic of Power.

These three examples vividly demonstrate the latitude that a Justice possesses when it comes to recusal concerns. By Machiavellian norms, that latitude is profitable. Those norms recommend that when recusal is of little or no moment, there is much to be gained in touting one's ethical virtues. By contrast, when recusal stands to thwart self-advantage, there is much to be gained in ignoring ethical platitudes. And as always, the extraordinary Justice must appear to be above reproach. Admittedly, there may be times when a jurist forgets about a conflict, and fails to disclose it[23]. But such omissions are quickly forgiven and forgotten. If one must err, let him take his example from Justice Ruth Bader Ginsburg (who has never recused herself), rather than from Justice Elena Kagan (who does so frequently).[24] And let him never succumb to demands for allegiance to a fixed code of conduct.

It is better to embrace the virtues of partiality than the vices of impartiality.

Chapter 4

The Use and Misuse of the Politics
of Personality

Who is the Justice of the Future? Who will master our 26 lessons (and yet others)? Who has the will and the way to see beyond today? Who can overcome law's lie? And who is prepared to make daring moves?

Obedience to the law is little more than a slavish submission to tradition or custom, to a group's way of judging life and those in it. And each group in its own time and manner forges its own customs, which when codified and constitutionalized become law. There is no HIGHER law; there is only the law of the lowlands, the law born of habit, fear, and obedience . . . or so the argument goes. The law of the Roman polytheists was no better than that of the Christian monotheists or vice-versa. Even so, we might think (if only offhandedly) of lawmakers (which includes Justices) as demi-Gods. They decide cases, then fashion doctrines, and then constitute it all under the label of the "Supreme Law of the Land." In our secular world, they are our high priests. Authority rests with authors, and legitimacy is conformity to the will of others.

The Justice of the future is *self*-controlled. He refuses to be controlled by others, though he may find it useful to appear otherwise. Thus understood, the lessons of *The Judge* are essentially lessons in self-control – of a certain kind, of course. Under the dominion of law, the Principle of Power is sublimated and the Will of the Self is obliterated, but only if one allows it to be so. The Self must not lose control; the Self must master the law and not be mastered by it; the Self must also be master over others, but carefully.

A Justice must understand that, when his or her colleagues claim fidelity to THE LAW, it is imprudent to follow their example *in action* but not *in word*. This is so because such loyalty does not really inform their actions, or if it does it is one that can be manipulated by a clever Justice. Hence, the Justice of the future must learn to think differently, not as others would have him or her do, but as he or she would do. To do this, however, a Justice must learn to lie, and to cloak his or her will in terms fitting the conscience of colleagues. By the same token, the mass of people needs lies to live, and one of those untruths is the lie of the law. So here, too, the skills of deception are important.

If it is to be realized, the Power Principle must traffic in the politics of personality. This brand of politics best informs interactions with one's colleagues. Its effective use is complex, and can backfire if one lacks sufficient knowledge or acts without sufficient tact. To that end, one must *display* the courtesy and gentility of a Lewis Powell combined with the objectivity and learnedness of a John Marshall Harlan, II. So, too, one must be able to build coalitions with the skill of an Earl Warren or a William Brennan. And one must be a leader at times (e.g., Charles Evan Hughes) while appearing to be a follower at other times (e.g., Louis Brandeis[+]+ or Potter Stewart). And then there are those Justices who pitch their fame to the future (e.g., Oliver Wendell Holmes[++]++).

No one formula fits all courts and all circumstances. Still, there are certain examples of what *not* to do.

❧

I thought Felix was going to hit me today, he got so mad.
> – *Justice Hugo Black*[1]

All Frankfurter does is talk, talk, talk. He drives you crazy.
> – *Chief Justice Earl Warren*[2]

+. Here the reference is to Justice Brandeis' concurrence in *Whitney v. California,* 274 U.S. 357 (1927). See Ronald Collins & David Skover, "Curious Concurrence: Justice Brandeis' Vote in *Whitney v. California,*" *Supreme Court Review* 2005: 333.

++. Certainly, Holmes did have his savvy side, as when he appeased his conservative colleagues by ruling against the rights claimant in *Schenck v. United States,* 249 U.S. 47 (1919), while at the same time restructuring the law of the First Amendment. In the process, he changed existing law and paved the way for the free-speech law of the future.

When Justice Benjamin Cardozo died in 1938, Attorney General Homer Cummings wrote in his diary that "Cardozo was not only a great Justice, but a great character, a great person and a great soul, [someone] held in reverence by multitudes of people. [W]hoever followed him, no matter how good a man he might be, would suffer by comparison."[3] How true that proved to be in the case of Felix Frankfurter, the successor to the mild-mannered and humble Cardozo who was greatly admired by his colleagues. Unlike the collegial Cardozo, when it came to the politics of personality Frankfurter was a disaster.

He was arrogant, combative, spiteful, and manipulative (but not in effective ways). Positioning himself as the modern exemplar of judicial restraint, Frankfurter lectured his colleagues on the importance of James Bradley Thayer's 1893 *Harvard Law Review* article.[4] If they had not read it, he "made certain they received a copy."[5] In oral arguments he sometimes acted as if his colleagues were not in the courtroom. Thus, he occasionally "consumed large segments of time with questions, exasperating counsel and other Justices. Frankfurter once interrupted a lawyer ninety-three times during a 120-minute oral argument."[6] In conference he regularly pontificated to infuriating lengths. He often came to conference "with piles of books, and on his turn to talk, would pound the table, read from the books, throw them around and create a great disturbance. . . . At, times, when another was talking, he would break in, make a derisive comment, and shout down the speaker."[7]

"During his years on the Court, Frankfurter served with four Chief Justices and nineteen associate Justices."[8] In his relations with them, the Vienna-born jurist could be combative, sycophantic, dismissive, and conceited. Though acrimony was already in the air during many of the Frankfurter years, he often made a bad situation worse. This was especially true in his belligerent dealings (both in private and in print) with Justice William O. Douglas (who welcomed a fight)[9] and to a lesser extent with Justice Hugo Black.[10] Sometimes it was personal; other times it was simply Frankfurter acting as the relentless professor who grills anyone holding an opposing opinion.[†] In any event, such hostilities only compounded the personality problems Frankfurter created for himself. In one sense, it was to be expected given Frankfurter's psychological profile.[11] In another sense, it was a bit unexpected if only because

Frankfurter traveled in many circles, both inside and outside of the judicial world, and placed a premium on networking. And at the Court his rapport with his law clerks was rather congenial. [12]

His image of himself was larger than life, though he could be very small-minded. Ironically, when he was nominated, Felix Frankfurter was to be the chosen son who "would lead the incipient Roosevelt Court in a constitutional revolution."[13] That never happened. Instead, he helped to divide the Court as he reveled in his contempt for those whose views did not comport with his Harvard-trained intellect. Predictably, "[h]istory has not been kind to [him] . . . there is now almost a universal consensus that Frankfurter the Justice was a failure."[14] Or as another historian of the Court put it: "Frankfurter ranks as one of the great disappointments in modern times."[15] Such assessments were not owing to his lack of knowledge; quite the contrary, he was most learned. As erudite as he was, Felix Frankfurter never mastered the art of the politics of personality.

❧

Why have we devoted so much attention to Justice Frankfurter and his failings? Fair question. We have done so for several reasons. First, as suggested in our Prologue, being Machiavellian is not easy; it requires the exceptional talents of a particular kind of Justice. (More could be said about this, but for now our discussion of Felix Frankfurter will suffice.) Second, the Frankfurter example well illustrates that mere knowledge of the law, even when considerable, is not enough unless put to one's tactical advantage. Third, appearing humble can be advantageous, whereas egotistical displays are usually counterproductive. Frankfurter (like Justice Antonin Scalia) discounted this lesson to his disadvantage. Fourth, though being secretive and duplicitous certainly has its benefits, one must always take care not to appear so. On this score, Frankfurter failed. Fifth, personal conflicts are to be avoided at almost all costs;

---

†. "He was the most unscrupulous debater alive; there were no holds barred." Alexander Bickel, quoted in Leonard Baker, *Brandeis & Frankfurter: A Dual Biography* (New York, NY: Harper & Row, 1989), p. 415.

typically, much is to be lost and little, if anything, gained from such clashes. And finally, one must be constantly attentive to tailoring the politics of personality to suit the demands both of the moment and, to the extent possible, of the days to come.

Sometimes it is best to be silent; then again, sometimes it is advantageous to be outspoken. Sometimes it is prudent to be a leader; sometimes it is wise to be a follower (but only to one's benefit). Sometimes one must put secret plots in motion; sometimes either one's good fortune or another's bad luck will suffice. In this respect, Felix Frankfurter was exceptional in his service to honor the will and secure the fame of Justice Oliver Wendell Holmes (see the Epilogue) and Justice Louis Brandeis.[16] Incredibly, he could not do it for himself.

Some Justices simply do not care about how they are perceived by their colleagues. Some do not care much about success. They are neither tactical nor ambassadorial. They are content to be contentious.[17] Take, for example, President Woodrow Wilson's 1914 appointee, James Clark McReynolds. *Time* magazine branded him "puritanical, intolerably rude, savagely sarcastic, incredibly reactionary, and anti-Semitic."[18] According to his biographer, McReynolds "disliked . . . compromise judgments and often disagreed with his colleagues, to whom he was frequently abrasive and rude."[19] When he passed away on August 24, 1946, McReynolds "died a very lonely death in a hospital – without a single friend or relative at his bedside. He was buried in Kentucky, but no member of the Court attended his funeral."[20] No surprise.

As the McReynolds example reveals, every now and then it is impossible to circumvent conflict. It comes straight at you, sometimes even with ideological flags flying and rhetorical guns blazing.†+ In such situations, one must either wait for a more opportune time to strike back or respond convincingly as Justice Harlan did in *Plessy v. Ferguson*,[21] or as Justice Holmes did in *Lochner v. New York*,[22] or as Justice Cardozo did in *Carter v. Carter Coal Company*,[23] or as Justice Stevens did in *Bowers*

---

†. See, for example, Justice Scalia's predictable and *ad hominem* dissent in *Obergefell v. Hodges*, 135 S. Ct. 2071 (2015) (same-sex marriage case). Such opinions have drawn a predictably critical response, even from some on the bench. See Richard Posner and Eric Segall, "Justice Scalia's Majoritarian Theocracy," *New York Times*, 2 December 2015.

v. Hardwick.[24] Though each lost the battle, in time they all won the war. Time, by contrast, rarely favors the James Clark McReynolds of the judicial world.

The brutish McReynolds, nonetheless, did have something in common with the sophisticated Frankfurter. Relatively speaking, they killed whatever potential they had. True, in the case of McReynolds it seemed more striking. Even so, since Frankfurter's potential was greater, his fall from judicial greatness was commensurately greater.

It is as ironic as it is true: If the exceptional Justice is to be his own master, he must sometimes assume the agreeable role of a Benjamin Cardozo (demure), an Owen Roberts (quiet and unassuming[25]), a Lewis Powell (gentlemanly), or a David Souter (polite). In other words, and to harken back to how we began our tract, a Justice must be hypocritical and strive to appear objective, judicious, and collegial.

Granting that, let us not move too far down this primrose path of kind-heartedness, or even the mere appearance of it. For all of this brings us back to an old Machiavellian query: "is it better to be loved than feared, or vice versa?"[26] Of course, and as was noted in *The Prince*, most would prefer both. It is, however, quite difficult to "accommodate these qualities." Hence, "if you have to make a choice, to be feared is much safer than to be loved."[27] And why? Because "[p]eople are less concerned with offending a man who makes himself loved than one who makes himself feared."[28] Two qualifications come into play here: First, if the fear card is to be played, there must be a "strong justification and a manifest cause"[29] for doing so; and second, what is most important is that one "take pains not to be hated."[30]

And just how can a Justice be strong and not hated? First, one should not use a heavy hand too often; it invites unnecessary animus. Second, one's strength should derive first from intellect and analytical power, properly applied. Marshall, Story, Taney, Holmes, Brandeis, and Rehnquist, among others, all enjoyed success in real part owning to their cerebral prowess. Third, sometimes one will hold the upper hand in a case in which a fifth vote is needed. In such situations, and to the extent possible and prudent, one should not shy away from making demands (as we noted in Chapter 14).

By and large, anyone who works at the Court realizes there will be good days and bad ones; there will be occasions when power is seized and other days when it is relinquished. One need not travel the corridors from chamber to chamber in order to make amends with those on the other side of the vote. In fact, that can be counterproductive. It is enough that one simply avoid hatred, that one let time heal the wounds of judicial wars. At other times, it is best to leave well enough alone, and then savor *Fortuna's* gifts.

Chapter 5

Fortuna

The Role of Chance in Deciding Cases

Fortune, good night. Smile once more, turn thy wheel.

– Shakespeare, *King Lear*[1]

Power is the principle, but Fate can ruin the best of plans. Maxims matter, but there is no tactic, however well followed, that can always elude the Unforeseen. It is possible to improve one's plight if one acts carefully, and one can sometimes evade disaster by being strategic. The lessons set out in this book speak to that concern. In that regard, circumstances may change the tactical equation, for better or worse. Moreover, the success of any of our lessons depends on how they are used and by whom – there is no magic in our method. Hence, in this chapter we think it wise to say a few more words about *Fortuna*, and how best to work with or around it.

The astute Judge is ever mindful of this admonition: Never assume that tomorrow will be the same as today. Of course, it may be, and it may even be for a long time. But that should never be taken as a given when it comes to plotting one's judicial behavior. Times change, people change, circumstances change, and then, too, there is the Grim Reaper's harvest. In short, nothing outlasts Change. Given that, one must be prepared for the unexpected, for the collapse of the finest of plans, and even for a bad outcome. Yet, sometimes *Fortuna* smiles and bestows the best of unforeseen benefits. When misfortune strikes, a backup plan is prudent whenever possible. And if that fails, the stratagem must be to seize whatever opportunity or diminish whatever loss one can in the chaos of the moment. If, however, Chance is kind, the potential to tap into the Power Principle may be unlimited. When that occurs, one should proceed forcefully but tactically, and plot out a plan that will be advantageous today and more significant tomorrow.

Fortuna often determines what cases come to the Court, when they come, how they come, whether they are reviewed, and whether they proceed to judgment.[†] And then there is the role of Fate in the Court's conference and in the journey from the assignment of an opinion to its announcement. Admittedly, there is a general level of predictability – in some matters more so than others – but circumstances can change at any time and for any reason. As the prudent Justice knows, in a few unusual cases one can put the wheel of Chance into motion, and this to one's advantage. It is rare, of course, to have that opportunity. In such circumstances, if things fail, one can fault Fate, whereas if they succeed one can stand back and reap the fruits of good fortune.

❧

September 6, 1901 is one of the most important dates in American constitutional history, though few think of it as such. On that day Leon Czolgosz attempted to assassinate President William McKinley at the Pan-American Exposition in Buffalo, New York. Though the President would live several more days, the two shots the anarchist fired ultimately killed him and thereby put in motion a string of events that led to Oliver Wendell Holmes, Jr. becoming the fifty-eighth Justice on the Supreme Court.

As the summer of 1901 wound down, it became apparent to President McKinley and others that Justice Horace Gray was ill and was likely to retire soon. So the President turned to his friend John Davis Long, then Secretary of the Navy, for advice. Though Secretary Long had nominated Holmes to the Massachusetts bench when he

---

†. The Article III doctrine of mootness can steal a case away anytime. Therefore, it is always wise to be attentive to its possibility. See e.g. *DeFunis v. Odegaard*, 416 U.S. 312 (1974). Or there may be jurisdictional issues that end a case before it his decided. See e.g. *Nike v. Kasky*, 539 U.S. 654 (2003).

was governor, he did not recommend him for the Supreme Court. Instead, Long urged the President to nominate Alfred Hemenway, his law partner. And Hemenway was prepared to accept the position if and when offered. But as it turned out, Horace's delay in retiring combined with President McKinley's assassination changed everything.

Fate played its hand, and when it did Henry Cabot Lodge, a U.S. senator from Massachusetts and one of Theodore Roosevelt's close friends, recommended Holmes for Gray's seat when the ailing Justice stepped down in July 1902. Roosevelt acted on Lodge's suggestion and nominated Holmes. By December the Senate confirmed Holmes unanimously. As ironic as it was, Oliver Wendell Holmes owed his justiceship to a crazed anarchist.[2]

For all his renown – a famous father, Harvard credentials, Civil War hero, acclaimed speeches and articles, authorship of the highly regarded *The Common Law* (1881), and Chief Justice of the Massachusetts Supreme Judicial Court – Oliver Wendell Holmes could not secure a seat on the United States Supreme Court. He needed something more; he needed Leon Czolgosz, the madman who paved the path for Holmes's road to glory (see Chapter 26).

≪ゝ

Justice Pierce Butler was one of the "Four Horsemen" (in addition to James Clark McReynolds, George Sutherland, and Willis Van Devanter). With some help from Chief Justice Howard Taft, the "Four Horsemen" kept Justices Holmes and Brandeis at bay in free speech cases such as *Gitlow v. New York* (1925)[3] and *United States v. Schwimmer* (1929).[4] The Four were foes of free speech.[5] By that measure, when in 1929 Jay Near set out to petition the Supreme Court in a seedy defamation case, there was good reason to believe that Justice Butler and his conservatives colleagues would prevail again, which meant Jay Near's First Amendment claim would lose.

Butler had done his fair share to keep free-speech freedoms closeted during his tenure on the Court. Admirable as Oliver Wendell Holmes's dissent was in *Abrams v. United States* (1919),[6] it received no constitutional traction as long as Pierce Butler and his fellow "horsemen" had their way. By 1929, Butler gloated while Holmes and Brandeis waited. And then *Fortuna* turned: Chief Justice William Howard Taft and Justice Edward T. Sanford both died in March of 1930. In First Amendment terms, it was a constitutional game changer if the new appointees (Charles Evan Hughes as Chief Justice and Owen Roberts as Associate Justice) were of the Holmes and Brandeis persuasion in free speech matters. Were that to happen, the strength of the Four Horsemen might be diminished.

The new Chief Justice Hughes tipped his hand, although subtly, at the memorial service of his two deceased colleagues. While most may have missed his real message, it probably did not escape the attention of Pierce Butler. "The figures of today," said Hughes in open Court, "like those of yesterday, will soon be replaced, and the best endeavors, striking as they may be in their immediate aspect, will soon form but the backdrop of another picture."[7] Put bluntly, Butler's view of the First Amendment would soon be replaced by a new "picture" of that world. And that picture would be painted, and with bold strokes, by Charles Evan Hughes. To that end, and within an hour or so of his memorial remarks, the Chief Justice triumphantly read from his opinion for the Court in *Near v. Minnesota*.[8] The vote was 5-4 with the conservative quartet in dissent; Justice Butler wrote for himself and the three other malcontents.

Hughes was not satisfied with securing the vote of Justice Roberts (no small feat); he was also determined to render a groundbreaking First Amendment opinion, one that could withstand the test of time. In this, he succeeded with masterful conceptual strokes; he reworked the constitutional architecture of the First Amendment's guaranty of press freedoms.[9]

A disgruntled Justice Butler complained bitterly.[10] But his view has been "virtually ignored by history,"[11] whereas Chief Justice Hughes's bold opinion became a mainstay of First Amendment law. Better still, and true to that fame, the *Near* opinion made Hughes the darling of the liberal and conservative press, which is a much coveted honor. "The immediate reaction to the decision was overwhelmingly positive. The nation's press was gratified and relieved. Many newspapers reiterated the view that "the decision of Chief Justice Hughes will go down in history as one of the great triumphs of free thought."[12] As for Pierce Butler, he was too cabined in his conservative bloc to do much more than he did.

✍

Chief Justice Frederick Vinson died unexpectedly on September 8, 1953. Why is that important? The answer: *Brown v. Board of Education* was first argued on December 9, 1952. The case had yet to be decided when Vinson passed away. And then Earl Warren took his seat on the Court a month or so after Vinson's death. Two months into Warren's term, *Brown* was reargued on December 8, 1953. The case was handed down the following May with the new Chief Justice writing for the Court. The banner headline read: "School Segregation Outlawed: Chief Justice Reads Historic Decision; Vote was Unanimous."[13]

Now think of it, and its possible permutations. Had a blood clot not blocked Vinson's coronary artery,[14] *Brown* might have gone the other way. [15] Then again, had Vinson lived he might have surprised many[16] and written a unanimous opinion for the Court declaring racial segregation unconstitutional.[17] If that had occurred, Fred Vinson would be remembered as a constitutional hero rather than as a constitutional villain, which is how he is often portrayed.[18] "Authorship of *Brown*," it has been aptly noted, "would have given Vinson instant historical immortality, guaranteeing his place among the nation's most significant Chief Justices."[19] Moreover, had all that happened, the famed "Warren Court" as we know it would not have existed, and there is even some credible doubt that Earl Warren would have ever been nominated to be Chief Justice.[20]

All of this did not occur, however, because the unexpected happened: Fred Vinson died and Earl Warren replaced him. Whereas Vinson thought *Brown* was complex and was thus hesitant to the end, Warren thought it was simple and was thus resolute from the outset: "I don't remember having any great doubts," he recalled years later, "about which way it should go. It seemed to me a comparatively simple case."[21] With that confident mindset, Warren proceeded slowly and cautiously at the start and confidently and boldly thereafter. He took control, combining diplomacy with resolve to achieve his "moral" end.

The new Chief Justice extended the discussion of the case to allow more days to build consensus. "The delay gave Warren time to negotiate, to search for common ground. He was to use the politician's tool of compromise in a temple where acts were ostensibly measured against the inflexible yardsticks of The Law."[22] Next, he sized up his votes: He had Justices Black, Douglas, Minton and Burton, but he wanted unanimity. What about Justices Reed, Clark, Frankfurter, and Jackson? He needed them to sign onto his opinion. With masterful skill,[23] Warren took the necessary steps to see that the Court spoke with one voice – his. Like Justice Holmes, but in his own special way, Warren grabbed the case "by the throat rather than by the tail."[24] He succeeded . . . and the rest, as they say, is history. In other words, *Fortuna* was kind to Earl Warren and he used that good luck to his celebrated advantage.[25]

There is one other lesson to be learned here: The prudent Justice should always be mindful of his or her health, and not yield to Eternity sooner than needed. Fred Vinson's "health was not good – he was overweight and a chain smoker."[26] He was 63 when a blood clot took his life. In those days they called it fate; today we call it avoidable, or largely so. If one hopes to move an agenda in any self-serving way, let him or her take health cues from the likes of Oliver Wendell Holmes (who retired at age 90), or Hugo Black (who retired at age 85), or William Brennan (who stepped down at age 90). After all, why spend so much time plotting one's judicial future if it is going to be cut short sooner than might be?

&

Death and circumstance can produce the best opportunities or the worst of possibilities. In the case of the former, the lesson is to be like Charles Evan Hughes or Earl Warren – to seize the day and move the earth. In the case of the latter, the lesson is to avoid being like Pierce Butler – when the world changes, either move with it or plot to change its future axis. And when *Fortuna* smiles – as in the case of Oliver Wendell Holmes and his elevation to the Court – start to plan how to best spend the bounty that has come to you.

Chapter 6

When and Why to Avoid a Case

Naim v. Naim is famous as the case that never was.

– Richard Delgado[1]

Justice Felix Frankfurter believed in judicial restraint. He did so to the point that his judiciousness sometimes betrayed the liberalism that won him fame before he joined the Court in 1939. Nonetheless, he is said to have played a role[2] in navigating the way that ultimately led to the Court's unanimous vote in *Brown v. Board of Education* (1954).[3] There his judicial moderation bowed to the cause of social justice.

Justice John Marshall Harlan, II was a cautious man, a moderate Justice. His grandfather, John Marshall Harlan was a far less restrained jurist. The first Harlan was the Justice who penned the famous dissents in the *Civil Rights Cases* (1883)[4] and *Plessy v. Ferguson* (1896)[5] – both much-heralded opinions in the history of racial justice in America. His moderation notwithstanding, the second Harlan proudly lent his vote to the controversial ruling in *Brown*.

The Texas-born Justice Tom Clark, yet another moderate, likewise cast an approving vote in *Brown*, and this consistent with his pro-civil rights record before he came to the Court[6] and his opinions once he donned a black robe.[7]

Three Justices, three judicial moderates, and three men who cared deeply about the Constitution's promise of equality of treatment. And yet, when it came to honoring that promise in two discrimination cases before the Court shortly after *Brown*, all three men hesitated; all three men voted not to hear those cases. Of course, their liberal brethren disagreed, if only silently. While some have criticized the timidity of the moderate trio,[8] their inaction is a lesson in prudence, a lesson of when a case ought to be avoided. Time and circumstances vindicated them, both then and now.

In the long run – twelve years later[9] – it all turned out well for the cause of racial justice. Yet in the short run, the stunning courage that was *Brown* yielded to the sober prudence exemplified in *Jackson v. Alabama*[10] and *Naim v. Naim*.[11] The lesson: Sometimes dodging a case may be more important than deciding one.

ৎ

> *Marriage is a personal matter on which the NAACP takes no position.*
> – NAACP Executive Secretary Roy Wilkins, September 1955[12]

The months and years immediately following *Brown* and *Brown (II)*[13] were times of triumph and tribulation. While the victory in *Brown* provided the legal platform for constitutional attacks on segregation and racial discrimination, it also carried with it the all too real prospect of acrimonious and violent backlash, often state-supported. It is in that maelstrom that *Jackson v. Alabama* and *Naim v. Naim* came before the Court – two cases that challenged the constitutionality of laws prohibiting miscegenation. Faithfully applied, the promise of *Brown* and the logic underlying it should have resolved the claims raised in both controversies.

In considering the relevance of *Brown* and its application to the miscegenation cases, it is useful to remember what the state of the law had been pre-*Brown*. In 1883, in a case named *Pace v. Alabama*,[14] the Supreme Court upheld the validity of Alabama's anti-miscegenation statute. Writing for a unanimous Court, Justice Stephen Field held that criminal prosecutions for miscegenation did not violate the Equal Protection Clause of the Fourteenth Amendment since whites and people of color were both subject to prosecution. Hence, *Pace* controlled when Linnie Jackson, a woman of color, was convicted for her sexual relationship with a white man. Similarly, when Han Say Naim, a Chinese sailor, married a white woman and later sought to challenge

Virginia's anti-miscegenation law, *Pace* controlled. The question before the Warren Court in both cases was whether *Pace* could be reconciled with *Brown*. In other words, could eugenic laws mandating the separation of the races be constitutional in light of *Brown*?[15]

As fate had it, Linnie Jackson's case came to the Court after *Brown* was decided but before *Brown (II)* was handed down.[16] Her chance to extend *Brown* thus occurred at the very moment when the Warren Court was trying mightily to enforce *Brown*. The result: Review denied[17] – no opinion, no dissents, just review denied. Now it was Mr. Naim's turn.

When the briefs were filed in *Naim*, the petitioner had successfully elicited the support of liberal groups, including the American Civil Liberties Union, the American Jewish Congress, the Association on American Indian Affairs, the Association of Immigration and Nationality Lawyers, and the Japanese-American Citizens League.[18] The most important group, however, was missing – the National Association for the Advancement of Colored People (NAACP). Why had it not filed a brief?[19] Why had it decided not to challenge Virginia's Racial Integrity Act? And why had it forsaken the chance to extend the promise of *Brown*?[20] These were all questions that any astute member of the Warren Court would have asked himself. Surely, the Justices must have noticed the striking absence of the name Thurgood Marshall (the hero of *Brown*) on any of the briefs presented to them in *Jackson* and *Naim*. As it turned out, the omission was intentional – a fact that buttresses the jurisprudential savvy of Justice Frankfurter and his colleagues.

Given the legal posture of the *Naim* case, the Court could either dismiss it for lack of any real and substantial federal question or it could assume jurisdiction and set the case for oral argument. Four votes were needed to do the latter. When the matter came before them during a November 1955 conference, Justice Frankfurter began by taking the high ground. "I candidly face the fact that what I call moral considerations far outweigh the technical considerations in noting jurisdiction," he conceded. "The moral considerations are those raised by the bearing of adjudicating this question [of] the Court's responsibility in not thwarting or seriously handicapping the enforcement of [our] decision in the segregation cases."[21] The promise of *Brown* had to be realized; it could not be marginalized. Translated, this meant that there was more at stake than the merits of Han Say Naim's case; there was the issue of the future power of the Court and its ability to have *Brown* followed. Mindful of that, Frankfurter admonished his brethren: "To throw a decision of this Court . . . into the vortex of the present disquietude would . . . seriously . . . embarrass the carrying out of the Court's decree of last May"[22] in *Brown*. On balance, the Court's honor and the future of *Brown* outweighed any claim, however meritorious, raised by Mr. Naim.

As it turned out, Han Say Naim's claim proved problematic; there was a fly in the jurisdictional ointment, or so Felix Frankfurter argued. "So far as I recall," he informed his colleagues, "this is the first time since I've been here that I am confronted with the task of resolving a conflict between moral and technical legal considerations."[23] Conveniently, those purported legal considerations made it impossible for Justice Frankfurter to address those troubling moral considerations head-on. Together with Justice Clark, Frankfurter prepared a *per curiam* opinion urging that the case be remanded to the Virginia courts in light of a factual problem in the record. His colleagues then voted 7-2 in support of the Frankfurter-Clark *per curiam*. Frankfurter was relieved. The Chief Justice and Justice Black were not; they dissented.[24] Though Black was agitated and Warren furious, in the end they withdrew their dissents. By all appearances, then, the Court had unanimously decided not to hear the case. The Virginia judgment was vacated and the matter remanded back to the state courts for "action not inconsistent with this opinion."[25] Thanks to Frankfurter, the Justices had fashioned a "make-weight excuse to avoid dealing with the miscegenation issue so soon after the school segregation cases."[26]

What makes *Naim v. Naim* such a valuable case study in the art of judicial power politics is the fact that, time and again, it constrained the reach of principle while expanding the limits of pragmatism, and this as the pot of opposition boiled. Helpful as learned calculation is in such circumstances, it can only do so much. Thus, for all of Felix Frankfurter's measured moves, he had to confront the specter of bold countermoves. And so it came to pass when the Virginia Supreme Court of Appeals rebuffed the Justices: "The decree of the trial court and the decree of this court affirming it have become final so far as these courts are concerned."[27] The South had risen again. "In effect, the Virginia Supreme Court of Appeals 'nullified' the order of the United States Supreme Court."[28] It made for banner headline material back in the cradle of the Confederacy: "Virginia Rejects Order of U.S. Supreme Court" is how the editors of *Richmond News Leader* titled their story.[29] Chief Justice Warren was livid: "That's what you get when you turn your ass to the grandstand."[30]

What to do next? Should the Nine charge ahead, hear the case, and strike down all miscegenation laws, such as Virginia's Racial Integrity Act? Or should they retreat? Pride suggested the former, prudence the latter. After some back-and-forth in conferences, the Justices split 5-4 not to hear the case.[31] This time it looked like the dissenters would dig in and go public with their displeasure. Still, "[d]espite a strongly worded dissent [that] Warren had his clerk draft, the opinion went out as another *per curiam* decision."[32] Again, the Court appeared unanimous; its words were cast in the cold language of indifferent legalese: "The motion to recall the mandate and to set the case down for oral argument upon the merits, or, in the alternative, to recall and amend the mandate is denied. The decision of the Supreme Court of Appeals of Virginia . . . in response to our order . . . leaves the case devoid of a properly presented federal question."[33]

"Although Warren and Black believed the Court had evaded its responsibility and Warren characterized the *Naim* opinion as 'total bullshit,' another Justice summed up the rest of the Court's view with respect to desegregation and anti-miscegenation: 'One bombshell at a time is enough.'"[34] It is said that those were Felix Frankfurter's words.[35] But they might as well have been those of any Justice who understands the practical limits of judicial power, and who realizes that to preserve power one must sometimes not deploy it. True to that canon, and despite all their heart-wrenching differences and the moral and constitutional imperatives that confronted them, every member of the Warren Court kept stoically silent in both *Jackson v. Alabama* and *Naim v. Naim*. The logic of "dispute-avoidance strategy"[36] had won the day. Moderation had prevailed over intemperance, though not without some real-world consequences in the lives of Linnie Jackson, Han Say Naim, and others like them.[37]

❧

Naim reveals the complex interplay of eugenical ideology, constitutional
    jurisprudence, the internal politics of the Supreme Court, and the
    Supreme Court's relationship to American society.

                             — *Gregory Michael Dorr*[38]

To be sure, the struggle within the Court over *Jackson* and *Naim* was complicated. It pitted the Court's liberals against its moderates and conservatives; it revived the judicial activism versus judicial restraint controversy; it highlighted dicey issues of federalism in a post-*Brown* period; and it presented the Justices with the question of how much deference they should accord to state sovereignty when eugenics were asserted as a legitimate regulatory interest. As important as those concerns were, they played out against the backdrop of the politics of prerogative, namely, the perceived need to proceed with a measure of realist caution. It was, after all, that same prerogative that produced *Brown*'s "with all deliberate speed" mantra, a judicial formula that delayed the demands of principle in the name of pragmatism.

Alexander Bickel was someone who understood the relationship between principle and pragmatism; he recognized the importance of timing; and he knew how to maneuver men around the shoals of perilous endeavors. As a young law clerk to Felix Frankfurter in the Court's 1952–53 term, Bickel prepared a historic memorandum for the Justice urging that *Brown* be reargued. It was an act that changed the course of history. Years later, when Bickel was a law professor at Yale Law School, he offered some opinions concerning the Warren Court's handling of *Naim*. "The Court," he wrote, discounted the "interest of the moving party [and] dismissed outright a case raising the constitutionality of a state anti-miscegenation statute."[39] It did so notwithstanding the fact that "a judgment legitimating such statutes would have been unthinkable given the principle of the *School Segregation Cases* and of the decisions made in their aftermath."[40] Hence, on the merits, Han Say Naim had more than a colorable case. But the merits were not what mattered most; there was prudence. Professor Bickel asked rhetorically:

[W]ould it have been wise, at a time when the Court had just pro-
nounced its new integration principle, when it was subject to scur-
rilous attack by men who predicted that integration of the schools
would lead directly to the "mongrelization of the race" and that
this was the result the Court had really willed, would it have been
wise, just then, in the first case of its sort, on an issue that the
Negro community as a whole can hardly be said to be pressing
hard at the moment, to declare that the states may not prohibit
racial intermarriage?[41]

The very idea of ducking the issue irritated Professor Herbert
Wechsler. The Court's action in *Naim v. Naim* was "wholly without basis
in law."[42] Whether or not true, what difference did that make? None.

Critical comments such as those of Herbert Wechsler may be fine
pedantic academic musings, the kind savored in ivory towers. But they
reveal a disquieting ignorance of the realism of judicial decisionmaking,
one that demonstrates why such counsel should be ignored. Besides, who
but a few pointy-headed intellectuals remembers *Jackson v. Alabama* and
Naim v. Naim? After all, those were the cases that never were.

⨎

Though he was silent in *Jackson* and *Naim*, Chief Justice Warren was
gloriously outspoken in *Loving v. Virginia* (1967),[43] which outlawed anti-
miscegenation laws. The moral: victory belongs to those who seize the
moment only when it is advantageous to do so. That was one lesson Felix
Frankfurter understood well and one that Chief Justice Earl Warren
came to understand better. Though Frankfurter was little blamed or
credited for his strategic roles in *Jackson* and *Naim*, he managed to steer
the Court away from the misfortune that might have found its way to the
Justices' chambers had righteous rashness prevailed.

Chapter 7

Carpe Diem:

When to Embrace a Case

There is a time for everything – a time to wait, a time to strike, a time to retreat. In principle, it is no different in law than it is in war. Julius Caesar's conquest of Gaul in 58 B.C. is a testament to the importance of timing; it was, after all, a move that helped to establish the dominance of Rome over Western civilization. To be effective in any campaign, time and opportunity must mix well. The tactical stars must be aligned. In law that means that a case coming to the Court must match with the desired cause. Of course, that may take time. One must thus be patient and prudent. One has to allow for the unexpected, those instances when the moment seems to ask for the taking but proves to be no more than an illusion.

Sometimes mistakes are made in the rush to hear cases presented to the Justices by cert.-pool memos fed to them by novice law clerks. For example, a "great" First Amendment case like *Nike v. Kasky*[1] can implode due to some unforeseen procedural problem. Or a "great" affirmative action case can vanish into oblivion because of a mootness problem like the one in *DeFunis v. Odegaard*.[2] Or a "great" harmless error case, such as *Vasquez v. United States*,[3] can evaporate if oral arguments prove it to be the wrong vehicle for the issue before the Court.[4] With the 10,000 or so petitions presented to the nine Justices every year, it is amazing that they have the time to do much of anything. Consequently, it is easy to become careless and overlook things. In other words, there are certain cases that are tempting to embrace but which should not be heard owing to some legal defect.

Obergefell v. Hodges[5] was the right case at the right time. It is the landmark case that was decades in the making. It is not a case that would have been ripe for victory in the Warren, Burger, or Rehnquist Court eras. The cause of gay rights wed to the idea of marriage was one that required a union of cultural progress and legal timing. While armchair generals battled over the niceties of the best legal theories to recognize same-sex marriage rights, more savvy minds waited for the perfect moment when the time was right, the facts were right, and the votes in the Court were right. In many ways, the *how* of the legal equation was less important than the *when*. That "when" moment came in *Obergefell*, and when it did, seizing it was far more important than deciding how to justify the reasoning of the result. In cases like *Obergefell*, the public will judge a Justice more by the result obtained than by the legal logic employed to get there. Justice Anthony Kennedy realized that; Chief Justice John Roberts did not. The former seized a great opportunity whereas the latter forfeited one.

◈

For almost a half century before *Obergefell* was decided, the Supreme Court struggled with constitutional issues of gay rights and/or same-sex marriage – from *Baker v. Nelson*[6] in 1972 to *United States v. Windsor*[7] and *Hollingsworth v. Perry*[8] in 2013.[9] Against that backdrop *Obergefell v. Hodges*[10] was a timely and sweeping challenge. Fourteen homosexual couples (and two gay men whose partners had died) brought federal court actions in four States to challenge same-sex marriage bans as violative of federal Due Process and Equal Protection rights. Not since *Baker*'s perfunctory ruling had the Supreme Court agreed to review such marriage claims by petitioners with standing to raise them. In the intervening 43 years, however, the political landscape and social environment had changed dramatically.

By January 16, 2015 – the day that the Court announced its grant of certiorari in the *Obergefell* case – 36 States and the District of Columbia had already validated and recognized same-sex marriages.[11] In effect, more than 70 percent of Americans lived in areas where gay couples could marry.[12] And whereas in 1996 public opinion polls indicated that only 27 percent of the nation favored the legalization of gay marriage, by the time of *Obergefell* that approval number had risen to well above 50 percent.[13] The pendulum had swung, the time was ripe, and now Anthony Kennedy had the right controversy before him; he only needed to grasp the jurisprudential prize to ensure his lofty place in gay rights history.

On June 26, 2015, the Supreme Court released *Obergefell v. Hodges*. An expectant nation read the moving words penned by Justice Kennedy and joined by his four liberal colleagues, Justices Ginsburg, Breyer, Sotomayor, and Kagan. "The history of marriage is one of both continuity and change," Kennedy explained. "Changed understandings of marriage are characteristic of a Nation where new dimensions of freedom become apparent to new generations."[14] Charting the evolving constitutional course of gay and lesbian rights, Kennedy argued that "the basic reasons why the right to marry has been long protected"[15] compelled the conclusion that same-sex couples should be entitled to that right. Accordingly, both the Due Process and Equal Protection guarantees of the Fourteenth Amendment required states to grant same-sex couples the rights of civil marriage on the same terms as opposite-sex couples and to recognize the validity of same-sex marriages performed in other states. Before concluding, Kennedy firmly addressed the dissenting argument that the Court is not a legislature: "While the Constitution contemplates that democracy is the appropriate process for change, individuals who are harmed need not await legislative action before asserting a fundamental right."[16] Finally, Anthony Kennedy waxed poetic: "No union is more profound than marriage, for it embodies the highest ideals of love, fidelity, devotion, sacrifice, and family. . . . It would misunderstand these men and women to say they disrespect the idea of marriage. . . . They ask for equal dignity in the eyes of the law. The Constitution grants them that right."[17]

It was a proud moment for Justice Kennedy. The editorial board of *The New York Times* praised his handiwork as "a profound and inspiring opinion expanding human rights across America." The editorial concluded: "Justice Kennedy's opinion will affect the course of American history, and it will change lives starting now."[18] President Barack Obama praised the ruling as "a 'thunderbolt' of justice."[19] And even more tempered commentators recognized the obvious: "Over time, voters have a say in the kind of justice the court dispenses. The odds are good that most of them will think the court got this one right."[20] All considered, Anthony Kennedy could count on that as he seized the day.

∽

Justice Kennedy has been said to be a fox; other times he prefers to be a hedgehog.[21] Isaiah Berlin's philosophical pitches aside,[22] there is truth here, or at least there is warrant to so believe. Unlike the late Justice Antonin Scalia, Justice Kennedy is not formulaic; he is fluid. And unlike Scalia, he is not combative; he prefers compromise. Some portray him as "heavy on rhetoric and light on legal reasoning,"[23] and yet others depict him as Hamlet-like in his occasional indecision. Moreover, in "certain circles it has become a sign of sophistication to speak of Justice . . . Kennedy with a knowing condescension."[24] Say of him what you will, criticize him or mock him, but do not underestimate him. His successes in *Romer v. Evans,*[25] *Lawrence v. Texas,*[26] *United States v. Windsor,*[27] and *Obergefell* have revolutionized constitutional law and our culture itself. Of course, *Obergefell* marks the high point in his constitutional calculations. One might even say that time was on his side . . . but there was more.

Fortuna opened a door for Anthony Kennedy. The timing of *Obergefell* assured him not only the result he wanted, but also provided him with another opportunity to fortify his Dignity Principle. To that end, he was able to:

1. Destabilize *Washington v. Glucksberg's*[28] command that any Due Process liberty interest must be "deeply rooted in the nation's history,"[29] a norm that would have defeated the right protected in *Obergefell;*
2. Enhance the jurisprudential connection between Equal Protection and Due Process in the service of a Dignity Principle (and thereby help to revive "the work that the Privileges and Immunities Clauses was originally designed to do");[30]

3. Solidify the notion that the harm suffered by a particular group "need not have been *deliberately* designed to harm the excluded group if its oppressive and unjustified effects have become clear in light of current experience and understanding;"[31]

4. Align the Dignity Principle with the State Sovereignty Principle so as to define the latter "less as an end in itself than as a means to the end of protecting the liberties of those who reside in those states – both their *negative* liberties from oppressive regulation and their *positive* liberties to take part in politically accountable self-government;"[32] and

5. Reinforce the notion that it is permissible (even desirable) not to rely on any single clause of the Bill of Rights but to invoke instead "the broader postulates of our constitutional order." [33]

Seen in that light, "*Obergefell* is an important landmark,"[34] one that helps to legitimize intra-textual decision-making even in the absence of any explicit textual declaration of a constitutional right. Hence, it might be said that Kennedy ushered in a new day in constitutional law, and thereby began a constitutional and cultural dialogue that could last for decades.[35] Furthermore, the *Obergefell* opinion lends itself to international human rights attention,[36] a readily exportable model of justice.

৶

Chief Justice John Roberts is an honorable man. He cares deeply about public respect for the Supreme Court. Such qualities were on admirable display in his majority opinion in *Hollingsworth v. Perry*. He began by declaring: "The public is currently engaged in an active political debate over whether same-sex couples should be allowed to marry."[37] After a learned discussion of the principle of law at stake in the case, he succinctly framed the holding: "We have never before upheld the standing of a private party to defend the constitutionality of a state statute when state officials have chosen not to. We decline to do so for the first time here."[38] The result: The federal district court judgment in favor of the Petitioners was sustained, meaning that same-sex marriage was legal in California. Soon thereafter, Kristin Perry and Sandra Stier, the original plaintiffs in the case, married; California's Attorney General Kamala Harris offici-ated at the ceremony. That was followed by the couple's appearance in a San Francisco Pride Parade – there they joyously rode atop the back seat of a convertible waving to an exuberant crowd. What a glorious day! And to think that John Roberts – the Law's gatekeeper – made it all possible.

What Chief Justice Roberts did in *Hollingsworth* was also the smart move, the tactical move, and the move that was at once conservative and liberal. Unlike the dissenters – Justices Anthony Kennedy, Samuel Alito, Clarence Thomas and Sonia Sotomayor – Roberts was in no rush to judgment if it meant liberalizing the law of standing. The idea that third-party busybodies might assert Article III standing when the State declined to intervene was nothing short of bizarre. To follow the exam-ple of the dissenters would pave the path of liberalized access to the fed-eral courts – something staunch conservatives abhorred. Furthermore, the *Hollingsworth* ruling left "in place laws banning same-sex marriage around the nation, and the court declined to say whether there was a constitutional right to such unions."[39] The *Hollingsworth* opinion, how-ever, also had its progressive side, as Justices Ruth Bader Ginsburg, Stephen Breyer and Elena Kagan (all liberals) surely understood when they joined the Chief Justice's opinion. After all, it not only culminated in the recognition of same-sex marriage in California, but further inten-sified the favorable momentum for same-sex marriage generally.

Whatever else, *Hollingsworth v. Perry* was not a case to be embraced on the merits. For all the reasons given, John Roberts's maneuvers there were brilliant. It was a perfect moment and he seized it. Given that, why in the world did he dissent in *Obergefell*? The savvy he displayed in *Hollingsworth* was greatly undermined by the imprudence he displayed in *Obergefell*. The former was a shrewd move, the latter a misguided one.

Let us be blunt: John Roberts made a disastrous mistake when he dis-sented in *Obergefell*. Never mind that the majority opinion was ill-reasoned or that it revived an "old discredited judicial tradition of writing a judge's own social perspectives into the Constitution."[40] Never mind how Roberts so judiciously parsed the real question in the case, or how convincingly he spoke of the workings of law in a truly democratic society. And never mind that the Chief Justice, unlike the savage Scalia, was temperate and even gentle in his dissent: "Many people will rejoice at this decision," he wrote with great compassion, "and I begrudge none of their celebration."[41] The only thing that really counted was how he voted – and his vote cut against the grain of a social justice movement too great to derail.

John Roberts was on the wrong side of history. It is that simple. Nothing else mattered. Anthony Kennedy successfully seized a transcendent moment. He outmaneuvered the Chief Justice, and in the process buttressed his own power and secured a coveted place for himself in the annals of liberty.

Like Roger Taney in *Dred Scott v. Sandford*[42] and Byron White in *Bowers v. Hardwick*[43], Roberts swam against the tide of EQUALITY. He looked back in history, to "Kalahari bushmen"[44] and their notions of marriage, when he should have looked forward in time. Two years earlier, he had tempted fate when he wrote for a slim majority of the Court in a ruling[45] diminishing the value of the Voting Rights Act. After *Obergefell* that fate was largely sealed: John Roberts was the man who stood as an obstacle in the doorway of Equality.

Once *Obergefell* came down, "there were wild scenes of celebrations on the sidewalk outside the Supreme Court."[46] Cameras captured the moments for history as the nightly newscasts spread the triumphant word. Though it was a momentous day in America, the Chief Justice left his chambers and drove home a defeated man. His flaw: He stood so high on "principle" that his fall from future fame would be all the harder. This is especially ironic since John Roberts, extraordinary as his skills could be, should have known better. In all likelihood, time will not forgive him – nor should it.

෯

Power and glory sometimes wait for one to embrace them. It is all a matter of timing. And when the time is ripe, one has to do little more than pick the fruits of fame. That is the lesson of *Obergefell v. Hodges*. It is one that Anthony Kennedy knew well and executed admirably. By stark contrast, John Roberts learned that lesson in *Hollingsworth* but then forgot it in *Obergefell*. He placed an idealized principle above realist reasoning, and in the process lost sight of what was in his own best interest. Call it principled folly.

Chapter 8

Tactical Tools

Using Procedure to One's Advantage

Generalizations about the law of standing are largely worthless.

-- William O. Douglas[1]

[Standing is] a word game played by secret rules.

-- John Harlan, II[2]

If ever there were a legal doctrine ripe for robbing, ready for manipulation, and supremely right for partisan purposes, it is the law of standing. Depending on the day, it is a fixed or flexible rule. Depending on the makeup of the Court, it is a principle to be honored or breached. And depending on the Justice and the case, it is one of those canons of law that can be dispensed with at one's will.

The liberal Warren Court expanded the law of standing[3]; the more centrist Burger Court tightened the doctrine in some areas[4] but not in others[5]; the conservative Rehnquist Court reined it in[6]; and the equally conservative Roberts Court sometimes further cabined the rule.[7] Let us therefore call this accordion-like brand of decision-making for what it is: partisan brinkmanship. Never mind the rules and rationales – if one wishes to hear a case or not, there will always be enough decisional leeway to secure the outcome. Hence, a Machiavellian Justice must understand how best to use this tactical tool. After all, what is procedure if not another way to secure one's advantage? By that measure, procedure is a path to power.

As judges proclaim, lawyers argue, and law students learn, the doctrine of standing serves various weighty and honorable purposes:

- It ensures that courts decide only real and concrete controversies rather than feigned or hypothetical lawsuits.
- It certifies that judicial decisions will further only the rights of truly interested parties and not the ideological concerns of bystanders.
- It reinforces separation of powers principles and promotes judicial self-restraint by preventing the judiciary from intervening in policymaking arenas better suited to the politically accountable branches of government.[8]

This is all well and fine, provided one never takes those arguments too seriously so as to limit his or her judicial power. While such purposes might be hailed rhetorically when it is beneficial to do so, the extraordinary Judge must be prepared to abandon them, surreptitiously if necessary, when they run counter to his or her greater interests. And this is easily done, since the devil is always in the details, and the law of standing is renowned for its multi-variant, self-serving, and always detailed distinctions.

The splendor of standing is that any partisan can profit from its malleability. *Massachusetts v. Environmental Protection Agency*[9] is an outstanding example of a liberal majority's successful efforts to further its ideological agenda by enlarging procedural boundaries. When the EPA refused to regulate automobile emissions as "greenhouse gases" under the Clean Air Act, Massachusetts sued the agency. To establish standing, the State argued that the EPA's decision contributed to global warming, which elevated ocean levels and, in turn, worsened the erosion of the State's coastal lands.

An ideologically divided 5-4 Court held that Massachusetts had sufficiently satisfied the standing doctrine's causality and redressability requirements, even though it was apparent that EPA's regulation of automobile emissions alone would not prevent global warming. Writing for the Court, Justice John Paul Stevens reasoned: "The risk of catastrophic harm, though remote, is nevertheless real. That risk would be reduced to some extent if [Massachusetts] received the relief [it seeks.]"[10] Moreover, Stevens justified the loosened causality analysis by arguing that, as a sovereign State, Massachusetts was "entitled to special solicitude"[11] under the standing doctrine.

The Court's capacious interpretation of standing requirements provoked a stinging dissent by Chief Justice Roberts, joined by Justices Scalia, Thomas, and Alito. "Relaxing Article III standing requirements because asserted injuries are pressed by a State," the Chief Justice contended, "has no basis in our jurisprudence."[12] Not only did the Court's precedents fail to "provide any support for the notion that Article III somehow implicitly treats public and private litigants differently,"[13] Roberts claimed, but "our cases cast significant doubt on a State's standing to assert a quasi-sovereign interest . . . against the Federal Government."[14] All such talk of "special solicitude" for Massachusetts was taken by the dissenters as "an implicit concession" that the State could not prove standing "on traditional terms."[15]

Given that, the Chief Justice and his colleagues argued vociferously against the liberal manipulation of standing rules. "Global warming is a phenomenon 'harmful to humanity at large,'" he reasoned, "and the redress petitioners seek is focused no more on them than on the public generally – it is literally to change the atmosphere around the world."[16] Not only was personal injury-in-fact speculative, but the same was true of the majority's treatment of the causation and redressability requirements. With proverbial flourish, the Chief Justice concluded: "Schoolchildren know that a kingdom might be lost 'all for the want of a horseshoe nail,'" but "realities make it pure conjecture to suppose that EPA regulation of new automobile emissions will *likely* prevent the loss of Massachusetts coastal land."[17]

Stare decisis may have been on the dissenters' side; doctrinal rules may have supported their arguments; and logic may have favored their conclusions. All of that was irrelevant. The liberal majority had the necessary five votes supported by facile distinctions. Justice Stevens and his colleagues understood how the standing game is played, and they did so with aplomb.

ॡ

The standing doctrine, of course, is often the darling of conservatives. Consider, for example, *Flast v. Cohen*,[18] a liberal Warren Court ruling that allowed any federal taxpayer to claim standing to challenge congressional appropriations to private religious schools. But its days were limited. *Valley Forge Christian College v. Americans United*[19] allowed conservatives to confine *Flast* to its particular facts. The Burger Court conservatives were constitutionally comfortable with the federal government's transfer of its property to a private religious institution. They reached into their procedural tool bag and pulled out a standing argument, one resting on a slender analyticaldistinction from *Flast*. Little wonder that in this 5-4 case, Justice William Brennan, writing in dissent, was outraged: "there is an impulse to decide difficult questions of substantive law obliquely in the course of opinions purporting to do nothing more than determine what the Court labels 'standing'; this accounts for the phenomenon of opinions, such as the one today, that tend merely to obfuscate, rather than inform, our understanding of the meaning of rights under law."[20]

Brennan was clearly correct, but so what? His ideological adversaries trumped their liberal colleagues by way of the standing card. And they did it again years later in *Arizona v. Christian School Tuition Organization v. Winn*,[21] another 5-4 ruling in which a revised and yet more nuanced standing argument was invoked to lower the First Amendment wall of separation between church and state. The result, lamented Justice Elena Kagan in dissent, was to "diminish the Establishment Clause's force and meaning."[22] Precisely. And that was the point.

As these and many other such cases reveal, the law of standing can be tapped in ways that allow procedure to triumph over substance. And that tends to be something suited to the partisan preferences of conservatives. By the same Machiavellian token, when the doctrine is expanded, it suits the partisan preferences of liberals in shaping ever more social policy.

Chapter 9

Oral Arguments

What to Say and How

*[T]he secret to successful advocacy is simply to get
the Court to ask your opponent more questions. . . .
[O]ral argument is the first time you begin to get a sense of what
your colleagues think of the case through their questions. . . .
Oral argument matters, but not just because of what the lawyers
have to say. It is the organizing point for the entire judicial process.*
— John G. Roberts, Jr. (2005)[1]

There was a time – long before truncated Court proceedings, computerized law, amicus briefs, and bevies of law clerks – when oral arguments in the Supreme Court really mattered. Daniel Webster's fame and success, after all, hinged on them. This was evidenced by his stellar four-hour performance in *Dartmouth College v. Woodward* (1819).[2] "Contemporaries reported that many in the room were in tears. [Even the cerebral] Chief Justice John Marshall himself was moved, and Webster won a decision in favor of the college."[3] Back then oral arguments went on for days; now each side typically has thirty minutes. Back then the Justices were far more dependent on what lawyers said in the course of their arguments. Today, the Justices are far more informed, often more so than some of the seasoned appellate lawyers who argue before them. What value, then, do oral arguments have in a modern setting? More to the point, how might such arguments help the cause of a Justice?

It is said that oral arguments seldom determine a case's outcome.[4] Whether true or not, they can help tease out an argument, test the soundness of a claim, reveal some blind spot in a contention, or help "focus the minds of the Justices and present the possibility for fresh perspectives on a case."[5] Additionally, a "good oralist," Justice Blackmun once noted, "can add a lot to a case and help us in our later analysis of what the case is all about. Many times confusion [in the brief] is clarified by what the lawyers have to say."[6] Sometimes, an insightful question is one that raises an important issue not covered in the parties' briefs. Hence, some questions benefit a Justice for informational purposes, other times for ideological purposes, or tactical purposes, or various other motivational purposes.[7] And oral arguments provide an arena for the egos of the Justices; they permit a Justice to show off for the press and public.[8]

Beyond providing a venue for obtaining information and a platform for hearing oneself speak, what good are oral arguments to a Justice hoping to mine some personal advantage? To that end, what helps and what does not? What questions are best to ask and why? Which ones should be avoided and why? Is it better to be Antonin Scalia-like and pepper counsel with many, often combative, questions? Or Elena Kagan-like and be polite and probative? Or Felix Frankfurter-like and be erudite? Or Hugo Black-like and be persistent though soft spoken? Or courteous like John Paul Stevens? Or perhaps dramatic like Anthony Kennedy? Or first-out-of-the-gate and rapid-fire like Sandra Day O'Connor? Or caustic like Samuel Alito? Or Clarence Thomas-like and remain virtually silent?

The answer to such questions varies with the context, the audience, and the particular objectives a Justice has in mind. Given these criteria, sometimes it may be best to be Thomas-like and remain silent for strategic reasons, whereas at other times it may be wise to be probative like Justice Kagan for informational reasons. Contextually speaking, there is another matter to consider – the relative skill of the lawyer arguing before the Court. Moreover, there are other factors that weigh heavily on the result in a case, things such as a Justice's "ideological orientations, strategic considerations resulting in intracourt bargaining over opinion drafts, legal norms, contextual factors such as workload, and case characteristics."[9]

All that said, a few lessons might be discerned from what some of the Justices have said and what they have not said. Moreover, there are examples of what should be avoided, if only because such actions may prove counterproductive.

✌

Justice William Brennan was a renowned jurist who had a significant impact on American law. He was savvy when it came to judicial strategies. Yet his record in oral arguments is somewhat difficult to evaluate. For example, in four days of legal argument in *Miranda v. Arizona*[10] (the famous Fifth Amendment "right to remain silent" case) and its companion cases, Justice Brennan spoke only once. In *Roth v. United States*[11] (the landmark obscenity case) and in *Texas v. Johnson*[12] (the flag-burning case), he asked no questions. By contrast, in two days of oral arguments in *New York Times Co. v. Sullivan*[13] (the seminal First Amendment case that reconfigured defamation law), Brennan spoke 71 times, and in four days of oral arguments in *Baker v. Carr*[14] (the well-known reapportionment case) he spoke 114 times. Finally, in *Mapp v. Ohio*[15] (the noted Fourth Amendment exclusionary rule case), he spoke 24 times. In all of those cases, Brennan voted with the majority; and save for *Miranda* and *Mapp*, he wrote for the Court, either by way of a majority or plurality opinion.

This sampling suggests that neither the importance of a case nor its ultimate authorship was determinative when it came to Brennan's questioning during oral arguments.[16] So how are we to think about all this? One answer is to consider it from Chief Justice Roberts's perspective highlighted above: Ask many critical questions in the hope of putting the lawyers arguing an unfavorable position (from the perspective of a jurist) on the defensive. That may help to explain Brennan's active engagement in the *Sullivan, Baker,* and *Mapp* oral arguments. But sometimes it is best to keep silent and be Clarence-Thomas like. That may have been Brennan's strategy in the *Roth* and *Johnson* arguments. Likewise, it may explain Roberts's virtual silence[17] in *King v. Burwell,*[18] the controversial Patient Protection and Affordable Care Act case in which the Chief Justice wrote the majority opinion.

Oral arguments sometimes provide a Justice with an opportunity to get a clearer idea of how his or her colleagues may analyze a case. That can be helpful when it comes to the Court's conference afterwards. Here the tactic is to sit, listen, take notes and begin to develop ideas. This silent or largely silent posture may also help conceal one's own approach to deciding a case, which may be useful at the time when opinions are assigned. Another commonplace practice is to demonstrate "an even-handed effort to probe the strengths and weaknesses of each party's case, and any appearances to the contrary result from Justices' playing devil's advocate."[19] Here, too, the impression is that one is hiding the ball not only from the lawyers and press, but also from one's colleagues. Justice Anthony Kennedy is a regular practitioner of this style of oral argument. Sometimes he surprises, but as often as not he proves predictable despite his conflicted posturing.

Whether one is active or passive, aggressive or measured, the idea is to obtain the information one needs and to stack the conceptual deck before the Court's Conference. While that is nowhere as easy as it sounds, there are instances when what a Justice says in open Court can be a game changer. Consider, for example, the oral arguments in *United States v. Jones*,[20] a Fourth Amendment GPS tracking device case. During an exchange between Chief Justice Roberts and Deputy Solicitor General Michael Dreeben, a telling point was made by way of a simple question:

> *Chief Justice Roberts* : "You think there would . . . not be a search if you put a GPS device on all of our cars, monitored our movements for a month? You think you're entitled to do that under your theory?"
>
> *Mr. Dreeben* : "The Justices of this Court?"
>
> *Chief Justice* ROBERTS : "Yes." [Laughter]
>
> *Mr. Dreeben* : "Under our theory and under this Court's cases, the Justices of this Court when driving on public roadways have no greater expectation . . ."
>
> *Chief Justice Roberts* : "So your answer is yes, you could tomorrow decide [to] put a GPS device on every one of our cars, follow us for a month . . . ."[21]

When the *Jones* decision was released, the judgment was 9-0 against the government. "The Supreme Court," wrote Adam Liptak of the *New York Times*, "ruled unanimously that the police violated the Constitution when they placed a Global Positioning System tracking device on a suspect's car and monitored its movements for 28 days."[22] Whether the government might have lost in any event does not refute an obvious point: After Mr. Dreeben's reply to the Chief Justice's cunning question, the government's case hung by the thinnest of threads.[23]

∽

Justice Breyer . . . is the Talmudic scholar of hypotheticals.

– Art Lien[24]

Breyer is the Court's most frequent practitioner of the hypothetical question, a conjurer of images that are unusual and occasionally bizarre.

– Mark Sherman[25]

While it may be difficult to discern exactly which questions to raise and when, there are, nonetheless, certain examples of when not to do so, or when doing so can only be justified in the name of ineffective vanity. Perhaps one of the best examples, but by no means the only one, is how Justice Stephen Breyer (a congenial jurist) often conducts himself during oral arguments. For whatever reasons, Justice Breyer (a former Harvard Law professor) seems not have grasped an important fact: a courtroom is not a classroom. While his dizzying displays of Socratic talent may be well suited for teaching purposes, they can be quite counterproductive for purposes of oral arguments in the Supreme Court. At best, they serve no purpose; at worst, they tire and tax one's colleagues to one's disadvantage.

In July of 1994, then-Judge Breyer testified before the Senate Committee on the Judiciary in connection with his nomination to the

Supreme Court. In answering a question posed by Senator Howard Metzenbaum, Judge Breyer could not resist the temptation to spin a hypothetical:

> Let's say—and I will use a hypothetical, I don't like to use that here, because I know this isn't a classroom and I know these are serious matters and I don't like to be professorial, frankly, but I think in this instance, maybe thinking of, say, they turn this wheel around and they charged 8 cents for the electricity, and that might help. They then transmit it across a wire. They then sell it to themselves, because they are in the retail operation, too. And they sold it, let us say, for 10 cents. So they make it for 8 cents and they sell it to themselves for 10 cents, and the price to the consumer is 10 cents. Now, the plaintiff in this case came along and said, you see, 8 cents is what we have to pay for it, because they sold a little bit to independent retailers, too, and that plaintiff was an independent retailer. And that independent retailer . . . . [26]

Justice Breyer's hypothetically-speaking mindset often informs his manner at the Court. "Justice Breyer," Lyle Denniston has rightly observed, "occasionally runs the hypothetical too far out, and it becomes as complex as the underlying legal concept he is trying to make intelligible."[27] As Court watchers well know, the hypothetical (typically long and complicated) is Breyer's signature move. Of course, other examples might have been selected (say, Breyer's hypotheticals in *McCutcheon v. FEC*[28]), but that is an assignment for a more extended discussion. For now, it is enough to note that, more than anything else, such posturing draws unwelcome attention to oneself rather than being of any use to one's colleagues or to the practicing bar.[29]

૭

However else a skilled Justice might conduct himself during oral arguments, in the most important cases one utopian ideal must be forsaken: the idea of coming to the arguments with an open mind and engaging in a forthright and principled way in the hope of first discovering and then honoring the rule of law. While it may make for an inspiring Law Day speech – the kind that our extraordinary Justice would publicly deliver but secretly despise – it does not help advance one's cause. To that end, we offer the following advice.

The modern practice is for a Justice to come "prepared" to oral arguments with a bench memo composed by his or her law clerks. While convenient, such "preparation" will not usually serve a Justice of more than average skill very well. William Rehnquist knew that, and thus did not rely on clerk-prepared "Cliff Notes."[30] Such counsel is especially important for complex or controversial cases.

Additionally, a zinger question can be most important, particularly if a Justice's colleagues are open-minded or somewhat so. Moreover, as in *Mapp v. Ohio*, a Justice can lure counsel into conceding what may prove to be an important point.[31] In response to the right questions, a lawyer may also agree to narrow a point or confine the relief sought to a specified type of remedy.[32] A well-placed question can solicit an important response relating to any possible legal or policy impediments to the desired result in a case. All such questions, when tactically and tactfully raised, can prove most useful to a clever Justice. On the whole, it is better for a Justice to appear disinterested, probative, and open-minded than talkative and combative. In that regard, to be Scalia-like may make for stimulating theater but one risks alienating Justices like Blackmun and Kennedy[33] – jurists who sometimes provided a vital fifth vote.

Speaking less can be important for any variety of strategic reasons already mentioned. An additional benefit is that when a relatively silent Justice speaks, his colleagues, the press, and the public are more likely to notice and pay attention. Recall Justice Clarence Thomas's remarks in *Virginia v. Black*,[34] a racial intimidation case involving a cross-burning in an African American's yard. In that context, Justice Thomas was not timid: "Now, it's my understanding that we had almost 100 years of lynching and activity in the South by the Knights of Camellia . . . and the Ku Klux Klan, and this was a reign of terror and the cross was a symbol of that reign of terror. [I]sn't that significantly greater than intimidation or a threat."[35] That statement may well have helped to shape the 7-2 outcome in that case, which rejected the First Amendment defense.

During oral arguments, questioning by analogy may prove quite beneficial. For instance, consider Justice Felix Frankfurter's question to John W. Davis (counsel for Appellees) in the *Brown v. Board of Education* case. "Mr. Davis," asked Frankfurter, "do you think that 'equal' is a less fluid term that 'commerce between the states'?"[36] Essentially, Frankfurter was suggesting that "equality of the laws" might be no less elastic than the open-ended commerce clause. Such questions have the potential to turn a case further in one's desired direction. Avoid spinning Breyer-like hypotheticals. They are a waste of time and opportunity. And don't show one's hand like Warren Burger did in *Cohen v. California*[37] – the "fuck the draft" First Amendment case – when the overly priggish Chief Justice asked counsel to omit a statement of the facts.[38] The counsel ignored the admonition.[39] When the case came down with a 5-4 vote, Burger was on the losing side. During oral arguments, he traded in prudery rather than in the kind of clever argument that might have influenced one or more Justices to vote with him.

There will occasions, although few, where it might be advantageous to "play to the crowd," as it were. It should be done to draw favorable attention to a Justice only in situations where he or she stands to win public favor. To be effective, such maneuvers should appear impromptu, even though much forethought ought to have been given.

Finally, remember: Oral arguments are the only time when one's moves are openly visible to the press and public. Take heed.

Chapter 10

When to Lose a Case and Win a Cause

The name William J. Brennan is synonymous with First Amendment liberty. A roll call of his opinions for the Court safeguarding rights of speech, press, and association includes such blockbusters as *NAACP v. Button* (1963),[1] *New York Times Co. v. Sullivan* (1964),[2] *Dombrowski v. Pfister* (1965),[3]*Nebraska Press Association v. Stuart* (1976),[4] *Carey v. Brown* (1980),[5] and *Texas v. Johnson* (1989).[6] Not only the substance but also the style of his writing became a classic part of First Amendment vernacular. *Sullivan,* "perhaps the most important free speech opinion ever written,"[7] inaugurated "the principle that debate on public issues should be uninhibited, robust, and wide open."[8] And *Dombrowski,* describing the dangers of overbroad regulations of expression, coined the phrase "chilling effect." By the time that he retired, Brennan had participated in 252 free speech cases, and according to Professor Geoffrey Stone's count, the Justice had "accepted the free speech claim" in 221 cases (88%), whereas the Court's majority did so in only 148.[9] It is no exaggeration, then, to contend that, in the realm of America's first freedoms, William Brennan was a giant.

But in one case – one very famous case – the Justice authored a majority opinion that *rejected* a First Amendment claim, and this over the forceful dissent of his fellow liberal colleagues. He upheld a criminal conviction and endorsed the state's power to enforce public notions of propriety and decency. His signature insistence on constitutional tolerance for social dissent and counter-cultural expression was nowhere on uninhibited display in that decision.

Why would he forfeit his free speech credentials in this scenario? Why would he align himself with the Court's more prudish conservative bloc? The answer: An astute Justice would realize that sometimes it is necessary to take one step backward in order eventually to advance several steps forward. After all, to paraphrase a venerated Machiavellian lesson, a wise ruler ought never keep faith when, by doing so, it would disserve his short-run or long-run interests.[10] As with princes, even so with judges.

∽

> *State and federal governments should be able*
> *to protect themselves against depravity.*
>
> *– Earl Warren (1957)[11]*

Prior to 1957, the Supreme Court understood the First Amendment to grant protection to speech that possessed social value, but to deny all protection to less valued speech. Among the unprotected categories was sexually explicit expression. In the seminal case of *Chaplinsky v. New Hampshire* (1942),[12] obscenity and lewdness were listed along with profanity, libel, and fighting words as unprotected forms of speech because "such expressions are no essential part of any exposition of ideas, and are of such slight social value as a step to truth that any benefit that may be derived from them is certainly outweighed by the social interest in order and morality."[13] *Chaplinsky's* rationale reigned without opposition in the obscenity domain for the next 15 years, even though the post-World War II industry of pornographic literature and imagery increasingly defied traditional sexual mores.

In 1957, however, the Supreme Court agreed to hear a First Amendment challenge[14] to the federal government's suppression of obscenity in the case of *Roth v. United States*.[15] Sam Roth, a New York publisher of risqué literature, was convicted, sentenced to five years in prison, and fined $5,000 for having sent an "obscene, lewd, lascivious, and filthy"[16] publication called *American Aphrodite* through the U.S. mails. On appeal, Roth stipulated to having violated the federal obscenity law, but argued that the statute abridged his First Amendment liberties of speech and press.

It was a mere 32 days after he was confirmed by the Senate when William Brennan took his seat on the Supreme Court to hear oral arguments in case no. 582, *Roth v. United States*. He was the junior player sitting alongside constitutional titans – William O. Douglas, Hugo Black, John Harlan, Earl Warren, and Brennan's former Harvard Law School professor, Felix Frankfurter. The Court chamber where the oral arguments took place was a monumental paean to the law's grandeur – a dignified chamber that was the antithesis of "smut" of the kind traded in by the Petitioner.

Under the majestic 44-foot ceiling supported by 24 columns of Italian marble, the constitutional dialogue began. As it did, Justices Tom Clark and William O. Douglas quietly distributed pornographic materials to their colleagues on the bench, out of the sight of those in the Court gallery, of course.[17] Prior to oral arguments, the Justice Department had shipped those materials under seal to the Court to demonstrate the kind of filth that would be legitimized if the Justices reversed Sam Roth's conviction for advertising and selling obscenity. In the very elevated quarters where decorum and propriety were the rule, some of the Justices eyed "stroke" mags as they listened to the nuances of American procedural and constitutional law. The very presence of such "filth" in this chamber must have disgusted the Chief Justice and several of his brethren.

Justice Felix Frankfurter was a pretentious jurist who wore his Harvard credentials on his lapel. He dominated the dialogue. The constitutionally conservative Justice peppered the parties with procedural, evidentiary, and jurisdictional questions. With professorial fervor, he tried repeatedly to pin Roth's counsel down to exactly what his position was on the legal status of obscene materials. The more he asked, the worse it got. Exasperated, the Justice said: "You can't just swim in the midst of the Pacific Ocean in these matters. You've got to get some footing on some . . . *terra firma*."[18]

Throughout the oral arguments on *Roth*, the timid Brennan spoke not at all. When all was said and done, what had been highly technical oral arguments about the point at which a sexualized expression crossed the constitutional line from protected to unprotected speech made it easy for the audience to drift off and stare at the sculpted marble panels surrounding the chamber. Though the outcome of the case seemed sure enough, no one could have predicted the landmark status it would later attain.

Bad facts make for bad law. And that maxim was busily at work during the Court's conference in *Roth*. Save for the First Amendment absolutists (the Douglas and Black duo) and Justice Harlan, no one else defended Sam Roth. One after another, Justices lined up against him: Earl Warren, Tom Clark, Harold Burton, and Charles Whittaker. And then there was Felix Frankfurter, who pushed hard to defend the Court's earlier anti-free speech precedents and place obscenity beyond the First Amendment's pale.[19] In an internal memorandum, he stressed: "The more I thought about this case the clearer it became that it should be decided on a narrow ground on which the whole Court, such is my strong hope, can agree."[20] By stark contrast, Brennan had earlier stated a contrary view when it came to the Court's handling of sexual expression cases: He thought "this should have the *full dress treatment*."[21] How, then, to reconcile these warring positions?

For whatever reasons, the Chief Justice assigned *Roth* to Justice Brennan, who was on board as to the result in the case: Sam Roth's conviction for mailing obscene circulars and advertising an obscene book was affirmed. But Brennan's opinion was far more sophisticated than suggested by the 6-3 ruling. His opinion for the Court read like a tribute to the Roman god Janus, the great gatekeeper with two faces gazing in opposite directions. There was the conservative face – the one that would please censors and frighten libertarians. "[T]his Court has always assumed," Brennan declared," that obscenity is not protected by the freedoms of speech and press."[22] In a passage that surely must have pleased Warren and Frankfurter, among others, Brennan added: "[I]mplicit in the history of the First Amendment is the rejection of obscenity as utterly without socially redeeming importance."[23] Better still, there was a blow to those who used blue vernacular. Justice Brennan repeated in full the *Chaplinsky* dictate that governmental prevention of "the lewd and obscene" had never been thought to pose constitutional problems because "such utterances are no essential part of the exposition of ideas, and are of such slight social value as a step to truth that any benefit that may be derived from them is clearly outweighed by the social interest in order and morality."[24] Obscenity was, by definition, worthless – no analysis, no clear-and-present danger discussion, and no balancing necessary. For prosecutors, that meant that if they succeeded in branding a book, movie, play, or poem "obscene," that was typically the end of the matter: Off to the mug-shot room with the moral offenders.

That said, "Brennan had no intention of facilitating censorship and suppression. . . . [I]n the second half of *Roth* he set out to ensure that the very constitutional framework he had just outlined would remain restrictive and careful in its application, preventing any future [Anthony] Comstocks from asserting power." [25] That is where *Roth's* liberal face came into the picture: it smiled on those who defended sexual expression in literature and the arts. Brennan provided language that inspired such an assessment: "[S]ex and obscenity are not synonymous."[26] Obscene material, he continued, is "material having a tendency to excite lustful thoughts."[27] And then Brennan delivered a blow to those who sought to outlaw blue vernacular: "All ideas having even the *slightest importance* – unorthodox ideas, controversial ideas, even ideas hateful to the prevailing climate of opinion – have the *full protection* of the guaranties, unless excludable because they encroach upon the limited area of more important interests."[28]

The upshot? Messages about sex were no longer categorically obscene. There was also a strong suggestion in the opinion that a finding of obscenity hinged on evidence that a work pushed libidinal buttons. Finally, when messages about sex commingled with social commentary, they ranked higher on the First Amendment scale.

Legally, the most important portion of the *Roth* opinion, the words that would find their way into numerous state and federal obscenity laws, was Justice Brennan's famous formula for determining obscenity. That formula repudiated the 1868 *Hicklin* test,[29] which sent many who traded in any kind of sexual expression to jail. Brennan's new test was far more liberal:

1. "[W]hether to the average person,
2. applying contemporary community standards,

3. the dominant theme of the material taken as a whole
4. appeals to prurient interest."[30]

With its four qualifying prongs, the new First Amendment obscenity test might prove promising in the hands of judges sensitive to the nuances of the law and the literary, artistic, political, or social value of the entirety of a work that contains sexually explicit, unorthodox, and controversial passages or images.

That, then, was Justice Brennan's Janus-like *Roth* opinion. It was an opinion that pleased conservatives and liberals alike, even as it troubled them.

৯

What is striking about Justice Brennan's *Roth* opinion and the "constitutional borderline [it] secured"[31] is the skill with which he navigated the shoals of conflict. On the one hand, there was the move to please the conservatives, including the Chief Justice in this case. Importantly, the writing of the majority opinion was not left to any of them, and that gave Brennan a significant opportunity to craft a different kind of opinion than either the Chief Justice or Justice Frankfurter would have written. Earl Warren's majority opinion would have championed a rule that denied First Amendment protection where there was any evidence of "commercial exploitation of the morbid and shameful craving for materials with prurient effect."[32] As Warren saw it, it all boiled down to unprotected conduct. If Frankfurter were at the helm, his opinion would not have been very speech protective, if at all. Recall that it was Frankfurter who championed a ruling based on a "narrow ground"; he favored the status quo of then existing obscenity law; he perverted the application of the prior restraint doctrine in an obscenity case;[33] and while the *Roth* ruling was pending, he handed Brennan a long memo arguing that obscenity was, historically speaking, beyond the purview of any constitutional protection – end of matter.[34] There would no bifurcation, no Janus-like quality to any opinion drafted by either Warren or Frankfurter. That left Justice Harlan and his standard: a speech-protective standard for federal law cases, but a non-protective standard for state law cases.

Brennan was aware of an obvious fact: There were never more than two votes for the libertarian First Amendment absolutist approach. And what were the chances that any of the Justices might applaud Harlan's novel constitutional logic? Bottom line: Nothing could be gained for Brennan by the idle act of joining the opinion of Douglas and Black or that of Harlan.

Conversely, it was quite a feat for Brennan to have his conservative colleagues reaffirm opposition to the *Hicklin* test; it was remarkable that he convinced them to sign onto the notion that obscenity and sexual expression are not always synonymous; it was significant that he persuaded them to vote for an obscenity test that focused on the dominant theme of material taken as a whole; and it was incredible that he influenced his conservative brethren to accept the concept that *all* ideas, including ideas relating to sex, enjoy "full protection," even those with "the slightest importance." In more pious quarters, such accomplishments were viewed with disdain: *Roth* "miss[ed] the nub of the whole matter: morality."[35] And that miss, no doubt, was quite intentional.

It has been said that "Brennan's jurisprudence 'embraced a technique of conceding in principle to the government's power to pursue its objective, while simultaneously making it extraordinarily difficult for the government to do so.' *Roth* certainly fit this mold." [36] Or to cast it another way: "If the first half of *Roth* was hasty and conservative, the second liberal half announced itself boldly."[37]

Whatever William Brennan's actual intentions, his *Roth* opinion stands as a Machiavellian testament as to how to make the best of a bad situation and why it is sometimes important to sacrifice a case in order to win a cause. Might his opinion have been more speech protective? Yes, of course, but not in that case at that time. Did his views evolve beyond what he had said and done in *Roth*?[38] Surely, but so what? Might the test that Brennan articulated in *Roth* have saved the Petitioner if applied to him were the case remanded? Perhaps.[39] And after *Roth*, did lower courts apply the precedent in both liberal[40] and conservative[41] ways? Yes. But at the time that he issued his Janus-like opinion, that was the very best that William Brennan could have anticipated.

In Defense of Unprincipled Decisionmaking

Throughout his life Justice Douglas was a controversial figure. . . . Much of the legal academic elite indicted him for failing to follow "neutral principles."

– Thomas Emerson[1]

He was not a great Justice, although he did have at least one great moment. While he cared little about nuance, he could be quite creative. And he was willing to set the principles of law aside whenever they proved inconvenient. Whatever his shortcomings, they ought not be branded as failings, at least not when they were aligned with the perfect case at the perfect moment. Such a moment came in 1965, and Justice William O. Douglas was savvy enough to seize it and inventive enough to find a constitutional right where none had existed. In the process, he changed the law of the land and gave birth to a cultural movement yearning to be born. Though some Justices had conceptual reservations and others strong objections, in the end Douglas convinced four of his brethren to sign his majority opinion and three more to join the judgment of the Court. The case was a seminal one – *Griswold v. Connecticut*[2] – and it helped to spawn a sexual rights revolution that continues to this day.

Justice Douglas has long been a whipping boy for those who preach the gospel of principled decisionmaking. His *Griswold* opinion stands as the example *par excellence* of judicial overreaching. His critics contend – and not without some merit – that he plucked a constitutional right out of thin air, one that later invited other specious claims to be made in the name of abortion and gay rights. "Wild Bill," as he was popularly known, was entirely unconcerned with all of this. For him, what counted was that the nation's sexual mores would never be the same after *Griswold*. Equally important, that precedent has been reaffirmed time and again, and remains sound law.

The lesson to be learned: legal principles are dispensable. Had Justice Douglas and his colleagues kowtowed to the dictates of principle, the magnificent constitutional right of privacy would not have been recognized and the culture of contraception would not have pressed forward so rapidly and thoroughly. In this way and others, he pushed the boundaries of morality beyond Anthony Comstock's repressive prudery; he pushed constitutional law into the brave new world of unenumerated rights; he pushed the national government into a domain once reserved to the states; and he pushed himself onto the pages of history. Think of it: he did all of this in one swift knock-out blow to principle.

&

If ever there were facts that cried out for legal redress, they were patently evident in the *Griswold* controversy. Estelle Griswold, the executive director of the Planned Parenthood League of Connecticut, and Dr. C. Lee Buxon, the League's medical director and the chair of Yale Medical School's Department of Obstetrics and Gynecology, had given information and prescribed a contraceptive to a married woman. They were arrested, convicted, and fined for violating an 1879 Connecticut Comstock law that prohibited the use of any drug or medical device to prevent conception. Even in 1965, such a prosecution seemed heavy handed. Nonetheless, the Connecticut high court upheld the convictions.[3] Yale Law School Professor Thomas Emerson came to the rescue of the criminal defendants and appealed to the Supreme Court.

In striking down the Connecticut law and overturning the defendants' convictions, the reasoning of the *Griswold* majority opinion was an exercise in judicial acrobatics. Justice Douglas agilely somersaulted through the Constitution's text, touching on this or that amendment to identify aspects of individual privacy. He fearlessly walked a narrow tightrope in announcing a new and general right of privacy, all the while repudiating the kind of judicial activism once espoused by conservative justices interpreting the Due Process clauses during the pre-New Deal era.[4] He nimbly tumbled with modern sexual mores as he reinforced contemporary expectations as to the sanctity of the marital bedroom. With these moves and more, Douglas vigorously advanced his unique "penumbral theory" of constitutional interpretation – and he did so in an opinion consisting of a mere 1,852 words.

Essentially, there were three stages to Justice Douglas's constitutional craftwork. First, he contended that several specific guarantees in the Bill of Rights implicitly protect dimensions of privacy, zones of privacy interests that he labelled "emanations" or "penumbras." In this regard, Douglas built on an earlier dissent he had penned in another Connecticut contraceptives case in which he sketched out his views on a personal right to privacy. That law, he wrote, deprived married couples of "liberty without due process of law. . . . 'Liberty' is a conception that sometimes gains content from the emanations of other specific guarantees . . . or from experience with the requirements of a free society."[5] The seeds were in the soil, but they had yet to break out of the earth and into the light of day. Perhaps mindful of that dissent, during oral arguments in *Griswold* Professor Emerson argued that the appellants "rely on the Third, Fourth, and Fifth Amendments, insofar as they embody a concept of a right of privacy."[6]

Against that backdrop, Douglas's penumbral analysis took shape. Among the emanations that the Justice portrayed were the rights of association contained in the penumbra of the First Amendment; the prohibitions against the quartering of soldiers "in any house" in time of peace as a facet of privacy in the Third Amendment; the "right of the people to be secure in their persons, houses, papers, and effects, against unreasonable searches and seizures" in the text of the Fourth Amendment; the zone of testimonial privacy created by the Fifth Amendment's Self-Incrimination Clause; and the Ninth Amendment's guarantee of "retained" rights that have not been explicitly enumerated.[7] For the dissenters, however, these contentions lacked logical force. Tellingly,

Justice Potter Stewart observed: "In the course of its opinion, the Court refers to no [fewer] than six Amendments to the Constitution . . . . But the Court does not say which of these Amendments, if any, it thinks is infringed by this Connecticut law."[8] The canny William Douglas had an answer to this criticism, however, one delivered in the next stage of his opinion.

With a daring demonstrated by only the most intrepid jurists, Justice Douglas performed a breath-taking conceptual act. Having recognized specific constitutional rights that partake of privacy, he moved to a higher level of abstraction to discover a general and more complete right of privacy. That is, even without clearly signaling such an analytical shift, he created from the separate zones of privacy lying in the peripheries of the various amendments an independent, autonomous, and broad right of privacy. Having formulated that novel constitutional guarantee, he proceeded to locate the use of contraceptives by a married couple as squarely within its parameters.

Finally, Justice Douglas applied his penumbral theory to swiftly adjudge the unconstitutionality of the Connecticut statute. In "forbidding the use of contraceptives, rather than regulating their manufacture or sale," the jurist reasoned, the law "seeks to achieve its goals by means having a maximum destructive impact" upon the most "intimate relation of husband and wife." With rhetorical drama, Douglas asked a question that answered itself: "Would we allow the police to search the sacred precincts of marital bedrooms for telltale signs of the use of contraceptives? The very idea is repulsive to the notions of privacy surrounding the marriage relationship."[9] Concluding with an astute eye to connecting constitutional tradition to contemporary morality, the Justice rhapsodized on the individual and societal significance of privacy and sexual relations in marriage. "We deal with a right of privacy older than the Bill of Rights," he declared. "Marriage is a coming together for better or for worse, hopefully enduring, and intimate to the degree of being sacred. . . . [I]t is an association for as noble a purpose as any involved in our prior decisions."[10]

By many measures, what Douglas had done was nothing short of interpretative bravado, a willingness to be audacious in the absence of any constitutional cover. By his sophistic reasoning, the Justice accomplished something extraordinary. He used the text of the Constitution to catapult his grand penumbral theory, which was in reality no more than a revised version of the old concept of reading substantive rights into the procedural due process clause. It was a case of constitutional camouflage. The very next day, his photograph graced the front page of the *New York Times* accompanying the headline: "7-to-2 Ruling Establishes Marriage Privileges – Stirs Debate." It was a sign of both praise and criticism, which was just the kind of sign the rebellious Justice relished.[11]

Of course, Justice Douglas was not one to allow such criticisms, no matter how mean or merited, to trouble him. He was too unorthodox to pay any mind to what orthodox thinkers said. Besides, the future would smile on his work, both during and after his life. Time and again, a majority of the Supreme Court constitutionally reaffirmed his *Griswold* opinion in subsequent cases involving contraception,[12] abortion,[13] free speech,[14] and gay rights.[15] On the latter score, at first there was resistance when a bare majority of the Court in *Bowers v. Hardwick*[16] attempted to roll back the right of privacy in a consensual homosexual sodomy case. But the effort ultimately proved unsuccessful; *Bowers* was reversed seventeen years later in *Lawrence v. Texas*.[17] Time and again, Justice Kennedy referenced *Griswold* approvingly, and in ways that favored the conceptual and operational expansion of the privacy right that it vouchsafed. Similarly, in recognizing a constitutional right to same-sex marriage, a majority of the Court in *Obergefell v. Hodges*[18] smiled kindly on Justice Douglas's privacy right and the idea of "individual dignity and autonomy" implicit in it.

❧

In the end, penumbras, not precedent, were the governing principle; unenumerated rights became a canon of our constitutional creed; and *Griswold v. Connecticut* endured as a precedent with immense staying power. Moreover, as Judge Robert Bork so bitterly discovered in his 1987 confirmation hearings (see Chapter 1), any Supreme Court nominee who disavows the wisdom of *Griswold* does so at his or her peril.

Griswold v. Connecticut is thus a precedent to be revered as a paradigmatic case in defense of the principle of unprincipled decision-making. Make of it what you will, but give credit to "Wild Bill" as the man who made history when he remade the law of the land . . . and without any apologies.

Chapter 12

How to Manipulate the Rule of Law

A lesson to be learned: objectivity is but a mask to hide one's bias.

Though some vilify him, Justice Antonin Scalia was worthy of high praise for his special skills as a resourceful jurist. Perhaps more than anyone else on his Court, Justice Scalia had a remarkable talent for manipulating the rule of law consistent with his own predilections. He did so, moreover, with freewheeling discretion masquerading as judicial restraint, and in ways at once crafty and complex. He knew how to parse the law's text so that its old meaning took on a new one, and this while pledging fidelity to the Founders. He knew, too, how to champion or condemn a case or cause when it was in his interests. No principle of law was so sacred as to be beyond his ability to rewrite it without openly appearing to do so. When he was dogmatic he proceeded with Papal-like confidence as if divinely inspired – the law was his religion. As a master of the vernacular, he enticed his readers to peer through his interpretive looking glass and behold a fantastical world with all the appearances of reality. In the process, strict construction became loose construction, though done with enough panache and conviction as to be believable.

The Harvard Law School-trained jurist was a far too modest man, if only because he portrayed himself as a mere interpreter (or an oracle) of the law rather than as its grand manipulator. Swearing devotion to the dictionary, he traded its meanings for his, and then pledged allegiance to the words of our Founders. In all of this, he was but a servant, one ever faithful to the will of our constitutional Fathers. While such modesty was undeserved, it was justifiable nonetheless given the Justice's judicial mission.

Originalsm, textualism, historicism – they were all isms perfectly suited to Justice Scalia's conservative constitutional jurisprudence. With interpretive cleverness that rivaled that of the great sophists of antiquity or the modern-day likes of Jacques Derrida, Justice Scalia adroitly changed the law of the land when he wrote for the Court in *District of Columbia v. Heller*.[1] The forty-six pages of the *Heller* majority opinion are a wondrous example of how to manipulate the law while claiming to honor it. Furthermore, what is so marvelous about the opinion is Justice Scalia's admirable willingness and remarkable ability to breach his own constitutional creed in order to obtain the desired result in the case. On that score alone, he would have won more than an approving nod from his great Italian ancestor, Niccolò Machiavelli.

In order to savor the virtuosity of Justice Scalia's constitutional handiwork in *Heller*, we return to the text of that opinion in order to first explain it, and then defend it against some of the charges leveled by jealous judges and pointy-headed scholars unschooled in the artful ways of Master Scalia.

∽

Heller has swept away [all] counsels of caution.
–Judge Harvey J. Wilkinson[2]

Scalia turned Heller into a textualist and originalist tour de force. Literally, word by word, Scalia deconstructed the meaning of the Second Amendment.
– Jeffrey Toobin[3]

The Second Amendment to the Constitution reads: "A well regulated Militia, being necessary to the security of a free State, the right of the people to keep and bear Arms, shall not be infringed." The organization, structure, and meaning of those twenty-seven words was the battleground on which Antonin Scalia and his liberal adversaries struggled to win an interpretative war over the law of gun control.

In this conflict, Fate had dealt the wily Justice an extremely good hand insofar as the facts of the *Heller* case were concerned. The District of Columbia regulated the use of handguns in a particularly Draconian manner; its law was the strictest in the nation, making it virtually impossible for any homeowner to procure a license for a handgun, and restricting any such handgun from being kept in an operational state even for purposes of self-defense. These facts assisted Scalia in converting the apparent straightforwardness of the constitutional text and the precedents relating to it into an ambitious exercise in exegesis. Whether focusing on the amendment's language itself, its historical setting, or its doctrinal treatment, he ably invoked his preferred theories of textualism, originalism, and historicism to create a novel federal constitutional right.

Here is the constitutional gospel according to Scalia: judges are to "look for meaning in the governing text, ascribe to that text the meaning that it has borne from its inception, and reject judicial speculation about the drafters' extra-textually derived purposes and the desirability of the fair reading's anticipated consequences." That canon of construction was preached in his coauthored book, *Reading Law: The Interpretation of Legal Texts*,[4] and has come to be known as textual originalism. This methodology was applied both aggressively and ingeniously in his *Heller* majority opinion, from which four Justices dissented.

Does the "keep and bear Arms" provision of the Second Amendment refer to a collective right of a State militia or to an individual right of a citizen? Justice Scalia answered that question boldly – the amendment protected an individual's right to bear arms. His response relied on a series of exegetical steps. To begin, Scalia segregated the amendment's two clauses; he separated the "prefatory clause" referring to the militia from the "operative clause" referring to the right to bear arms. Then, he focused first on the meaning of the operative clause, and characterized the prefatory clause so as to comport with that meaning. Having thus loaded the interpretative dice, the Justice concluded that the prefatory clause was not meant to limit the reach of the operative clause; the militia's purposes were merely one important use of an individual's right to bear arms.

In his dissent, Justice John Paul Stevens took strong exception to all of this, claiming that the two clauses of the amendment should be read singularly so as to cabin the right to the militia's purposes. Circuit Judge Richard Posner agreed: The objective "of the first clause of the amendment, the militia clause, is to narrow the right that the second clause confers on 'the people.'"[5]

In this swirl of conflicting views, Justice Scalia created enough interpretative complexity so as to make his perspective seem plausible. And that was all that was needed to secure four other votes and to persuade future generations of lawyers and judges of the soundness of his claims. Never mind that his interpretation was not the most natural or obvious one; never mind that his parsing of the words created more confusion than clarity; and never mind that there were strong countervailing arguments. All that really mattered was an interpretation sophisticated enough to pigeonhole into his theory of textual originalism. On that score, the good Judge was on *terra firma*, or so he led all to believe.

Moving beyond the text, Justice Scalia turned to the background and contemporaneous history of the Second Amendment's drafting to support his individual rights interpretation. Among a myriad of sources considered by the majority and dissenting justices, they hotly debated the relevance and the significance of pre-constitutional history, amendments offered at the constitutional ratifying conventions, and the drafting of the Second Amendment.

By his reading of the historical materials, Justice Stevens called out his guileful brother for "unpersuasive" and "misguided" interpretations and even "irrelevant" reliance. Analyzing the debate, Judge Posner emphasized that the weight of historical evidence favored Stevens: "most professional historians reject the historical analysis in Scalia's opinion." Worse still, Posner asserted, "omitting contrary evidence turns out to be [Scalia's] favorite rhetorical device."[6] Moreover, the "range of historical references in the majority opinion is breathtaking, but it is not evidence of disinterested historical inquiry. It is evidence of the ability of well-staffed courts to produce snow jobs."[7]

Why should such condemnations concern the scheming Scalia? Let History PhDs groan and jurisprudes moan; he was not above the common practice of cherry-picking historical evidence as a convenient means to a commendable end. Besides, even his critic Posner had to concede that the "bits and pieces" of his "law office history" were sufficient for "a skillful rhetorician such as Scalia to write a plausible historical defense of his position."[8]

There was an additional argument, an important one. It concerned the doctrine of *stare decisis* – Latin for "to stand by things decided" – a rule by which the Court honors its precedents (see Chapter 13). It is typically viewed as a conservative doctrine, one designed to encourage judicial restraint. In *Heller, stare decisis* posed a problem for Justice Scalia; three Supreme Court precedents,[9] dating back to 1875, stood in his way. Those rulings portrayed the Second Amendment guarantee as a collective right to bear arms rather than the individual one Scalia hoped to empower. Though such precedents foreclosed judicial overreaching of the kind urged by the National Rifle Association, they were cautiously distinguishable. In this regard, Justice Scalia realized, like his liberal predecessors on the Warren Court, that the best way to cope with hostile precedents is either to ignore them entirely or to distinguish them, however disingenuously.

The earlier cases, after all, involved either the use of weapons by mobs and unorganized citizen militias or the use of certain types of weapons (e.g., sawed-off shotguns) typically wielded by criminals. As Justice Scalia was quick to point out, the facts in *Heller* were radically different: apart from its other constraints, the D.C. gun law prohibited the non-criminal use of ordinary firearms by law-abiding persons in their homes. By that measure, the Court's precedents did not control the result in this case. Here again, Justice Stevens was unimpressed; he branded such arguments as "feeble attempt[s]" to distinguish prior doctrine by way of fixating on facts rather than focusing on the Court's reasoning in the opinions. And here again, Scalia made a colorable argument – one tapped to trump the force of judicial restraint dictated by *stare decisis*.

While critiques of the *Heller* decision[10] make for good magazine cover and tantalizing blog posts, they add little to the real and binding bounty of the law as proclaimed by the Supreme Court of the land. Yes, there are responses to such criticisms.[11] But so what? Whatever one makes of Justice Scalia's constitutional craft, he secured three great achievements. He changed the law of the land, and in the process changed the culture of the country by giving constitutional cover to states and municipalities that had relaxed or might relax their gun control laws when pressed to do so by the N.R.A. He left enough play in the interpretative joints, however, to satisfy societal concerns of law and order.†+ And he buttressed his claim to constitutional greatness. Moreover, there is this: in constitutional law, all that matters in the war of words is the final word. Or as Justice Robert Jackson so wonderfully put it: "We are not final because we are infallible, but we are infallible only because we are final."[12]

∾

Heller is a testament to Antonin Scalia's prowess: to his ability to make the weaker argument the stronger; to his skill to manipulate the text and purposes of the law; to his propensity to pick-and-pluck historical evidence to his advantage; to his capacity to circumvent precedent; and to his talents to do all of this and much more with amazing rhetorical flair.

True, lofty-minded scholars and jurists have criticized him, and harshly. And whining liberals have condemned him, and frequently. No matter. Law like life can be messy. More importantly, history glorifies monuments and monumental moments, and forgets everything else. Hence, all remember the majesty of the great pyramids at Giza while only few recall the heaps of lives lost in erecting them. By that all-too-human rule of rationalization, Antonin Scalia's landmark opinion stands as a glorious monument exemplifying the gains to be reaped

---

†. Colonial history aside, and mindful of crime-control concerns, Justice Scalia recognized limitations on the constitutional right to bear arms. Perhaps such limitations explain why the Court has thus far declined to review any petitions contesting gun control laws.

if one is willing to manipulate the law while smugly claiming fidelity to it. Once *Heller* took its place in the palace of the supreme law, Scalia "secured his claim as King of the Originalists."[13] With more than a dollop of pride, he told National Public Radio's Nina Totenberg: "I think *Heller* is my legacy insofar as it is the best example of the technique of constitutional interpretation [that] I favor . . . ."[14] How true.

Chapter 13

When Precedents Are to be Honored (If Only Formally)

Over the course of his three-plus decades on the Supreme Court (the last 19 years in which he served as Chief Justice), William H. Rehnquist left his mark – and it was a bold one – on the law. In several significant ways, he epitomized the calculating Judge. He was temperate in manner and shrewd in execution, rather like a seasoned poker player. On the one hand, he realized the importance of staking out his ground early in any endeavor. On the other hand, he was patient enough to appreciate the value of the long view of things. He always chose his words carefully, and just as carefully manipulated the words of others. Though he was judicially conservative, he was personally conciliatory. His ideological stripes were similar to those of his more extremist colleagues, but he was not an apocalyptic crusader. Although some of his views might be radical, others could just as easily be measured when the circumstances warranted. His own inconsistencies did not trouble him; he did his best to make them opaque. All of this and more is known by his former clerks, some of whom now follow in their Master's judicial footsteps.

Much useful ink could be devoted to the skills William Rehnquist brought to his judicial job. But on this occasion, and for our immediate purposes, we have chosen to praise his "respect" for precedent, which he so wonderfully displayed in his 2000 opinion for the Court in *Dickerson v. United States*.[1] It was an opinion – a *Miranda v. Arizona*[2] opinion involving police warnings to those in criminal custody – that neither friend nor foe saw coming. The press was surprised, politicians shocked, and scholars dumbfounded. What a display of judicial restraint; what a fine example of respect for precedent; and what a shining example of non-partisanship. On that day, William Rehnquist rose high above the fray into the ether of justice impartially applied . . . or so it seemed.

What is instructive about Rehnquist's opinion is the amazing arc from his early days in the Office of Legal Counsel, to his early years on the Burger Court, to his time as Chief Justice, to his *Dickerson* opinion, and to what followed thereafter. It is a tale, all true, of a man who first opposed the landmark *Miranda* precedent, then helped to create new doctrinal exceptions to undermine it, then reaffirmed *Miranda* when he had the opportunity to overrule it, only thereafter to endorse the very anti-*Miranda* precedents he once helped to create. It is, of course, rather dizzying. But if one carefully follows the trail of his jurisprudential maneuvers, the lesson learned will be of considerable value to jurists able to do likewise.

∽

Stare decisis in constitutional law is pretty much a sham.
– William Rehnquist (1986)[3]

Every judge who faithfully applies the law honors the rule of *stare decisis* ("let the decision stand"). It is a rule deeply rooted in the Anglo-American system of jurisprudence. This doctrine holds that judges should look to past decisions for guidance in resolving new disputes *consistent with precedent.*

Of course, this is all textbook law – doctrine meant primarily for legal neophytes and mild-mannered jurists. No Justice who values power and seeks greatness can take the doctrine too seriously, even though such a jurist must appear to honor the rule and breach it outright only with calculated care.[†] Moreover, such a jurist knows all too well that there are many ways to circumvent the rule without violating it:

[†]. "A judge's influence depends on his decisions being treated as precedents by other judges. If he is cavalier about adhering to precedent in his own decisions, he weakens the doctrine of precedent and hence the likelihood that his own decisions will be followed by other judges." Richard Posner, *How Judges Think* (Cambridge, MA: Harvard University Press, 2008), p. 144 (footnote omitted).

- For starters, different facts can produce different results. Hence, how one characterizes the statement of facts in a case can have a significant effect on the rule applied. Besides, distinguishing cases is never that difficult.

- Additionally, there are so many precedents – some similar, others not – that one can cherry pick the precedent best suited to produce the desired result. One can also misapply precedent while claiming to hold true to it.

- Moreover, a Justice who can secure four votes can, over time and in enough cases, distinguish a disfavored precedent out of existence. In the process, viability is granted to a new body of precedents while the old ones gradually die off.

- Finally, if the Court's certiorari docket can be manipulated, then there is an added benefit: Cases favoring a preferred precedent can be selected for review (this to buttress it) along with cases disfavoring a disliked precedent (this to dismantle it).[4]

All of these moves and still others were certainly made by William Rehnquist in the long span of his tenure on the Court. He knew, for example, how to circle around precedents,[5] how to overrule precedents,[6] and even how to circumvent the rule of a case that overruled one of Rehnquist's own precedents.[7] But the best of his opportunist moves came in connection with what he did to dismantle Earl Warren's beloved opinion in *Miranda v. Arizona*. It is a long story, one that began in 1969. In order to avoiding being pedantic, we offer but an overview of that story, one sufficient for and adapted to our purposes.

&

No one was a fiercer critic of *Miranda* than William Rehnquist. The very idea that the Constitution mandated that criminals be coddled by the police and prosecutors, that they be made aware of their constitutional rights, and that any failure to comply with this judge-created mandate would result in the exclusion of relevant evidence – it all repulsed him. Put another way, this aspect, among others, of the Warren Court's criminal justice revolution demanded a counter-revolution. Rehnquist was happy to lead that charge.

However problematic the *Miranda* warnings' constitutional basis, there can be little doubt that the Warren Court viewed it as constitutionally required. Or as Chief Justice Warren put it: "Congress and the States are free to develop their own safeguards for the privilege, *so long as they are fully as effective as those described above* in informing accused persons of their right of silence and in affording a continuous opportunity to exercise it. In any event, however, *the issues presented are of constitutional dimensions and must be determined by the courts.*"[8]

By this linguistic measure, Congress acted unconstitutionally when it passed the Omnibus Crime Control Act of 1968. Specifically, 18 U.S.C. §3501 of that Act ventured to replace the *Miranda* rule requirements with a pre-*Miranda* standard of voluntariness.[9] Perhaps mindful of this constitutional overreach, federal prosecutors at the time did not attempt to use §3501. Even Rehnquist, back in 1969 when he served as an Assistant Attorney General in charge of the Office of Legal Counsel, seemed to share that view. In a memorandum to the Associate Deputy Attorney General (John Dean), Rehnquist took aim at *Miranda*: "The impact of *Miranda* and its progeny on the practices of law enforcement officials is far-reaching. . . . The Court, believing that the poor, disadvantaged criminal defendant should be made just as aware of the risk of incriminating himself as the rich, well-counseled criminal defendant, has undoubtedly put an additional hurdle in the way of convicting the guilty."[10] Critical as he was, Rehnquist did not recommend reliance on §3501; instead he proposed a constitutional amendment to overrule *Miranda*.[11] In other words, back in 1969 Rehnquist viewed *Miranda's* requirements as constitutionally required.

Ever resourceful, when William Rehnquist became Justice Rehnquist he quickly set out to deconstitutionalize *Miranda*. He seized an opportunity to do just that when he wrote for the Court in *Michigan v. Tucker* (1974).[12] Early in his opinion, and in a casual way, he declared: "We will . . . first consider whether the police conduct complained of directly infringed upon respondent's right against compulsory self-incrimination or whether it instead violated only the *prophylactic rules* developed to protect that right."[13] In a brilliant move, he divorced the "prophylactic rules" from the constitutional rule mandated by the Fifth Amendment. Building on that, he later added: "[W]e have already concluded that the police conduct at issue here *did not abridge respondent's constitutional privilege against compulsory self-incrimination, but departed only from the prophylactic standards* later laid down by this Court in *Miranda* to safeguard that privilege."[14] (Justice Douglas, writing in dissent, was asleep at the jurisprudential switch – he missed this breakthrough point.[15])

Justice Rehnquist upped the ante when he later wrote for the Court in *New York v. Quarles*[16] where he echoed what he wrote in *Tucker.* "The prophylactic *Miranda* warnings therefore are '*not themselves rights protected by the Constitution* but [are] instead measures to insure that the right against compulsory self-incrimination [is] protected.'"[17] The following year, in *Oregon v. Elstad*,[18] Justice Sandra Day O'Connor did her old Stanford Law School mate a favor – she added more staying power to Rehnquist's "prophylactic rules" rhetoric. After quoting *Tucker's* devious language twice, O'Connor declared: "If errors are made by law enforcement officers in administering the *prophylactic Miranda* procedures, *they should not breed the same irremediable consequences as police infringement of the Fifth Amendment itself.*"[19]

Thus, by 1985 – fifteen years before his *Dickerson* ruling – there were three Supreme Court opinions openly questioning the constitutional status of the *Miranda* warnings. As time passed, this deconstitutionalizing language found its way into several other Supreme Court opinions.[20] If one were to just stop there, Rehnquist would be deserving of a grand ovation for the clever moves he made in devaluing *Miranda* without formally overruling it. But there was more; there were the many cases in which the Court, aided by Rehnquist,[21] time and again either read *Miranda* narrowly or carved out exceptions[22] to the *Miranda* rule. Such tactics are known in the trade as, among other things,[23] "boiling the frog." The idea behind the metaphor is that if "you want to boil a frog, you put him in warm water and gradually turn up the heat; should you put him in boiling water at the start, he would jump out and you would have to put him back in and this time hold him down. Either way he would die."[24] And isn't that the point?

Rehnquist's constitutional handiwork, aided by his conservative colleagues, had a twofold effect: First, it helped deconstitutionalize *Miranda*; and second, it gave the police considerable leeway to work around *Miranda* while purporting to honor it. The overall result: The former encouraged a head-on challenge to *Miranda* and its constitutional viability, whereas the latter diminished the need for a head-on challenge. Either way, it was a win-win for William Rehnquist, which brings us to his famous "concession" in *Dickerson v. United States*, a case in which he bowed to *stare decisis* in order to pay respect to precedent.

৯

> *Considered in isolation, the language used in Tucker and its progeny that a violation of Miranda is not a violation of the Constitution could be read to support an inference that Miranda is not a constitutional rule.*
> – Government's brief in Dickerson v. United States.[25]

Those words reflected the prevailing view at the time when *Dickerson* came before the Court for review. That view held the day when the Court of Appeals for the Fourth Circuit ruled in the case, holding that *Miranda* waivers were not required when officers interrogate suspects already in custody. The circuit court based its ruling on §3501, which allowed for the admissibility of a defendant's statement if it was given voluntarily, regardless of whether the defendant waived his *Miranda* rights.[26] It seemed like the perfect case to come before the Rehnquist Court, one ripe for ideological consideration. But there was, as the Chief Justice surely knew, a fly in the jurisdictional ointment. In so many ways, *Dickerson* was a bogus controversy.

First and foremost, at the trial level the prosecutor never raised a §3501 challenge. So, too, on appeal, the government never raised that defense. Worse still, it openly refused to employ §3501. Rather, the issue was introduced by a conservative public interest group in a third-party *amicus* brief. That did not stop the Fourth Circuit from ruling as it did. When the matter came before the Supreme Court, the federal government again declined to invoke §3501 or defend it.[27] That drew the following response from the Chief Justice: "Because no party to the underlying litigation argued in favor of §3501's constitutionality in this Court, we invited Professor Paul Cassell to assist our deliberations by arguing in support of the judgment below."[28]

In light of all that, what is amazing is that the Court agreed to hear the case in the first place.[29] Why? On the one hand, the conservatives on the Court must have felt that fate was on their side, this was their moment . . . and to hell with the jurisdictional posture of the case. On the other hand, the liberals on the Court must have been delighted when they learned of the Chief's position . . . and to hell with the jurisdictional posture of the case. Meanwhile, the Chief must have smiled.

Given the judgment of the Fourth Circuit and the Court's grant of certiorari, many believed that Chief Justice Rehnquist would soon enough read *Miranda* its last rites.[30] After all, there was ample precedent to do so, precedent that undermined the constitutional status of the *Miranda* precedent. Viewed from that conceptual perch, the problem presented in *Dickerson* was a case of precedent warring against precedent. Thus, the question: What was actually the settled law in 2000? The law of the pristine *Miranda*? Or that of the degraded *Miranda*? Most thought the latter, and not without some justification.

No one saw it coming. When in *Dickerson* the Chief Justice had the chance to formally overrule *Miranda*, he demurred. Not surprisingly, this outraged Justice Scalia: "Those to whom judicial decisions are an unconnected series of judgments that produce either favored or disfavored results will doubtless greet today's decision as a paragon of moderation, since it declines to overrule *Miranda v. Arizona*."[31] A paragon of moderation? One wonders.

Consider, for example, what the Chief Justice said: "We hold that *Miranda*, being a *constitutional* decision of this Court, may not be in effect overruled by an Act of Congress, and we decline to overrule *Miranda* ourselves."[32] Fair enough, that seems moderate. But consider the next sentence: "We therefore hold that *Miranda and its progeny* in this Court govern the admissibility of statements made during custodial interrogation in both state and federal courts."[33] Is that equally moderate or rather mischievous?

Think of it: The first sentence of the holding makes it clear that the *Miranda* warnings are of constitutional dimension, whereas the second sentence speaks of the governing principle being dictated by *both Miranda* and "its progeny," which includes cases such as *Tucker, Quarles,* and *Elstad* – all decisions that contested *Miranda's* constitutional status. Notably, even if *Miranda* were indubitably of constitutional pedigree, we are admonished by Rehnquist that "[n]o constitutional rule is immutable, and the sort of *refinements* made by such cases are merely a normal part of constitutional law."[34] So, are all of the various attempts to deconstitutionalize *Miranda* or evade its mandates (only recall the boiling frog metaphor) mere "refinements"? Such statements are cunning, not moderate.

There is more. Consider this, for example: "Whether or not we would agree with *Miranda's* reasoning and its resulting rule, . . . the principles of stare decisis weigh heavily against overruling it *now*."[35] In other words, *Miranda's* day of reckoning may well come; it just didn't arrive in *Dickerson*. Finally, there is this ingenious line: "While the Court has overruled its precedents when subsequent cases have undermined their doctrinal underpinnings, that has not happened to *Miranda*. If anything, subsequent cases have reduced *Miranda's* impact on legitimate law enforcement while reaffirming the decision's core ruling."[36]

Two points here: First, contrary to what the Chief Justice would have us believe, many of the post-*Miranda* cases actually did undermine its doctrinal underpinnings. Second, while it is certainly true that many post-*Miranda* cases have indeed limited its impact, by that very fact such rulings have diminished, not preserved, *Miranda's* core. These rather esoteric points prompt the question: What exactly is *Miranda's* core?

At every turn, the Chief chose his words carefully – sometimes there were mixed messages, sometimes there were devious refinements, sometimes there were half-truths, and sometimes his real message was rather opaque. But who reads the fine print? The takeaway point, the one that made for big banner headlines, was this: REHNQUIST REAFFIRMS *MIRANDA* – the moderate Rehnquist, the judicious respecter of *stare*

decisis, the man who placed principle above politics. It was all so preposterous, yet all the more delicious because so many were conned.

Feeling the need to spit out yet more rhetorical venom, Justice Scalia
complained: "Today's judgment converts *Miranda* from a milestone of
judicial overreaching into the very Cheops' Pyramid (or perhaps the
Sphinx would be a better analogue) of judicial arrogance."[37] Really?
Such barbs, and the thinking behind them, make for good copy, but
they certainly don't make for prudent counsel that a more than ordinary
judge should heed.

There is another consideration to be noted here as well, one that
points back to John Marshall and *Marbury v. Madison* (Chapter 2). If
Chief Justice Rehnquist had upheld the constitutionality of §3501, he
would have given the impression that Congress's will could trump that
of the Court's, that judicial supremacy was really not supreme.[38] This
would have invited all sorts of problematic complications in future conflicts between the Court and Congress. No Justice – liberal or conservative, activist or minimalist – is willing to forsake the *Marbury* moment.
Think of it: Was formally overruling an already decimated *Miranda*
worth that? To ask the question is to answer it.

For those who thought *Miranda* was in safe harbor in light of
Dickenson, the Court's subsequent 5-4 ruling in *United States v. Patane*[39]
demonstrated that enemy combatants awaited its attempted mooring.
The issue in the case was whether a failure to give a suspect the *Miranda*
warnings requires the suppression of physical evidence derived from the
suspect's unwarned but voluntary statements. Predictably, the Court
found such evidence admissible, with the Chief Justice siding with
the majority. What is important for our purposes is not only this new
breach of the *Miranda* wall, but what Justice Thomas wrote in his plurality opinion, in which Rehnquist joined. Thomas asserted: "[B]ecause
. . . prophylactic rules (including the *Miranda* rule) necessarily sweep
beyond the actual protections of the Self-Incrimination Clause, . . .
any further extension of these rules must be justified by its necessity
for the protection of the actual right against compelled self-incrimination . . . . Indeed, at times the Court has declined to extend *Miranda*
even where it has perceived a need to protect the privilege against

self-incrimination. See, e.g., *Quarles* . . . ."[40] And there was this for good measure: "The *Dickerson* Court's reliance on our *Miranda* precedents [including *Elstad*] further demonstrates the continuing validity of those decisions." [41] Incredibly, and as Professor Yale Kamisar has aptly observed, in this "post-*Dickerson* confession case the two dissenters in *Dickerson* and the author of the majority opinion in *Dickerson*" came together – "strange bedfellows."[42]

There you have it – a window into the Chief Justice's mind.[43] For all of Justice Scalia's the-sky-is-falling rants in his *Dickerson* dissent, the world of criminal procedure seemed pretty much the same after *Dickerson* was decided as it did before. "Aside from invalidating §3501, did *Dickerson* accomplish anything?," Professor Kamisar asks.[44] Though his question was understandably rhetorical, the real answer relies on the vantage point from which one views the matter. By the Chief Justice's Machiavellian measure, *Dickerson* accomplished precisely what Rehnquist had hoped it would.

If one takes the long view and considers the trajectory of strategic moves from 1969 and Rehnquist's days at the Office of Legal Counsel, through his years on the Court busily dismantling *Miranda*, to his 2000 majority opinion in *Dickerson*, what the Chief Justice achieved was truly amazing. And to pull it off as he did – from assuming review over the *Dickerson* case to writing the opinion as he did to his post-*Dickerson* actions – was nothing short of brilliant.[45] And all of this while the *Miranda* frog boiled away.

Is precedent "infinitely malleable"?[46] Is it an "inexorable command"?[47] No, of course not, on both scores. But that is not owing to any normative principle. As William Rehnquist's strategic encounter with *Miranda* shows, the doctrine of *stare decisis*, as he shrewdly applied it, demonstrates how it can be put to one's advantage. Sometimes it will serve a Justice to honor the doctrine and even bolster it; others times he or she will want to circumvent it; and at still other times there will be an opportunity to take the doctrinal bull by the horns and overrule a case outright. By that tactical measure, there are many arrows for *stare decisis* in the quiver of the right Judge.[48]

If one listens carefully, he or she can hear the whispering echo: "*Stare decisis* in constitutional law is pretty much a sham." Yes indeed, a sham – a delusion, a pretense of seriousness, something that trades the reality of a thing for its appearance. Here again, William Rehnquist chose his words carefully.

Chapter 14

When to Take Command and Make Demands

If one wishes to be obeyed, it is necessary to know how to command.

– Niccolò Machiavelli[1]

Which is better: To be collegial or demanding? Neither. A prudent jurist must master both. Justice William Brennan[2] exemplified collegiality, whereas Justice James McReynolds[3] exemplified the opposite as a man who could offend everyone. Justice Felix Frankfurter[4] (ever the lecturing professor) ineffectively feigned collegiality, and was far too demanding to be productive in his dealings with his colleagues. Three jurists: One skilled and successful, one bigoted and mediocre, and one who wasted the great potential he had.

Chief Justice John Roberts and Justice Anthony Kennedy are both collegial jurists; they are gentlemen who care about the Court and their colleagues. They are not combative; they are not intimidating; they are not ill mannered. But when the cause is right and the case is ripe, they are experts at making the kind of demands that are difficult to refuse. While we cannot be certain of this (if only because we are not privy to their true intents), we feel safe in inferring it. But even if we misjudge them, we are nonetheless willing to use some of their opinions as examples to illustrate when a Justice should take command and make demands.

"Five votes. Five votes can do anything around here."[5] How true were Justice Brennan's wise words. To that end, collegiality always helps – the preferred allies are one's true friends, those who can be counted on, even when unsure, to deliver that decisive fifth vote. Of course, no Justice would ever admit to delivering a vote in the name of friendship. Then again, none would ever concede that power or politics (or vanity) ever influences the decision in a case. But such disclaimers come with the territory, and therefore can never be taken too seriously.

Sugar, however, does not always attract the extra votes one needs to secure a majority or, even more impressive, unanimity. Sometimes the mix has to be a little bitter. Or, to forsake the metaphor, sometimes one must demand compliance. Of course, this is always a risky endeavor. Hence, it must be done rarely, carefully, and not too fiercely (unless truly necessary). Never swing a mace when gently pushing a pressure point will suffice. To proceed more aggressively to invite disappointment, or even catastrophic failure.

A First Amendment decision authored by Chief Justice Roberts is illustrative. *McCullen v. Coakley*,[6] was an abortion-clinic protest case, a controversial one. The vote was 9-0, a surprising result. How did Roberts manage to obtain such unanimity? Our guess: The Chief Justice made demands of his liberal colleagues, demands seemingly impossible to reject. By that measure, *McCullen* shows the Chief Justice at his manipulative best. By studying the case, then, one can derive a sense of when and how to make demands and remain collegial.

◈

It was a sign: On its own motion, the Court in *McCullen* asked the parties to brief the question of whether *Hill v. Colorado*[7] should be overruled. In *Hill* the Court upheld, by a 6-3 margin, a Colorado law that created a 100-foot buffer zone around abortion clinic entrances, this to prevent protests, "education," or "counseling." Justice Antonin Scalia wrote a dissent (joined by Justice Clarence Thomas) as did Justice Anthony Kennedy. By the time *McCullen v. Coakley* came to the Court some fourteen years after *Hill*, four of the Justices (John Paul Stevens, David Souter, Sandra Day O'Connor, and Chief Justice Rehnquist) had left the Court and were replaced by two conservatives (Chief Justice Roberts and Justice Samuel Alito) and two liberals (Justices Sonia Sotomayor and Elena Kagan). What that meant is, by the time of *McCullen*, there were five potential votes to overrule *Hill* (the Chief Justice and Justices

Scalia, Kennedy, Thomas, and Alito). Since Justices Scalia and Kennedy had written forceful dissents in *Hill*, and since the Chief Justice was a likely ally, it seemed probable that *Hill* would either be formally overruled or functionally gutted. And *McCullen* – the facts of which involved a 35-foot buffer zone around the entrances, exits, and driveways of abortion clinics – was the case in which to do just that.

If *Hill* were overruled, it would surely be one of those ugly 5-4 scuffles, with the liberal dissenters carping about how women's *Roe* rights were being sacrificed once again on an ideological altar. But so what? After all, Justice Kennedy had already hopped off the pro-choice bandwagon when he moved from "saving" *Roe* in *Planned Parenthood v. Casey* (1992)[8] to undermining *Roe* in his opinion for the Court in *Gonzales v. Carhart* (2007).[9] Moreover, Kennedy was a big First Amendment man (as was the Chief Justice) and this was a First Amendment case. In other words, *McCullen* could be the payback moment for the conservatives, especially Justices Kennedy and Scalia. After all, reconciliation is agreeable, but retribution is delightful.

The oral arguments in *McCullen* fit predictably into the 5-4, liberal-vs-conservative template. Nina Totenberg, for one, said as much on NPR: "Inside the Supreme Court, the questioning was fast and furious, with the Justices apparently divided equally."[10] Adam Liptak of the *New York Times* saw it likewise: "The Supreme Court appeared evenly divided . . . as it heard arguments in a First Amendment challenge to a Massachusetts law that created buffer zones around abortion clinics in the state."[11]

There was one problem; it was captured in a *New York Times* headline on the case: "Crucial Voice Is Silent." According to Liptak: "[A] significant piece of data was missing: Chief Justice John G. Roberts, Jr., who almost certainly holds the crucial vote, asked no questions."[12] Ms. Totenberg echoed that point: "For the first time in memory, no questions from Chief Justice John Roberts."[13] No questions, silence, no indication from the "crucial vote." In light of the common view at the time, Roberts could well by the man who would determine which side would prevail in what was thought to be a 5-4 case. "Roberts may have been keeping his thoughts to himself," speculated Ken Jost, in order "to steer the Court toward a compromise position that protects free-speech rights on one side and women's rights to access to abortion on the other."[14] Compromise? How would that happen? And how would the Chief Justice steer around the likely 5-4 divide?

When judgment day came, the vote was 9-0. Incredible! The Court voted unanimously to strike down the Massachusetts abortion clinic buffer zone law. The Chief Justice wrote the majority opinion, followed by a concurrence by Justice Antonin Scalia (joined by Justices Kennedy and Clarence Thomas) and another by Justice Samuel Alito writing for himself. The split was over the rationale of the Court's reasoning, with the more conservative Justices wanting to overrule *Hill v. Colorado*. What was surprising, however, is that none of the liberal Justices dissented. Even more surprising was that none of them wrote a separate opinion. They were as silent immediately after the opinion came down as the Chief Justice was when the case was argued. Why?

≪ঔ

> *"It was not a compromise decision but a good decision to say yes, you can regulate, but it is speech so you have to be careful not to go too far,"* [Justice] Ginsburg told the Associated Press . . . , *referring to the case* [of] McCullen v. Coakley. *Many observers, including Ginsburg's biggest fans, were also disappointed that the longtime reproductive rights champion did not write in concurrence to affirm the importance of safe access to clinics.*[15]

No compromise? A "good decision"? What else could Justice Ginsburg say? How else could she explain away her vote and silence in *McCullen*? How else could she justify the fact that she and her three liberal colleagues joined forces with their conservative counterparts to further cripple the right guaranteed in *Roe v. Wade*? *McCullen* was, after all, the controversy in which the lawyers for Planned Parenthood told the Court: "This case arises against a backdrop of decades of harassment, intimidation, obstruction, and violence directed at staff, patients, and volunteers at PPLM's Facilities."[16] Furthermore, in *McCullen* the ACLU argued that the "Massachusetts statute is a facially valid time, place, and manner regulation."[17] Notably, as far as the First Amendment claim was concerned, Justice Ginsburg and her liberal colleagues gave little or no credence to the brief filed by the United States in support of the clinic: "The Massachusetts statute at issue in this case is content neutral, is narrowly tailored to significant governmental interests, and leaves open ample alternative channels of communication. Accordingly, it is a permissible time, place, or manner restriction under the First Amendment."[18]

Obviously, there was a compromise in *McCullen*. But what was it?

Start here: The decisive vote was that of the Chief Justice. Though the judgment was unanimous, the Justices divided on the rationale for the ruling. Thus, the majority could either read the First Amendment narrowly (and appease the liberals) or apply it broadly (and appease the conservatives). The way it turned out, the narrower rationale prevailed as exemplified by Chief Justice Robert's majority opinion. Justice Scalia was livid: "Today's opinion carries forward this Court's practice of giving abortion-rights advocates a pass when it comes to suppressing the free-speech rights of their opponents. There is an entirely separate, abridged edition of the First Amendment applicable to speech against abortion."[19] No matter, he was on the losing side of the five votes equation. "Get use to it,"[20] as Scalia was so fond of saying.

Chief Justice Roberts's strategy was brilliant. First, he secured a unanimous judgment in an abortion case – a remarkable feat in itself. That made him appear judicious. Second, though he did not formally overrule *Hill* (or even much discuss it), he nonetheless drafted his opinion to tap into *Hill's* reasoning while producing a different result. That demonstrated his shrewdness. Third, he managed to bring the four liberals along for the ride. That revealed his ability to work with those on the other side of the ideological divide. And most importantly, he did all of this without any of the liberals writing a separate opinion. That suggested his capacity to be demanding, albeit gingerly and quietly.

Why did the liberal four keep silent? Why didn't they write a concurrence and mention some of the advice tendered in the briefs filed by the United States, Planned Parenthood, the ACLU, the American College of Obstetricians and Gynecologists, the National Abortion Federation, and 31 other organizations, among others? Why not add a few qualifying words about the agonizing plight of women who try to go to Planned Parenthood's clinics? Why not clarify that the precedent established in *Hill v. Colorado* still stands solidly?

Conjecture: The Chief Justice had taken command. If so, did he demand the votes and secure the silence? Maybe yes, maybe no. We assume the former. But even if he had not, even if Fate had just played out that way without interference, he should have demanded compliance. And what price did he pay? There were the liberals: They could not be delighted with the outcome, though they would get over it – the alternative would have been far worse. There were the conservatives: Though they desired more, they got the judgment they wanted and a reworked application of *Hill's* reasoning[21]– here too, the alternative would have been far worse if the law were upheld. And finally, there was the logic of the law, of First Amendment law: Admittedly, it had been twisted a bit to fit the Chief Justice's reasoning[22] – then again, a case can always be distinguished in the future.

It was a long journey – John Roberts had traveled a considerable conceptual distance from the "balls-and-strikes" metaphor[23] he extolled in his confirmation hearing to the masterfully manipulative moves he exercised in *McCullen v. Coakley*. And yet he traveled it with marvelous skill.

Chapter 15

The Boldest Moves:

When and How to Make Them

Here is the point – the Machiavellian point . . . .
[H]ypocrisy of a certain kind is what the country desires of the Court.
— Frank I. Michelman[1]

Judging is different: Justices wear black robes; they act largely in private; they arrive at a result by impartial legal reasoning; they justify their opinions in print; and they remain above the fray. In other words, they are not politicians, they are not to be partisan, and they ought not enter such unruly controversies. For those reasons and others, when issues are openly political, highly charged, unamenable to the logic of the law, and jeopardize the Supreme Court's legitimacy, the best course of action is for the Justices to keep their jurisdictional distance and permit such conflicts to be resolved in the court of politics and public opinion.

There is some truth here, but not enough to persuade any Justice of more than ordinary talent and ambition. Though rare, sometimes the boldest judicial moves are ripe for the taking; sometimes political maneuvers can prevail; and sometimes the public both invites and accepts such actions. The question, then, is not whether to be partisan, but when and how; and the decisive concern is not whether to act politically, but how to appear otherwise. There are times when the Exceptional Justice must be bold and take a political controversy by the horns and make it succumb to his or her will.

It seems so ironic: One of the reasons that Alexander Hamilton argued in Federalist No. 78 that the judiciary would be "the least dangerous" branch[2] was the expectation that judges would act with "neither force nor will" typical of political officers of the federal government. But Hamilton could never have anticipated how ravenous the beast of judicial review (invigorated by his fellow Federalist John Marshall) would become. In contemporary American culture, the idea of judicial politics is a commonplace, if only because so many political controversies are adjudged. So much so that sometimes the judiciary can intervene in the most extraordinary conflicts of the most partisan natures. True, this is risky; admittedly, this could trigger severe political backlash; and possibly this could lead to institutional disgrace or individual impeachment and conviction. Then again, the rewards are proportional to the risks. Judicial supremacy is the fruit of bold and aggressive action, cleverly cultivated and cunningly harvested. The maxim is no less true of judges than it is of politicians: Power is as Power does.

Bold judicial power moves, however, need to be dressed up; they must masquerade as judicious. All of the legal trappings need to be on display. Lawyers must file well documented and carefully reasoned appellate briefs; the lawyers and Justices must engage in probative oral arguments; and the Justices must deliver opinions anchored in precedent and principle. That, at least, is the veneer; the real wood is otherwise. It is the stratagem behind a legal argument; it is the tactic that advances a Justice's *realpolitik*.

One of the key functions of the Supreme Court is to bring calm to a turbulent nation. When the democratic process fails, when politicians are at loggerheads, when executives are powerless to troubleshoot, and when societal strife is at a high pitch, the public may look to the majesty of the law and its keepers for guidance. "It could be that what Americans want above all else out of the Supreme Court is assurance that someone is there to bring the country to heel when chaos looms or politics threaten to get out of hand," Professor Michelman hypothesizes.[3] It is precisely at such trying times that the opportunity is rife for judicial action of the manipulative kind that preys on the public's vulnerability in order to advance one's political agenda. The best kind of judicial activism – the type that seems judicious but is disingenuous – is the kind that is invited.

Perhaps no Supreme Court case in American history exemplifies these Machiavellian moves more than *Bush v. Gore* (2000),[4] the ruling that effectively decided a presidential election . . . to the benefit of the Justices who prevailed. It was a triumph for hypocrisy.

✑

Political elections are the Devil's domain, the place where deals are made, votes bought, and outcomes rigged. The specter of such possibilities was very much in the air during the 2000 presidential election, the one that pitted George W. Bush against Al Gore. Division, divisiveness, and distrust were widespread as conservative TV and radio pundits faced off repeatedly against their liberal counterparts to the point that the line between news and commentary nearly vanished. In the process, political anxiety reached a high water mark as Americans sat fixed in front of their televisions waiting for election results. It all came down to Florida; what happened there would determine whether Bush or Gore would be the next president.

"The scramble for votes in Florida exposed what has long been the dark secret of the entire electoral process: significant inaccuracies and mistakes infect the actual process of recording and tabulating votes. In effect, elections have an unacknowledged 'margin of error.'"[5] Those infections, inaccuracies, and errors culminated in a constitutional crisis, one that first engaged the Florida Supreme Court and then the United States Supreme Court. The result was constitutional drama orchestrated by partisan performances. Working through the pandemonium, a narrow majority reaffirmed the Court's institutional supremacy, reconfigured doctrinal law, decided the election, and calmed an all too anxious nation. Given the fast-and-furious pace of events, it was easy to lose sight of the advantage that an extraordinary Justice might perceive as valuable to his or her agenda. Predictably, there was ideological bickering afterwards as liberals and conservatives squared off against one another as to the legitimacy of what the five conservative Justices had done. But like the common cold, it passed and Court business went on as usual . . . except for the new measure of power seized by those clever enough to do so.

The dizzying swirl of events that made certain Machiavellian moves possible and other moves unadvisable can be succintly summarized:

- *November 7, 2000*: When the polls closed on election night, the presidential race hung in the delicate balance of a virtual tie. The outcome in Florida would be the tie-breaker, and the first tabulation showed Governor Bush as the winner by fewer than 600 votes of the 6 million cast. As Florida law required, an automatic machine recount was conducted the next day, and Bush was still in the lead with 930 votes. Florida's Secretary of State Katherine Harris certified Bush the winner in Florida.

- *November 21, 2000*: After Al Gore and the Democratic Party filed a lawsuit against Harris, the Florida Supreme Court ruled unanimously that the Secretary had abused her discretion by refusing to accept late returns, and ordered that the deadline for submission of manual recounts be extended to November 26.[6] George Bush immediately filed a certiorari petition for expedited review in the Supreme Court to determine whether the Florida high court's order violated federal law.

- *December 4, 2000*: By a per curiam opinion in the case colloquially known as *Bush I*,[7] the Supreme Court vacated the Florida high court's judgment and remanded the case for further proceedings. In the interim, because Bush was still ahead in the vacated recount, Secretary of State Harris certified him the winner, and Gore returned to state court to challenge that decision.

- *December 8, 2000*: By a 4-3 vote, the Florida Supreme Court ordered a statewide manual recount of all "undervote ballots" (those counted by machine that did not register a vote).[8] On the next day, the Supreme Court voted 5-4 to stay the recount process and treated the application for stay as a petition for certiorari, which was granted.[9]

- *December 11, 2000*: The Florida Supreme Court issued its opinion on remand from *Bush I*.[10] Reaching precisely the same result, but citing only to legislative materials and rules of statutory interpretation, the Justices emphasized that "[l]egislative intent – as always – is the polestar" that guided its interpretation of the Florida Election Code. On the same day, oral arguments were heard in *Bush v. Gore (Bush II)*. In the sober and intense 90-minute session, the Court's focus turned on practical questions of constitutionally acceptable standards for a recount: "What standards were used to determine the intent of the voters? What were the implications of using different standards for different counties?"[11]

- *December 12, 2000*: The Supreme Court issued its decision in *Bush v. Gore*. The Per Curiam opinion was joined by Chief Justice Rehnquist and Associate Justices Scalia, O'Connor, Kennedy, and Thomas. Rehnquist also authored a concurring opinion, joined by Scalia and Thomas. Dissenting opinions were filed by Justice Stevens (joined by Justices Ginsburg and Breyer), Justice Souter (joined by Breyer), Justice Ginsberg (joined by Stevens and joined in part by Souter and Breyer). Holding that the use of standardless manual recounts violated the Equal Protection and Due Process Clauses of the Fourteenth Amendment, the *per curiam* Court reversed the Florida Supreme Court's judgment and recount order. With the termination of the recount process, Florida's 25 electoral votes were awarded the next day to George Bush. Al Gore officially conceded in a televised address.[12]

When the dust storm subsided and the 2000 presidential election – aptly tagged "the longest night"[13] – finally ended, what remained was a sharply divided Supreme Court ruling that broke new and controversial constitutional ground. In brief, the opinions divided into three conceptual categories:

Equal Protection and Due Process violations: Seven Justices (the five conservative majority Justices plus Souter and Breyer) agreed that the use of different standards of counting in the recount processes in different counties was constitutionally prohibited. The Equal Protection Clause holding broke new ground insofar as the Supreme Court's precedents concerned themselves with what happens before votes are cast.[14]

Article II §1 – state judicial violation of state legislative powers: Three Justices (Rehnquist, Scalia, and Thomas) reasoned that the Florida Supreme Court infringed upon the state legislature's authority by interpreting the Florida election laws in ways that distorted a fair construction of state legislative intent. The two remaining Justices in the majority (O'Connor and Kennedy) refused to join the Chief Justice's concurrence on this matter, and the four liberal Justices dissented.

5 U.S.C. §3 considerations for the remedy: Five Justices (the conservative majority Justices) agreed that the recount remedy ordered by the Florida Supreme Court threatened the legislature's purpose to take advantage of the "safe harbor" provisions of federal law. Since December 12 (the date of the decision) was the deadline for securing the "safe harbor," the Justices reversed the state high court's remedial order. The four liberal Justices opposed this ruling.

If one steps back to take a broader tactical view of the opinions and the breakdown among the Justices, a most revealing scenario jumps from the pages – one that cured the problem of conservative division and secured the appearance of unanimity. The majority Justices were divided among themselves. Three conservatives (Rehnquist, Scalia, and Thomas) aimed to ground the decision in Article II §1, whereas the other two (Kennedy and O'Connor) refused to sign onto that rationale. That left the Equal Protection analysis promoted in a draft opinion by Justices Kennedy and O'Connor.[15] If events had stopped at that point, there would have been no majority opinion; potentially, there would only have been a judgment of the Court, followed by the Art II opinion (Rehnquist, Scalia, Thomas), a conservative Equal Protection opinion (Kennedy and O'Connor), a liberal Equal Protection opinion (Souter and Breyer), and four dissenters contesting on different bases the outcome of the decision on remedial relief.

Such a scenario would have been a mess; it would have highlighted the conflict of conservatives vs. conservatives, of liberals vs. liberals, and of conservatives vs. liberals; it would have put into striking relief the incompetency of judicial intervention in presidential electoral politics. And that would have played into the liberal position, first declared in *Bush I*, that the Court should never have taken the case to begin with.

Housecleaning had to be done before the decision was announced to an anxious nation. First, the conservatives needed five conservative votes. Since Kennedy and O'Connor were unwilling to jump ship from their Equal Protection argument, that meant that their conservative brethren had to come on board. Almost as a bonus to the conservatives, two liberals came along for the ride; now, there were seven votes for a constitutional violation. A good measure of unanimity now secured, the Chief Justice could take things a step further. He insisted upon releasing the Kennedy-O'Connor majority ruling as a *per curiam* opinion,[16] this to give it the veneer of a unanimous decision, revealing an "air of consensus,"[17] as it were.

Yet more was needed to prevent the Equal Protection rationale from opening a Pandora's box. Unless the scope of the equality analysis were reined in considerably, the *Bush v. Gore* decision might invite future constitutional claims for structural reforms in electoral matters,[18] such as the need for uniformity in electronic machine technology in all voting districts.[19] Mindful of that, O'Connor demanded that the *per curiam* opinion include qualifying language: "Our consideration is limited to the present circumstances, for the problem of equal protection in election processes generally presents many complexities."[20] In other words, the Equal Protection holding was good for this case, and this case only; it was not to be employed to revolutionize the constitutional law of elections. [21]

In the midst of these confusing conceptual moves and voting alignments, Rehnquist and his conservative allies could publicly claim a level of judicial accord belied by their doctrinal divisions. They could even claim, as conservative pundits later did, that the vote in the case was 7-2. Never mind the 5-4 split on the "safe harbor" remedial ruling; never mind the disputed soundness of the Equal Protection arguments tendered by *per curiam* opinion. What mattered was the judgment, the one favoring George W. Bush. No wonder, then, that Justice John Paul Stevens subsequently declared: "The [*per curiam* opinion] by the majority of this Court can only lend credence to the most cynical appraisal of the work of judges throughout this land."[22]

&

> O'Connor and her husband were hosting a party when she heard
> Dan Rather on CBS call Florida for Democrat Al Gore. "This
> is terrible," she exclaimed, according to two eyewitnesses. (2000)[23]
> [The Supreme Court] took the case and decided it at a time when it
> was still a big election issue. Maybe the Court should have said,
> 'We're not going to take it, goodbye.' . . . Probably the Supreme
> Court added to the problem at the end of the day.
>   – Sandra Day O'Connor (2013)[24]

Law students are taught that the legal reasoning of a case counts for more than its results. If that were entirely true, the Court's politically disastrous opinion in *Dred Scott v. Sandford* (1857)[25] might be defended,[26] whereas the landmark opinion in *Brown. v. Board of Education* (1954)[27] might be criticized.[28] But as those cases reveal, results very much matter. Sometimes what the Court does is far more important than what it says. That is surely true of *Bush v. Gore*. Few, if any, of the six opinions in the case will be remembered. Few, if any, will likely have much influence on the law.[29] But so what?

Let us be clear: The opinions in *Bush v. Gore* are of no great consequence (unless some future Justices breathe creative life into one or more of them.). What is important, by the norms of tactical decision-making, is the result. While the Justices may have had any variety of reasons for doing what they did,[30] there is one reason that meshes especially well with the final judgment in the case. What was most important about the presidential election of 2000 was not so much how a Bush Administration would govern the nation, but rather how it might shape the federal judiciary in the future, especially the Supreme Court. The conservatives on the Court surely must have understood beforehand what liberals realized afterwards – that a victory for George W. Bush was the best way to perpetuate the legacy of the Rehnquist Court. Though true as a generalization, it was not necessarily true for each of the five conservatives then on the Court, if only because they were not all similarly situated when it came to their respective legacies. In that regard, consider the following sketches of the key judicial players in *Bush v. Gore*:

Chief Justice Rehnquist: Here was a man who then had a lot at stake. By the time of *Bush v. Gore* he had 14 years of jurisprudence under his Supreme Court belt. Rehnquist had made quite a constitutional mark for himself on everything from federalism to criminal justice, among other things. But he could not always count on five votes as Justice Kennedy and O'Connor would sometimes betray their conservative credentials in the name of centrist tactics. Translated: Why risk any further judicial losses at the hands of a liberal President? To vote as Rehnquist did was the smart move, the Machiavellian move.

Justice Scalia: Antonin Scalia was 64 when *Bush v. Gore* was decided; William Rehnquist was 76. Though Scalia much sought it, he had been passed up for the Chief Justice's position in 1986. If Rehnquist were to retire soon (and there were then reports that he might[31]), perhaps Scalia might yet lay claim to that coveted office. Moreover, if *Bush v. Gore* came out the right way, in "the next four years and possibly eight years President Bush, aided by legions of former and present members of the same Federalist Society that Scalia helped to create and support over the years, some of them still sitting in the Justice Department, would be sending conservative, possibly originalist-oriented jurists to the federal judiciary. Any vacancies on the Supreme Court would be filled with those who would tip the voting direction in Scalia's favor, and who might also follow his brand of textualism and originalism."[32] Translated: Voting as he did, Scalia increased the chances that some or all of those things would happen. That meant he had time enough to write textualist/originalist opinions such as *District of Columbia v. Heller,*[33] the guns-rights case.

Justice O'Connor: The world looked much different to Justice O'Conner in 2013 than it did in 2000. In time, she came to realize what she only vaguely suspected when *Bush v. Gore* came before the Court – that she had more to fear from a staunchly conservative bench than from a tepid liberal one. As it played out, O'Connor became increasingly alienated from the Republican Party and disenchanted with the jurisprudence of her fellow conservative Justices.[34] Translated: By her legacy lights, she voted the wrong way in *Bush v. Gore*. Hers was an unwise move.

Justice Kennedy: Here is a man who could stare into the water and fall in love with the image. His ego aside, Anthony Kennedy has nonetheless managed to do well playing the centrist card in various contexts, whether in abortion or gay rights cases. His mish-mash form of jurisprudence has had some measure of real success. But if some of his most notable opinions are to survive, they are not likely to do so at the hands of strong-willed conservatives.[35] Then again, he really cannot rely on liberal Justices to do his bidding either, since some of his other important opinions would be condemned by tough-minded liberals.[36] By those standards, *Bush v. Gore* was something of mixed blessing for Justice Kennedy, though it is nonetheless true that he votes more often with the Court's conservative bloc than with its liberal wing.[37] Translated: Unless another centrist comes to the Court, Kennedy stood to lose some clout and gain some clout by virtue of his vote in *Bush v. Gore*.

And what of the liberal dissenters? What might they have done? Well, Justice Breyer is said to "have sent his law clerks out on reconnaissance missions to identify potential converts from the majority."[38] But that balloon never floated because Justice O'Connor was firm in her vote. Instead of stressing legal doctrinal logic, however, Breyer could have played a much more Machiavellian card, one that might have switched O'Connor's mind. He had to convince her that her centrist jurisprudential legacy had more to lose than to gain with a Bush Court filled with the likes of Scalia and Thomas. Had O'Connor been led cunningly to see in 2000 what she eventually saw in 2013, *Bush v. Gore* may have come out the opposite way. Imagine that.

Justice Stevens, too, had made a pitch for Kennedy's vote, since he appeared (as always) to be on the fence.[39] That attempt likewise failed, if only because Kennedy seemed to have more to gain with casting his lot with the conservatives, who would secure his vote even at the expense of suffering his "self-dramatization."[40] Losing the case, however, did not mean that the four liberals might not have another option with possible future implications. Recall our earlier consideration of the Equal Protection argument in *Bush v. Gore* as laying the conceptual groundwork for structural changes in American voting law. In the short run, such arguments might influence election-law cases only in the lower courts; in the long run, they might even point toward the Supreme Court's intervention in federal election voting for a progressive agenda.

The Machiavellian lessons of Bush v. Gore: (1) Focus on the big picture, on what counts most to oneself; (2) Do not be afraid to act boldly; (3) Ignore potential conflict-of-interest problems and never recuse oneself from the case; (4) Secure at any cost five votes to obtain the desired result; (5) When searching for allies, do not necessarily confine oneself to the law; appeal, instead, to the heart of what matters to prospective allies; (6) Take whatever steps are available to feign unity; (7) Do not fret over doctrinal inconsistency; (8) Limit any potential liabilities in the majority opinion regardless of the illogic of doing so; and (9) Act and appear judicious, thereafter moving on as if nothing unusual occurred. This formula worked splendidly for William Rehnquist, sufficiently for Antonin Scalia (though he never became Chief Justice and never received new and faithful textualist allies), adequately for Anthony Kennedy, and unsuccessfully for Sandra Day O'Connor.

❧

July 19, 2005: It must have been a joyous day for the retired Chief Justice, who would be dead within two months. For on that occasion, John G. Roberts, Jr., one of Rehnquist's former law clerks (October Term 1980), was nominated by President George W. Bush to become Chief Justice. Of course, Rehnquist may have suspected that possibility years earlier when, several months after *Bush v. Gore* came down, the President nominated Roberts for a seat on the United States Court of Appeals for the District of Columbia. After Rehnquist died and Roberts was sworn in as his successor, the new Chief Justice said of his former boss: "The Chief is a towering figure in American law, one of a handful of great Chief Justices."[41] Indeed. Though John Roberts would forge his own jurisprudence, that of William Rehnquist was in fairly good hands with his former law clerk. Mission accomplished.

And to think that it all may have traced back to *Bush v. Gore*, where the judgment of the Court mattered far more than any of the opinions in the case, including Rehnquist's own. The name of the strategic game was not, after all, the precedential value of *Bush v. Gore*, or the soundness of its doctrinal analysis, or even any fame it might bring to any Justice. No, not at all. What was most important was the preservation of one's judicial legacy – that blanket of influence that would cover future generations for decades to come.[42] Measured by the yardstick of jurisprudential legacy, William Rehnquist did rather well, perhaps better than all the rest.

Chapter 16

On Writing

When Style Should Trump Substance

Language was Machiavelli's weapon.

– Angelo Codevilla[1]

Holmes was a great judge because he was a great literary artist.

– Richard Posner[2]

Style stands at the door: Whence comes this most peculiar of all visitors? Such words may please philosophers or prose writers, but they have no place in the law. Legal writing, after all, cabins creativity and binds us to its own rules. It bars style from the door, or so we have been led to believe. But do not believe it.

In truth, a few fitting words can trump the finest of legal arguments. Metaphors matter, analogies assist, and an active verb sometimes sways passive minds. Style is the sister of substance. For all the effort that is spent teaching law students about the logic of the law, the inescapable truth is otherwise: "The life of the law has not been logic." [3] It took a Supreme Court Justice in the person of Oliver Wendell Holmes to give that idea currency. There is the experience of life, the letter of the law, the reasons invoked to explain both, and the package in which it is all wrapped. We call that packaging *style*. Hence, how we style the law can determine its substance; it can make the mundane memorable; it can make the complex seem comprehensible; and it can turn a precedent around with the ease of a few well-selected words, and more.

"The sparkling, vivid, memorable opinion," it has been said, "is not chained to the immediate context of its creation. It can be pulled out and made exemplary of law's durable concerns." In that regard, the "literary judge wears best over time."[4] But being literary can also mean writing in simple and straightforward ways. Sometimes a few words will do. Consider Judge Richard Posner's forthrightness "Heterosexuals get drunk and pregnant, producing unwanted children; their reward is to be allowed to marry. Homosexual couples do not produce unwanted children; their reward is to be denied the right to marry. Go figure."[5]

Those who have moved the law in their direction know that style can save a weak argument; it can convince a confused mind; it can resolve a riddle; and it can even inform how we think about the law. When properly used, style can immortalize an idea or principle. And it serves all masters, be they Nietzsche or Holmes, Derrida or Breyer, Wittgenstein or Roberts, or Hobbes or Scalia.

A careful Justice is attentive to the need to craft an opinion in a certain way, sometimes in tandem with substance, sometimes despite it. Style can be a substitute for substance; it can be a way to circumvent substance; it can intentionally complicate substance; and it can even contradict substance. Style can be simple. Or it can be layered. Or it can draw from the well of metaphor. Or it can be alliterative. Or it can be a tool for veiling thoughts too controversial to be expressed directly. It can be anything provided that it serve the demands for which it is employed.

Holmes mastered metaphors, Warren traded in ambiguity, Black sparked passions, and Brennan used adjectives to breathe vigorous life into the law. Their work, whatever their actual intentions, exemplifies the various values of style.

Some believe that style begins where substance ends, but the wise understand that it begins where substance begins. In that sense, style may do what reason alone cannot. Think of it as a noble lie that gives the law its meaning, a meaning at once profound and perplexing. And it is just that quality that makes style indispensible to an extraordinary Judge, the one who knows when and how to wield the sword of style.

❧

Metaphors do more than explain the meaning of statutes and constitutional provisions. They also create their meaning.

– Louis J. Sirico, Jr.[6]

The value of metaphors & polished prose. Modern First Amendment law begins with Justice Holmes. He is the *pater* of that body of law because he crafted metaphors to do the work that precedent could not. The notion that the dangers of speech were to be measured by analogy to "falsely shouting fire in a theatre"[7] came from Holmes. The idea that role of the First Amendment was to permit ideas to be traded in a "market"[8] came from Holmes. Such metaphors informed his "clear and present danger"[9] and "imminent danger"[10] tests. Whatever the criticisms leveled against Holmes's metaphors and the tests linked to them,[11] they have left indelible marks on the law. Given that, it is ironic that Holmes once declared that it "is one of the misfortunes of the law that ideas become encysted in phrases, and thereafter for a long time cease to provoke further analysis."[12] The irony is that it is precisely that "misfortune" that provided Holmes's metaphors and tests with the staying power they have come to enjoy. Truer to the mark was Felix Frankfurter's assessment: "It is not reckless prophecy to assume that his famous dissenting opinion in the *Abrams* case will live as long as English prose retains its power to move."[13]

It is a testament to Holmes's writing skills that they secured a place for him on the Mount Olympus of law. Those same skills helped him to shape the modern law of free speech, even by way of dissenting opinions. In several important respects, his metaphors were his method.[14]

The importance of obscure phrases. The Court in *Brown v. Board of Education*[15] summoned history and precedent to serve the Equality Principle, which Earl Warren recast[16] to aid in the battle against school segregation. It was, most assuredly, a noble effort undertaken by nine courageous Justices. Of course, announcing a grand constitutional principle is one thing; putting it into practice is yet another. When it came to the latter, Warren and his colleagues[17] ducked into the alley of obscure phrases: "with all deliberate speed"[18] is how they put it. And what exactly does that signify? If one pondered the meaning of those words, the message was a mixed one: On the one had, to be "deliberate" is to be unhurried, measured, and/or to proceed with cautious resolve. On the other hand, to move with "speed" is to act in a hurry. Were Warren and his colleagues ordering Southern segregationists to first proceed with measured deliberation and only thereafter with dispatch? Or were they ordering them to act quickly and purposefully at the outset? Even if we assume the latter to be the case, what specifically does it mean to act with *speed*? How contextual was the test of speed in the segregationist setting of the 1950s? Full speed or gradual speed? Whatever else the phrase meant, it was different from what the lawyers for the NAACP wanted – a "forthwith" formula.[19] That is why Thurgood Marshall then stressed that there could be no "middle ground," and that *Brown I* would "mean nothing until [a] time limit is set." [20] But no time limit was set. Thus, "if *Brown I* was a clarion call, *Brown II's* ambivalence implicitly diminished the moral imperative of the first decision."[21] Indeed it did; hence the need for style to mask substance.

Our point: The Warren Court had to be evasive; it needed opaque words to do the work that neither legal reasoning nor a clear directive could do. The Court had to appear as if it were ordering immediate action while at the same time allowing for a measure of gradualism. Conflicting norms? Certainly. Yet that is what might be required, and that is where well crafted words come into play. Sometimes one's message must be obscure; sometimes it must appear to be what it is not; and sometimes one must write to different audiences in different ways, even within the same work. The lesson here is that every now and then the logic of the law must succumb to the experience of life, and when it does words matter, even fuzzy words.

The significance of rhetoric: Like Justice Benjamin Cardozo before him, Justice Hugo Black had a flair for words. The Alabama jurist was known as the "absolutist" of the First Amendment. There was nothing sophisticated about his homespun originalist/textualist approach to decisionmaking in this area. His First Amendment motto: "No law means no law."[22] Admittedly, it was tautological. And both liberals and conservatives called him on it repeatedly. Still, he was determined. One does not have to buy into Black's absolutism to recognize its value when combined with the rhetoric he employed to defend expressive liberty against McCarthy-era attacks. In 1951 he wrote passionately in defense of free speech:

> Public opinion being what it now is, few will protest the conviction of these Communist petitioners. There is hope, however, that in calmer times, when present pressures, passions and fears subside, this or some later Court will restore the First Amendment liberties to the high preferred place where they belong in a free society.[23]

To the same effect, but with even greater vigor, in yet another case he railed against the specter of men and women frightened to stand on their rights:

> Too many men are being driven to become government-fearing and time-serving because the Government is being permitted to strike out at those who are fearless enough to think as they please and say what they think. This trend must be halted if we are to keep faith with the Founders of our Nation and pass on to future generations of Americans the great heritage of freedom which they sacrificed so much to leave to us. The choice is clear to me. If we are to pass on that great heritage of freedom, we must return to the original language of the Bill of Rights. We must not be afraid to be free.[24]

Hugo Black was not effective doctrinally – he wrote few majority opinions in this area and his absolutism seldom garnered more than two votes on the Court. And it was true: Justices such as Frankfurter and Harlan usually got the better of the doctrinal argument. But that was not Black's domain. He was very effective in other ways; he played a significant role in liberalizing the culture (both legal and popular) of the First Amendment and thereby made the near-absolutism of the likes of William Brennan more palpable. In that respect, Hugo Black's rhetoric touched a nerve. The result was a Court more sensitive to First Amendment freedoms. Not surprisingly, Justice Black was labeled as "one of the great men of his generation."[25] If so, it was more because of the *pathos* of his words than because of the *logos* of his legal arguments. In the case of Hugo Black, it was a triumph of style over substance.

The worth of catch phrases. Like Holmes, William Brennan no doubt appreciated the value of important catch phrases. Such phrases are appropriately titled when they catch and hold the attention of readers; they help direct attention to a writer's purposes and divert attention away from oversights or omissions. When adroitly crafted, they are the artifacts that fill lawyers' briefs and law students' minds as they evolve into mainstays in legal thought.

The First Amendment reflects "a profound national commitment to the principle that debate on public issues should be uninhibited, robust, and wide-open." That phrase,[26] gracing Justice Brennan's opinion in *New York Times Co. v. Sullivan,*[27] has played significantly in reconfiguring and liberalizing the American law of free speech. Birthed in the context of a defamation case, this phrase has become the mantra of judges, lawyers, law students, and others. It not only added to the doctrinal value of *Sullivan,* it catapulted it into the sphere of landmark opinions.

৯

We stress: All advice is contextual, here as elsewhere in this book. What works in one situation might not work as well in another. That is why it is not helpful to the exceptional Justice to endorse a *general* approach to judicial writing.[28] True, there are times when one needs to be clear and concise, but there are times when one needs to be opaque and verbose. Writing must to be tailored to intended audiences and to one's objectives; otherwise, it is likely to be little more than an idle literary exercise.

How one writes depends on the audience: for other judges? / for lawyers? / for the press? / for the public? / for law professors? / or for no other reason than to secure five votes? Moreover, how one composes a concurrence or dissent may be quite different from how one drafts a majority opinion. Since many only read the beginning and the end of a long opinion (or merely the syllabus), there may be occasions when it is to one's benefit to write in a lackluster but thoughtful way, and to locate significant statements in the middle of an opinion, perhaps even in the center of an "unimportant" opinion. By the same token, sometimes it may be appropriate to invoke key "search" words (e.g., Google words), and then again sometimes not. It may even be helpful to buttress one's cause by using photographs in opinions, this in order to tap into the benefits (rational or emotional) of visuality. Thus, how one writes the law depends on who is reading it or why it is being written as it is.[29]

Careful writing counts. When done prudently, it can be one of the most important of assets. If a Justice aspires to greatness, if he desires to clutch more power, he must not do what modern Justices do – regularly assign opinion writing to law clerks. Whenever it matters, he must be an author, not a delegator. He must actively lead, not merely manage. Drafts of important opinions must begin with the Justice, not with the law clerks. So, too, the final edits must be done by the Justice, if only to insert those last-minute changes that can make a difference. For such reasons and others, the "shop model," as we brand it, poses a clear and present danger to any meaningful attempt to render an opinion to one's advantage.[30] (We say more about this in Chapter 18.)

Artfully crafted opinion writing is more time consuming, more thought demanding, more complicated and difficult to execute. That is why it wars with today's shop model of judicial writing. That model of law-clerk-driven writing tends to be lengthy, mundane, and orthodox – facts, issues, laws, "analysis," and conclusion – all replete with a full stock of quotations and tedious case citations. It typically substitutes careful writing and analysis for a stock-in-trade and cut-and-paste approach to "judicial" writing. Those Justices who regularly maintain the role of delegator subvert their native abilities to maximize whatever power and fame they might claim.

ℰ

Lest we be misunderstood, we do not discount the value of substance, important as style can be. Substance, obviously, is the matter with which a Justice works. How he or she shapes it, reconstitutes it, and offers it to colleagues and the public all count. In that regard, there may well be instances in which it serves a Justice best to be rigorous[31] and stilted in writing an opinion, even Kantian-like. Our sketch of styles, by no means complete, is premised on the notion that different circumstances necessitate different styles. Hence, metaphors worked well in Holmes's free speech opinions, opaqueness worked best in *Brown II*, rhetoric helped Justice Black market his constitutional absolutism, and catch phrases allowed Justice Brennan to reconfigure the jurisprudence of defamation and other areas of the law. In the end, both substance and style must be seen as tools by which a Justice molds the law to his or her will. Because of that, neither substance nor style need be valued in its own right – they are merely the means, one's *will* is the end.

By Machiavellian calculations, words are weapons; they can provide an important advantage in the struggle for dominance. Words can be manipulated so as to create new meanings or change old ones.[32] They do not describe reality; they define it. When used tactically, words can reorient jurisprudence in power-maximizing ways. Consequently, their value is their effectiveness. Or to cast it more metaphorically, "the best verbal flag is the one most saluted."[33]

Chapter 17

When It Is Wise to Write a Separate Opinion

I depart from the orders of others.

— Niccolò Machiavelli[1]

It has been said that the "most important internal effect of a system per-mitting dissents and concurrences is to improve the majority opinion."[2] While that may make for a fine line in a Constitution Day speech, it is never to be taken seriously by any Justice wed to amassing power and prestige. If the majority opinion and/or result does not benefit one's purposes, why bother to improve it *unless* in doing so one aims to under-mine that opinion? Or as Machiavelli put in in *The Prince*: "a prudent lord . . . cannot observe faith, nor should he, when such observance turns against him."[3] True.

We pause at the outset to highlight something important. Neither a separate opinion (a concurrence, for example) nor a dissent should be obsessed with setting the law right, preserving precedent, or enhanc-ing "values" such as the coherence of the law. That is too elevated a notion. It is a notion that needs to be pulled down to the realities of our modern world.

Judicial resistance of the kind we counsel often "gains power from its very opposition to whatever is established and inherited."[4] If a separate opinion or dissent is a point of departure; it is a break from some rule or norm. For our purposes, that breakaway is from law in its fixed form. That being so, the Justice of more than ordinary tal-ents will sometimes take exception to such formalistic views of the law – views at odds with the Power Principle best suited to one's ambitious enterprise.

One dissents when it is in his best interest, and not instead when it is in the best interest of THE LAW. Homage to the lofty demands of THE LAW is servitude. Or more aptly, it is to subjugate oneself to a fiction, to a lie in the service of another's will. The exceptional jurist, by Machiavellian contrast, aims to dethrone THE LAW as King; but it is a quiet revolt, a very quiet one.

As a general principle, law (like religion) steals power. Otherwise, we would live by the caprice of chaos and anarchy.[5] Hence, law understood as a limiting principle is a gospel that must be preached from on high. To do so, it must be cast in elevated terms that seem to transcend the will of any individual or group. Hence, the notion of the *common good*. But actual allegiance to that good can be disadvantageous. It deprives one of power.

Dissent is the attempt to reclaim one's power, but in such a way as to make it appear otherwise, to appear elevated. In that regard, our Judge is not an anarchist. He or she appreciates the importance of THE LAW and endorses it at every public turn. Thus, the Judge befriends the moral principle in public, but the amoral one in private; openly hails the common good, but acts to serve one's personal good. Does the resulting hypocrisy trouble our jurist? No. For he or she understands all too well that neither law nor morality could hope to exist without it. The goal is to master hypocrisy.

Of course, it may be best to strive to have someone else do one's bidding. Thus, it may be smart to first venture to influence the author of a majority opinion so as to secure an advantage. Failing that, however, one of the main purposes of a separate opinion or dissent is to undercut the majority opinion – right down to its roots if need be – in order to uplift one's own agenda, albeit suitably draped in the garb of THE LAW. In all of this, the Judge, like Machiavelli's Prince, must "learn to be able not to be good, and to use this [knowledge or] not to use it according to necessity."[6] Necessity, after all, makes even the pious sin; it can override the noblest of principles.

৩

One considers a separate opinion because he or she has been unable to secure some outcome, or doctrinal principle, or majority-opinion authorship. The reason for writing is ether because there is something to be lost by remaining silent or something to be gained by speaking out. Too many modern Justices do not appreciate this as they produce concurrences or dissents with robotic regularity, as if the world awaited their worthless wisdom. In the 2009-2010 Term, for example, "there was at least one concurring opinion in 77 percent of unanimous rulings."[7] That said, a concurrence can be tactically important *if* one's objective is to blur and/or blunt the impact of a majority opinion. By the same strategic measure, when unanimity is attained at the price of securing votes, one's opportunity to slip something into a majority opinion is great – it may be no more than a few obscure words in an abstruse sentence.

A majority opinion controls the law of today, but a tactfully crafted separate opinion can control the law of tomorrow. How long "today" lasts and when "tomorrow" comes are other matters.[8] Still, in its capsulized form our lesson is simple: When one is on the wrong side of a majority vote, sometimes it is best to cut one's losses by writing either a concurrence or a dissent. This counsel is, to be sure, linked to what we said in Chapter 7 on when to embrace controversy, and to what is urged in Chapter 16 concerning writing style. For now, we focus on the lesson at hand.

Next, let us say a few words on when it is *imprudent* to write a separate opinion. Such opinions, especially dissents, should be shunned when they are done with Twitter-like frequency as Justice William O. Douglas ("wild Bill") did in the 783 dissents he released between 1939 and 1975 (an average of 21.7 per term).[9] Howling at the moon may suit a wild wolf, but it is of no use to a cunning fox. Here, frequency is not synonymous with influence; in fact, it may actually diminish it.

Furthermore, it is ill advised to write dissents whenever they serve no real purpose other than to vent one's anger and/or to mock the majority gratuitously. While spectacle may make for good theater, it tends to devalue one's jurisprudential stock and, worse still, it unnecessarily creates an adversarial relationship with one's colleagues whose votes will be needed come tomorrow. Justice Oliver Wendell Holmes appreciated that. Hence, and by stark contrast, he wrote his seminal dissent in *Lochner v. New York*[10] in a somewhat restrained tone, but with enough finesse and flair to prove influential in the long run.

One more thing to avoid: the self-righteous separate opinion. This is the kind of opinion written when one is intoxicated with his or her self-importance and feels driven to pontificate pompously from on high. One such example, among many, is Chief Justice Warren Burger's 1986 concurrence in *Bowers v. Hardwick*[11] where he proclaimed with God-fearing certainty: "To hold that the act of homosexual sodomy is somehow protected as a fundamental right would be to cast aside millennia of moral teaching."[12] Such scruples aside, the real moral here is plain: avoid such pointless moralizing. In much the same way, the self-righteous are notorious for being unnecessarily combative.[13] They are happy to burn the barn. And they do so for two reasons: first, they do appreciate the danger of their actions, and second, they do not care – as if recklessness were its own reward.

❧

Next, it is important to be aware of the various kinds of judicial dissent. A jurist may issue an *ex officio* dissent by what he or she says in public or writes in a book or article. Take, for example, Judge Learned Hand's 1958 book titled *The Bill of Rights*, wherein, among other things, the revered jurist registered a dignified (but unpersuasive) dissent[14] to the Warren Court's constitutional handiwork in *Brown v. Board of Education*.[15] Justice Antonin Scalia did something of the same, though in a more tactical and general way, in 1997 with the publication of his book *A Matter of Interpretation*, which took exception to many of the then prevalent canons of construction.[16]

Another form of judicial dissent is a dissent from a denial of certiorari – meaning that a Justice takes exception to the Court's unwillingness to hear a case. On the one hand, a tactic a Justice might use to win votes to hear a case is to circulate his or her dissent from a proposed denial of cert. This stratagem may be especially effective if other Justices sign on to it.[17] On the other hand, the aim may be to prompt future

Courts as to how to resolve an issue. A good example of that move is Justice John Paul Stevens' dissent (joined by Justices Souter, Ginsburg and Breyer) from a denial of *cert.* in the case of *In re Kevin Nigel Stanford* (2002),[18] which involved the denial of a habeas petition in the case of an execution of a defendant who at the time of the crime was under the age of 18. That dissent may well have shaped the opinion of the Governor of Kentucky who in 2003 commuted Stanford's sentence to life imprisonment without parole.[19] It may have also influenced the Court's ruling in *Roper v. Simmons* (2005),[20] in which the Justices declared by a 5-4 vote that such executions are unconstitutional, this despite a 1989 precedent[21] to the contrary.[†]

Implicit in all of the above is the notion of the threat of a dissent, regardless of whether that threat is actualized. Such a threat may be "useful for a Justice trying to persuade the majority to narrow its holding or tone down the language of its opinion."[22] To be effective, such threats

- must be uncommon;
- must prompt a real measure of alarm;
- must be supported by one or more Justices; and
- must be followed, when needed, by a commanding dissent.

Threats of this kind are also helpful when unanimity is sought or when a Justice's particular vote is desired. In such instances, however, care must be taken to give the appearance that one's threat is not spiteful, but rather the product of a serious and genuine difference of jurisprudential opinion. Nothing personal. In these instances, it may even be advantageous to feign dissent in the hope of changing a majority opinion so as to

---

†. An example of what *not* to do in a related kind of situation is well illustrated by Justice Clarence Thomas's lone vote to deny a stay in *June Medical Services v. Gee*, 579 U.S. __ (2016). The case involved the continued enforcement of a Louisiana anti-abortion law, one that imposed certain conditions on doctors who perform abortions. Over Justice Thomas's objection, the Court stayed a Fifth Circuit ruling affirming the law's constitutionality, this while a similar issue had just been argued before the Court in *Whole Woman's Health v. Hellerstedt*, 579 U.S. __ (2016). By this self-righteous move, Thomas stood to gain nothing other than the contempt that comes with the appearance of rank bias.

add a few innocent-looking but clever lines (of the Trojan Horse variety) to that opinion. Here as elsewhere, such moves must be infrequent.

Five-to-four opinions can provide a rare opportunity to secure one's advantage. Consider in this regard *Philip Morris USA v. Williams* (2007),[23] a wrongful death lung cancer case in which the issue was whether punitive damages were constitutionally excessive. The case was decided by a single vote. To say the least, Justice Stephen Breyer's majority opinion was not a model of jurisprudential clarity, and the dissenters hammered that point home. That fact alone could have given one of the other four Justices in the majority a welcome window of opportunity to draft a concurrence suited to his or her advantage. Such a concurrence should be circulated late, at the last minute. And then, all one has to do is provide a measure of clarity absent in the majority opinion. Justice Powell did something along those very lines in his concurrence in *Branzburg v. Hayes* (1972),[24] a reporters' privilege case. For many years thereafter, lawyers and judges[25] pivoted their interpretation of the law on that concurrence. Justice Powell employed a similar tactic in his concurrence in *Zurcher v. Stanford Daily* (1978),[26] a 5-3 police search of a press newsroom case.

ॐ

Maxim: Do not blindly honor *stare decisis* (see Chapter 13). It is a fool's doctrine if it prompts one to yield power to another. Worse still, one's adversaries know this; they will only invoke the doctrine when it suits them, otherwise they will do all in their interpretive power to skirt it. So when precedents stack up, and when the wall of existing law is too high to conquer, one can dissent. One can call for a new paradigm, a novel way of looking at the legal world. That's where the right dissent, written in the right way, and delivered at the right time, can steer around *stare decisis*.

Maxim: Distort – be tactical, not principled. Justice Robert Jackson put it well: "The technique of the dissenter often is to exaggerate the holding of the Court beyond the meaning of the majority and then to blast away at the excess. So that the poor lawyer with a similar case does not know whether the majority meant what it seemed to say or what the minority said it meant." [27]

Maxim: Plant the seeds of discontent, but ones that may actually grow. It is not enough to dissent; one must point the way to some attainable goal, some realizable tomorrow. Kathleen Sullivan (a learned constitutional scholar and talented litigator) put it in warring terms: "Great Supreme Court dissents lie like buried ammunition for future generations to unearth when the time comes."[28] Few have mastered this skill with more success than Justice Oliver Wendell Holmes, who never let *stare decisis* stand in his pragmatic way. Holmes was as shrewd as he was sage. Still, he needed time to come to his jurisprudential rescue. And it did with the advent of the judicial crisis of the late 1930s and the emergence in the 1960s of a spirited commitment to free speech. Beyond that, Holmes also savored realist bravado. In 1924, he wrote to Harold Laski: "One of the advantages of a dissent is that one can say what one thinks without having to blunt the edges and cut off the corners to suit someone else."[29] There is truth there, but it is a truth that is useful only if one adapts it to his or her benefit. And, to be sure, Holmes did issue his share of dissents that enhanced the value of his jurisprudential brand both in his life and posthumously.[30]

Against the general backdrop of those three maxims, we offer some additional advice by way of short sketches that illustrate when it is wise to write a separate opinion. These are opinions authored by:

1. James Iredell dissenting in *Chisholm v. Georgia* [31]
2. Louis Brandeis concurring in *Whitney v. California*[32] and
3. Robert Jackson concurring in *Youngstown Sheet & Tube Co. v. Sawyer.*[33]

The three separate opinions[†] reveal how one can sometimes lose the case of today and yet win the cause of tomorrow. Or as in chess, one

---

1. [†] John Marshall Harlan's dissent in *Plessy v. Ferguson*, 163 U.S. 537, 552 (Harlan, J., dissenting), could be added to this list, insofar as the Justice's realistic understanding of white supremacist politics trumped any formalistic fidelity to the separate-but-equal doctrine.

can sometimes gain a strategic advantage by setting up the board for future moves. By either measure, the ultimate "checkmate" may best be secured.

James Iredell: Pragmatism trumps principle: During the 1787 Constitutional debates, eminent Federalists such as Alexander Hamilton[34] and James Madison[35] assured the States that out-of-state creditors could not sue them in a federal court without their consent for payment of their Revolutionary War debts. Despite these assurances, the Supreme Court ruled to the contrary in *Chisolm v. Georgia* (1793).[36] Four Justices gave a principled textual interpretation of Article III to find such jurisdiction. Unlike his brethren, Justice James Iredell understood that it was political suicide for the federal judges to subject the financially strapped States to their contractual obligations. His dissenting opinion read Article III in a pragmatic fashion that conditioned federal jurisdiction in state-citizen diversity actions upon an explicit grant of authority by Congress, which had not yet been provided. In response to a fast and furious groundswell of State opposition to the *Chisholm* ruling, Congress quickly drafted the Eleventh Amendment, which effectively overruled the case. Within a few years, the Amendment was ratified, and Iredell was vindicated.

Louis Brandeis: Eloquence trumps results: On May 16, 1927, a unanimous Supreme Court affirmed California's conviction of Charlotte Anita Whitney for criminal syndicalism.[37] After the Court's ruling, the fifty-nine-year-old social activist faced fourteen years in prison. Though it is often overlooked, Justice Brandeis agreed with that judgment, but did so by way of a curious concurrence.[38] What made it so is that, although it was a concurring opinion, it read as a formidable dissent. In stirring prose, the Justice declared: "Those who won our independence believed that the final end of the State was to make men free to develop their faculties, and that, in its government, the deliberative forces should prevail over the arbitrary." Building on that theme, he added: "Fear of serious injury cannot alone justify suppression of free speech and assembly. Men feared witches and burnt women. It is the function of speech to free men from the bondage of irrational fears."[39] Beyond its eloquence, the Brandeis concurrence provided multiple justifications for safeguarding expressive liberties – though unfortunately not those of Ms. Whitney. Her conviction nothwithstanding, the Brandeis opinion has been lauded as "arguably the most important essay ever written, on or off the bench, on the First Amendment,"[40] and it ranks as one of the most frequently cited opinions written by a Supreme Court Justice.[41]

Robert Jackson: Ordered framework trumps disordered confusion: For decades, courts and commentators have given more weight to Justice Robert Jackson's concurrence in *Youngstown Sheet & Tube Co. v. Sawyer* (1952)[42] than to any of the other opinions in the case.[43] The *Youngstown* decision invalidated President Truman's executive order that directed the Secretary of Commerce to seize and operate most of America's steel mills in the face of a nationwide strike during the Korean War. Although six separate Court opinions agreed that President Truman's order violated his Article II powers, Justice Jackson's opinion alone became highly influential for future analyses of presidential claims of inherent or emergency authority. Not surprisingly, his concurrence has been labeled "the best judicial opinion ever written on the vexing question of the President's constitutional powers."[44] Why did Jackson's concurrence win such renown? The answer: It stood above the conceptual morass. Jackson furnished a structural framework – a tripartite one – that clearly and coherently tendered needed guidance for analyzing the strength of presidential authority to act with or without congressional approval. For that, his concurrence has been hailed as one of the "most highly regarded opinions in the twentieth Century."[45]

✍

These, then, are some tactics for the extraordinary Judge who deems it necessary to write a separate opinion. As always, their efficient use depends on circumstances. If such an opinion does not crack open a window of opportunity, it deserves not to be written.

Chapter 18

Law Clerks

When and How to Use Them

Falsities and diplomacies aside, Supreme Court law clerks are both a blessing and a curse. They are the former because the bureaucracy of the institution is such that work without them would be Herculean. The judicial world has changed much since Justice Horace Gray hired the first Supreme Court law clerk in 1882. There are more clerks, more staff, and far more things to read and write. Today, the nearly 10,000 certiorari petitions submitted each term alone are too much for any single set of eyes to scan and mind to process. True, the Justices decide fewer cases theses days, but their majority opinions tend to be longer and the number of separate opinions is on the increase. Reading cert. memos, bench memos and briefs, preparing for oral arguments, doing the requisite research, writing drafts of one's own opinions and critiquing those of others, and ultimately readying and editing one's own opinions for publication all take considerable time. In those ways and others, a Justice needs four clerks. Hence, these young assistants (typically from distinguished law schools such as Harvard, Yale, Stanford, Chicago, and Columbia) serve an important role. They can also be of service, perhaps more so, *after* they conclude their work at the Court, as they continue to champion their Justices' causes.

Necessity, however, can also be the mother of ruin. Caught in the bureaucratic maze and succumbing to the new normal, too many Justices assume the role of delegators, managers, or shop supervisors. They collaborate with their law clerks; their work product is a team effort. Thus has it come to the point that "the admitted practice of the Justices [is] to assign the drafting of opinions to their law clerks."[1] The trend is to cede "the task of composing their words to their clerks."[2] In some instances, "Justices have issued wholly clerk-written opinions as their own."[3] It all culminates in a collegial, "efficient," and egalitarian atmosphere where everyone makes his or her contribution to the cause of Justice. This is ideal in liberal theory, though disastrous in actual practice. If that is the naive mindset, it is one well suited to mediocre Justices who invite exploitation. This provides a welcome window of opportunity for an extraordinary Justice. Put brazenly: One does not seize power by ceding it; one does act secretly by acting openly; and one does not plot an opinion by delegating it. First and foremost, one must be one's own master.

The trick is how best to use one's law clerks, how to harness their work in one's service, and how to cast the image of an honest judicial broker even as one deceives the clerks and others in one's employ. A Justice must command respect as the leader of his or her chambers. Moreover, secrecy must be the working imperative; integrity the perceived norm; and loyalty to a Justice's person and cause the guiding principle. After that, and consistent with that, fidelity to *The Code of Conduct for Law Clerks of the Supreme Court*[4] should be imperative.

✺

Justice William O. Douglas is reputed to have said that "[l]aw clerks are the lowest form of animal life."[5] The eccentric jurist had little use and often no patience for his law clerks. He openly displayed his disdain for them. This, to be sure, is not the way to treat law clerks. Gratuitous or mindless cruelty is imprudent and invites strife, or makes clerks indifferent to their boss's well being. Instead, a Justice must appear to be kindhearted, but also firm. By carrot or stick, the clerks must understand that Authority rests first and fully with their Justice.

A Justice must also have a solemn pact that the secrecy of the chambers remains forever sacrosanct.[†] This requires more than adherence to the law clerks' *Code of Conduct*. It requires that the clerks understand

---

†. Of course, this rule of secrecy does not apply to the Justice. Hence, he or she may dispense with it to the extent that it proves helpful, as in the case of the release of one's private papers. See Chapter 25.

that even their own work product be viewed as that of the Justice. Thus, law clerks must be dissuaded from seeking future fame for drafting some passage or opinion. Fame must yield to fidelity. A Justice must convey that imperative, albeit subtly. For example, he or she might say: "I noticed that Richard Posner, who once clerked for Justice Brennan, now claims to have written *NAACP v. Button*,[6] among other opinions. Can you believe that? I have long felt that such statements, even if true, are a breach of faith. You know, Eugene Gressman, who clerked for Justice Frank Murphy, did much the same and took credit for writing Murphy's famous dissent in the *Korematsu* case."[7] Or on another occasion some casual comment might be made to this effect: "What would ever prompt a clerk to betray his boss like that?" Such prompts, when done cautiously, should suffice, provided a Justice selects clerks with care.

If loyalty is the measure, then wise hiring is the mode. This cannot be left to chance or to selection based simply on the best paper credentials. When it comes to the Supreme Court, there will always be a bounty of candidates with superior qualifications from Ivy League schools. Hence, merit alone cannot be the determinative consideration. Since a Justice needs allies, the "best and the brightest" should be selected with that in mind. To that end, a handful of trusted appellate judges[8] and law professors[9] ought to be enlisted to send along those who can best serve a Justice. Beyond that, other applications should not be considered, though they must be accepted for the sake of appearances. Moreover, favors ought not be granted to please those who direct potential clerks to a Justice, though it may be useful to give that impression on occasion. By the same token, diversity should count only when it serves the interests of a Justice and should not be a factor beyond that. In all of this, attention must be paid to avoid junior-league Niccolòs[10] who may connive to serve their interests at their Justices' expense. This is why one cannot "yield great and excessive power to immature, ideologically driven clerks, who in turn use that power to manipulate their bosses and the institution."[11] There can, after all, be but one fox in the henhouse.

A law clerk must delight in being selected, not just due to the honor of working in the Marble Palace. Rather, a clerk should view his or her selection "as an invitation to life, to a wider [and] richer life,"[12] one like no other. And that emotive sentiment ought to be cultivated during the clerkship and afterwards in professional and social ways. In other words, the clerkship experience should be seen as the beginning of a special lifelong bond, one in which the Justices invest in their clerks to help them however they might. That generosity, of course, will further buttress the clerks' fidelity to their revered Justice. For that reason, a Justice might present each of his or her law clerks before their service concludes with a signed photograph, one inscribed with the Latin line: *Erat tam mirabile* ("It was so wonderful").

Law clerks are not mere stenographers, though sometimes they are that. They are not mere research assistants, though on many occasions they are that, too. And they are not one's associate-in-chambers,[13] though there may be instances in which a semblance of that responsibility might be prudently entrusted to them. Nor are they publicists, though there will be times when their communication skills might prove helpful. And then there is the use to which Felix Frankfurter (a largely failed exemplar of Machiavellian lessons) sometimes put his clerks: he tapped them to act as spies on his colleagues. Other times Frankfurter would lobby the clerks serving his Brethren in the hope that they might in turn influence their Justice to Frankfurter's advantage.[14] Of course, when these practices became known, his colleagues were outraged. Justice Douglas complained that Frankfurter "used his law clerks as flying squadrons against the law clerks of other Justices and even against the Justices themselves."[15] While such tactics may have merit, they are so fraught with perilous repercussions that it is best, by and large, to avoid them or to let information flow from the law clerks' circle in the normal course.

⤚

Tony Mauro is right: "[L]aw clerks are crucial, if not downright indispensible, to the work of the nation's highest court."[16] But here is the rub: What exactly is the work they should do? As already indicated, law clerks can serve in a variety of capacities. And since all clerks are not all created equal, their assignments will differ from clerk to clerk, from assignment to assignment, and from year to year. What is key is that, if and when any delegation occurs, it is done out of informed necessity and meaningful oversight. Thus, there may be situations when a Justice deems it best to be more involved in reviewing cert. petitions[17] and less involved in the drafting of an opinion.

Ever since 1972, and at the suggestion of Justice Lewis Powell, most of the Justices have pooled their clerks, "dividing up all of the filings and having a single clerk's certiorari memo then circulate to all of those participating in the 'cert. pool.' "[18] When it comes to these memos – the ones that instruct the Justices whether to hear a case or not – "recent research shows a strong correlation between cert. pool law clerks' recommendations and whether the Court grants or denies a case."[19] Only Justices John Paul Stevens (now retired) and Samuel Alito have opted out of the pool,[20] and wisely so. According to Professor David O'Brien, "[f]ormer law clerks [estimate] that the preparation of a cert. memo may take anywhere from fifteen minutes to, in a rare case, a full day.,,, When the memos from the cert. pool are circulated, each justice typically has one of his or her clerks go over each memo and make a recommendation on whether the case should be granted or denied. Each clerk in the pool writes roughly 250 cert. memos per term."[21] Translated: Screening the cert. petitions takes a lot of time and work. Hence, the tendency to delegate.

Such actions, however, have their costs. For one thing, by and large they allow the clerks to set the Court's agenda. Moreover, and as Professors Artemus Ward and David Weiden have noted, there is "evidence of pool writers injecting partisanship and strategy into a function that was designed to be objective."[22] In light of this, and given the importance o the Court's docket, a Justice should follow the examples of Justices Stevens and Alito and monitor the cert. petitions with the kind of thoughtfulness most conducive to a Justice's interests. In other words, do not rely on the eyes of others, especially when their interests may be counter to yours.

Sometimes a clerk is so exceptional and the demands of the moment so imperative that a Justice will deem it wise to consign a major undertaking to a young assistant. Such was the case in 1953 when Justice Frankfurter asked his clerk, Alexander Bickel, to prepare a memorandum for him on the legislative history of the Fourteenth Amendment as it pertained to segregation. Young Bickel's 90-page memo found that history to be inconclusive. With that, the case of *Brown v. Board of*

Education was scheduled for reargument.[23] What followed proved to be groundbreaking.

Similarly, one will sometimes have a clerk with substantive and stylistic skills so extraordinary that it may be prudent to permit an added measure of drafting leeway. That was the case with Justice Brennan and Stephen Barnett, his clerk who worked on the seminal *New Yorks Times, Inc. v. Sullivan*[24] case. For it was Barnett who crafted[25] the famous words: "Thus we consider this case against the background of a profound national commitment to the principle that debate on public issues should be uninhibited, robust, and wide-open, and that it may well include vehement, caustic, and sometimes unpleasantly sharp attacks on government and public officials."[26] And those words served Brennan very well for a very long time. The Bickel memo assisted Frankfurter in attaining his goal and the Barnett contributions aided Brennan in achieving his objective. When judiciously supervised, and always attentive to one's end game, such support from law clerks may prove most advantageous.

By contrast, law clerk influence can be significant when the timing of a case demands speedy results. Thus it has been correctly observed that when a Justice "is particularly busy, such as near the end of the term, he or she may be less willing or able to spend time revising a clerk's draft."[27] Justice Powell flagged precisely this difficulty in a memo to his law clerks: "One of the problems which we encountered last term was that I became the 'bottle neck' the last week in May, when several draft opinions hit my desk about the same time. This makes it a bit difficult for me to do the type of reviewing, revising, rewriting, and – above all – careful thinking about each opinion."[28] Every step must be taken to guard against such last minute "bottle neck" scenarios, which diminish a Justice's control of a case while maximizing that of the clerks, who then quite often set the agenda on their terms. Accordingly, calculated measures should be set into motion beforehand to ward off such circumstances. Moreover, if chaos reins in the other chambers owing to such "bottle neck," the attentive Justice is given more opportunity to be manipulative.

All of this leads to a larger issue: Who should author a Justice's opinion? Only a handful of federal circuit court judges write their own opinions,[29] and one of them openly disparages the practice of Supreme Court law clerks drafting opinions.[30] Should a Justice follow their example? Our answer: it depends. On the one hand, in all cases a Justice deems important, he or she should draft the opinion and leave the research and proofing to the clerks. On the other hand, sometimes the formulaic and innocent work of a clerk-authored opinion may prove sufficient, especially if the judgment in a case is unanimous. That is owing to the fact that such an opinion could be the ideal one in which to place an idea or line to be drawn upon at some future date. This Trojan-Horse approach, if done subtley, can benefit a Justice considerably. But this example should not be confused with the one in which a Justice routinely delegates much of his or her opinion-writing to law clerks. In that regard, one of Thurgood Marshall's clerks has noted that the Justice "depended *heavily* on his clerks for substantive recommendations and drafting."[31] (In the 1986 Term, "'he didn't write anything,'" one of his clerks recalled.[32]) Of course, Marshall was not alone in transferring so much of his work to his clerks. That is folly, even if such reliance has become more and more the institutional norm. Any Justice who follows that path cannot hope to maximize power or enhance reputation in any way short of luck.

◈

It is not so much who you are, but how you are perceived,
both in the short run and in the long run.

Despite his well-earned reputation as an accomplished civil-rights litigator, Thurgood Marshall's record as a Supreme Court Justice was not illustrious,[33] and not surprisingly so given what we have just observed. Still, he fared relatively well in the legacy department. Of course, there are different explanations for that. One has to do with a person who was in the Justice's employ during the 1972-73 Court Term. Hiring Mark Tushnet as his law clerk may have been one of the smartest things Justice Thurgood Marshall ever did. Was it because of the excellent cert. memos Tushnet prepared? Was it because of the oral arguments memo he might have prepared when *Roe v. Wade* (1973) was first argued and then reargued? [34] Was it because of the dissent he might have drafted for Justice Marshall in *San Antonio School District v. Rodriguez* (1973)?[35] However meritorious his service, the best thing that individual did for the Justice came *after* his tenure as a law clerk. Mark Tushnet, now a professor at Harvard Law School, is a respected constitutional scholar. In that capacity he benefitted his former boss by several of his impressive publications. His two-volume biography[36] of Thurgood Marshall surely elevated the Justice's stock in legal and popular minds. To much the same effect, there is the volume of the Justice's writings and speeches that Tushnet edited,[37] the book he wrote entitled *The NAACP's Legal Strategy Against Segregated Education*,[38] and the numerous scholarly articles[39] he wrote about Justice Marshall. All in all, Thurgood Marshall did rather well by the good professor . . . which is how it should be. Our main point: Clerks serve many purposes. One of those purposes is more important than all the rest – buttressing the Justice's reputation both during and after his or her life.

Chapter 19

How to Play to the Media

Perception is reality. Often perception counts most, save for the ruinous consequences of reality. And it is so important because perception, when managed, can shape reality. It is a truism: For all practical purposes, we are what others perceive us to be. That is why a savvy Justice must know how to play to the media, if only because the media are the public's looking lens. Reality is channeled through the prism of their news reports and broadcasts.[†]

Try as he might have, Chief Justice Warren Burger[1] never learned that lesson. He either did not care about courting the media or did the wrong things at the wrong times and with the wrong people. He failed miserably in his attempts to win over a press corps hostile to him, and had troubles from the start. First and foremost, he was the darling of Richard Nixon – the president the press loved to hate. Burger was not only on board with Nixon's "strict constructionism," he was the main man for the President's hoped-for judicial counterrevolution.[2] What made it problematic was how Burger flaunted it so early, so often, and so heedlessly. For example, not long after becoming Chief Justice, this successor to Earl Warren agreed to an interview with Fred Graham of

---

[†]. In this regard, Professor Walter Murphy wisely counseled a Justice to "encourage his friends among reporters and popular writers to support in print his policies, or he might make friends with influential writers." Then again, he cautioned a Justice to remember that "in all matters of political strategy there are dangers in dealing with writers. . . . [A] Justice would have to be most cautious in whom he approached, usually limiting himself to those who would be most apt to agree with him already. There is the further possibility that a writer might use the Justice rather than vice versa, and even the greater danger of a story boomeranging to hurt the Justice." Walter F. Murphy, *Elements of Judicial Strategy* (Chicago, IL: University of Chicago Press, 1964), pp. 128-129. Though such tactical advice is surely sound, its relevance is partially eclipsed in this chapter given the main stratagem recommended here.

the *New York Times* – a reporter enamored of the Warren Court's activist commitment to social justice. In that interview the new Chief Justice admonished young lawyers not to turn to the courts for societal reform; under Burger's rule there would be great "disappointments"[3] if they did. It was folly to say so publicly, even if he fully believed what he said.

Typically, a new Chief Justice is wise to keep a relatively low profile and to feel the way into the perceptions of the press, public, and colleagues. Though William Rehnquist was more conservative than Burger, he was far more cautious in how he handled his task of forming perceptions. If the liberal press did not like him, at least they respected him. He cut his losses. That could not be said of Burger. Worse still, Burger did little to change that.

Warren Burger and Harry Blackmun were close friends; they were both Nixon appointees; and in the early days of the Burger Court the press tagged them the "Minnesota twins." And yet, when asked if he was a "strict constructionist," the newly nominated Harry Blackmun replied: "I've been called a liberal and a conservative. Labels are deceiving."[4] Smart. Blackmun realized early on the importance of perception, and the need to play to the press, up to a point anyway. Because of that, in time he brought himself out from under Burger's cloud and into the light of his own making. More than all else, it started on January 22, 1973,[5] the day the liberal press began to adore the Justice they once thought of as Nixon's pawn and Burger's puppet. By 1986, when the Court decided *Bowers v.* Hardwick[6] (a homosexual sodomy case), the chasm between the two was great, which only elevated Blackmun's image in the eyes of the liberal press. Throughout their time on the Court, Blackmun's liberalism was overstated and Burger's conservatism exaggerated, and it was precisely that perception that helped the former and harmed the latter. Incredibly, Burger placed his press stock in contrived interviews with *U.S. News & World Report* while Blackmun played to far bigger media players. Or as Thomas Sowell so well put it: "Nowhere has . . . judicial vanity been flattered more than in the *New York Times*, and no one laps it up more than Harry Blackmun."[7]

Warren Burger never knew how to befriend the press; Harry Blackmun did. Burger distained the Fourth Estate, while Blackmun tweaked his jurisprudence[8] just enough to curry press favor. Though neither was a great jurist, one moved away from fame while the other moved toward it. Much of it had to do with perception, with mastering the art of image.

There are, to be sure, many ways to befriend the media. To that end, a adept Justice might consider everything from artfully crafting opinions to impressively writing books, from carefully choosing one's words in oral arguments to prudently scripting one's appearances on television, from seizing the right moment in certain cases and avoiding the wrong one in other cases, and from skillfully conducting interviews with a select few in the media to secretly leaking things to the press. In most of these ways, the Chief Justice's practices failed him, whereas much the opposite was true for Justice Blackmun. But Burger's biggest mistake, the one that might have won the press over to him, was the way he mishandled a landmark case, *Roe v. Wade*.[9]

Here his mistake was so big that it should not be overlooked. Had he been more perceptive – and calculating in a productive way – he might have improved his plight; he might have won some of the press favor that flowed to Harry Blackmun. There would be time and opportunity enough to take things from there, but back in 1973 Warren Burger really needed something to transform his fate and improve his image in the eyes of the media. He failed to grasp that; he mismanaged his handling of *Roe*; and it never occurred to him how his botched attempts to be clever would be discovered and exposed by a judgmental press.

ꞩ

*The Chief strongly in favor of upholding the state
abortion laws, but not casting a clear vote.*
– Conference note, 1971 Term[10]

For all of Chief Justice Burger's many ideas, the ones he acted upon too often proved to be counterproductive or failed to advance his own career in any meaningful and memorable way. Take, for example, *Roe v. Wade*. He handled it poorly from the outset. It was one mistake after another, and they all pointed to disaster. For one thing, Burger assigned the majority opinion in *Roe* even though he was reportedly in the minority when the case was discussed in conference. He tried to be clever by hiding his nefarious actions in a cloud of ambiguity and confusion. Predictably, it angered his colleagues and made them even more suspicious of his motives. That said, when his acts were revealed it made for eye-popping reading in *The Brethren*, a behind-the-scenes account by *Washington Post* investigative reporters Bob Woodward and Scott Armstrong.[11] Nearly 30 pages were devoted to exposing the Court's internal handling of *Roe*. Page after page, readers were told of Burger's manipulative actions, along with the internal strife they caused. Blunder compounded blunder. Apparently, the Chief Justice assigned the *Roe* opinion to Harry Blackmun in order to prevent William O. Douglas, the Court's notorious liberal and senior Justice in the majority, from writing another opened-ended privacy opinion like the one he authored in *Griswold v. Connecticut* (See Chapter 11). To do that, Burger had to (1) work his way over to the majority side of the decisional divide, (2) assign the opinion to Blackmun, (3) schedule the case for re-argument, [12] (4) wait long and hard as Blackmun labored to craft an opinion that might win a majority, and (5) write his own mediocre concurring opinion.[13]

It was all such a foolish waste of time and effort. But Burger's most egregious mistake was his not reserving the majority opinion for himself. Since he ultimately voted with the majority, there were no moral or ethical constraints that might have restrained him. Besides, the many examples provided within this book make clear that morality when truly held is the enemy of power securely held.

So why did Warren Burger assign the *Roe* opinion to Harry Blackmun? Here is one answer:

> Burger assigned the [abortion] cases to Blackmun, who never knew exactly why. Certainly his medical background from his years at the Mayo Clinic made him a logical candidate. But the more likely reason was that Burger, whose political antennae made him better attuned than some other members of the Court to the inflammatory nature of the issue, believed he should count

on Blackmun to deliver narrowly focused opinions that would discharge the Court's duty without doing or saying anything more than necessary.[14]

Fact: Warren Burger's "political antennae" were defective, severely so.[†] He had his thoughts on the wrong concerns, his mind on the wrong Justice, and his eyes on the wrong prize. Obviously, writing the abortion opinions was risky; surely, there would be backlash; and clearly it would draw a lot of public attention. But that attention, especially coming from the liberal press, is exactly what Burger needed.

To resume: Why make Harry Blackmun the liberal save-the-day hero? Why let Harry Blackmun take all the credit for protecting women's rights to choose how to control their bodies? And why let Harry Blackmun burst out of the Nixon mold and begin to become his own self-thinking Justice? Good questions all – yet they were not ones that Warren Burger ever paused to consider. He was too busy trying to pacify Justice Douglas, please Justices White and Rehnquist (the dissenters), delay the release of the opinions in order not to upstage Nixon's second inauguration, and control Justice Blackmun, which only widened the personal distance between the two erstwhile friends.

Looking at the matter today, it may appear that Warren Burger was smart after all. Not really. He needed to improve his image then, at the time when it mattered most. For all the controversy generated by the abortion ruling, Blackmun fared far better with the press than did Burger. And that was due in good measure to *Roe*. And what about tomorrow, when the world of abortion politics might change? Simple: There were any variety of ways – from bold but qualified, to novel but cautious, to minimalist but protective[15] – that Burger might have crafted his opinion of the Court in order to secure a majority, safeguard his reputation, maneuver his way through future cases, and most importantly, win magnanimous kudos from the liberal press. Instead,

---

†. According to a Gallop poll "taken at the height of the 1972 presidential campaign . . . a substantial majority of the public, and more Republicans than Democrats, supported leaving the abortion decision up to a woman and her doctor." Linda Greenhouse and Reva Siegel, *Before Roe v. Wade* (New York, NY: Kaplan Publishing, 2010), p. 224. In other words, even at the time Burger would have had significant public support for a majority opinion in *Roe*.

he did the opposite: Warren Burger made Harry Blackmun the great protector of women's rights, and then Burger shifted his views to undermine the very right he once voted to safeguard.[16] What did all that win him? Nothing.

Justice Anthony Kennedy – a jurist skilled in cozying up to the press – could have taught Warren Burger a thing or two on how to play his hand in the abortion cases. Remember, it was Justice Kennedy who saved *Roe's* "core holding" when he lent his name to the joint opinion in *Planned Parenthood of Southeastern Pennsylvania v. Casey* (1992).[17] Years later, he swung the other way and wrote for the Court in diminishing *Roe's* constitutional core – the case was *Gonzales v. Carhart*.[18] And in 2016 he flipped once again in his majority opinion in *Whole Woman's Health v. Hellerstedt*.[19] Inconsistent? Possibly. Unprincipled? Probably.[20] Prudent? Certainly.

Our point: The main way Justices communicate with the press and public is by way of their judicial opinions. How Justices are perceived depends greatly on how they present themselves – how they vote, how they style their opinions, and how they manage to appear both judicious and just, which is quite a feat in itself. Contrary to the gospel the Justices routinely preach, their opinions do not speak for themselves. For that, the media – the Associated Press, or the *New York Times*, or Fox News – are their mouthpieces. Hence, a Justice must be attuned to where the bulk of media power resides. In one period the press may be overwhelming conservative (as in the heyday of the Hurst newspapers); in another it may be liberal (as in the *Times'* glory days). Whether and to what extent a Justice ventures to manipulate them depends much on how his or her power agenda comports with the media powers of the day. Even if the gulf between the two is wide, a Justice can nonetheless minimize negative publicity by presenting himself or herself as fair and above the fray.

Chief Justice Burger was egocentric enough to believe he could ignore such wisdom or create his own to replace it. The former cost him, the latter doomed him. He never realized that it took more than his imperial manner and crop of white hair to attain real and lasting greatness and power, and to become a Chief Justice in the order of John Marshall (see Chapter 2).

৯

Blackmun's close relationships with reporters help to account for the favorable coverage
he received . . . . [By contrast], Burger's efforts to influence news coverage were outweighed
by reporters' awareness of his general hostility toward the news media.

— Laurence Baum[21]

Warren Burger died in 1995. Even so, his official biography[22] lingers in limbo. He has long been forgotten. The memory of the author of major opinions on presidential power, separation of powers, free expression, press liberties, separation of church and state, electronic surveillance, and racial integration,[23] has been eclipsed by lesser Justices. And then there was his important work in overseeing the management of the federal courts[24] and his oversight of the Bicentennial of the Constitution. All impressive, yet all lost in the remote back alleys of history. Worse still, his hoped-for judicial "counter-revolution" never took deep root in the often centrist Burger Court. [25] Admittedly, there were other reasons for Burger's difficult plight. [26] Yet one of the most important of them was his inability to win over the media. So great was the liberal press bias against him that even his First Amendment rulings in their favor[27] could not alter their harsh opinion of him.

As for Harry Blackmun, Yale Law School conducted a 38-hour oral history interview series with him[28] – this to permit him better to control his legacy. True to that effort, Blackmun arranged for the Library of Congress to release his voluminous Court files – the ones in which he stored all the internal notes passed between the Justices, documents from every case, selected mail he received, and countless other documents. That bevy of information led to a book by former *New York Times'* veteran Supreme Court reporter Linda Greenhouse. The book, titled *Becoming Justice Blackmun: Harry Blackmun's Supreme Court Journey*, contained a revealing and well-documented portrait of the "Minnesota twins" and how they came to be separated. The *New York Times* review labeled it "a judicial Horatio Alger story and a tale of a remarkable transformation."[29] Greenhouse's flattering biographical profile[30] of Blackmun was followed by a longer work by another biographer[31] – a biography said to have faithfully "capture[d] Harry Blackmun, one of the late-twentieth century's most intriguing Supreme Court Justices, in all of his richness and complexity as the self-effacing lover of the underdog. Finally, we understand how 'Old Number 3' for Richard Nixon and the conservatives became instead 'Old Number 1' in the hearts of liberals everywhere."[32] Glorify Harry, belittle Burger – thus did much of the press coverage proceed.

The lesson is an old one, a Machiavellian one. Those who seek power must sometimes take chances in order to give great examples of themselves. Power is stirred in that cauldron. If one fails to try, nothing is gained. If one tries and fails, he or she will be no worse off than Warren Burger was. But one must be shrew; if one succeeds, then others might follow his or her lead (no matter the principles) or sing his or her praises (no matter the beliefs). Of course, some will not, but so what? The present and the future, after all, belong to the victors. They are the ones applauded in newspapers, congratulated on television, and glorified in books yet to be written.

There us a cautionary note here. The antithesis of such shrewdness was Justice Ruth Bader Ginsburg's gratuitous public criticisms made to the *New York Times* about then-Republican presidential candidate Donald Trump. By throwing herself into the political maelstrom, Ginsburg invited controversy – and it came.[33]

Chapter 20

Cameras in the Courtroom

Seizing the Future

*[T]he day may come when television will have become so commonplace
an affair in the daily life of the average person as to dissipate all reasonable
likelihood that its use in courtrooms may disparage the judicial process.*

-- Justice John Marshall Harlan, II (1965)[1]

An exceptional Justice realizes the value of breaking ranks, of abandoning tradition, and of forging ahead into the future in bold ways ... at least sometimes. Such a jurist will neither allow the status quo nor the collective voice of his her colleagues to thwart advantageous action. Admittedly, the ways of the past might counsel otherwise, and the circumstances of the present might deter such action. None of this, however, should stay the hand of the Justice who appreciates the inevitable: Time is on his or her side. It may be a long time, but that is a small price to pay for being prescient. Fame prefers leaders to followers. That said, such wisdom escapes the thinking of Justices who march in lockstep, oblivious that theirs is a road to nowhere. It is just such thinking that provides a perfect opportunity for the perceptive Justice to lay claim to the fame of the future.

⟡

Though it was false, Chief Justice Warren Burger delighted in saying: "The Supreme Court literally operates 'in a goldfish bowl.'"[2] In fact, the opposite largely is the case. Most Americans never see what happens in the Court's solemn chamber. Real transparency has never been the norm – the judicial goldfish bowl has always been opaque.

Chief Justice William Rehnquist was emphatic. He "repeatedly rebuffed requests from radio and television companies to broadcast oral arguments in important cases. After a consortium of broadcasters in 1989 demonstrated how cameras might be introduced into the Court, [Rehnquist] rejected the possibility of television coverage, explaining: 'A majority of the Court remains of the view that we should adhere to our past practice and not allow camera coverage of our proceedings.'"[3] Only Justices William Brennan and John Paul Stevens favored a break from tradition.[4]

A quarter of a century later, the Court's resolve remained unequivocal. Justice David Souter was vehement: "the day you see a camera come into our courtroom, it's going to roll over my dead body."[5] Justice Antonin Scalia thought the idea a precarious one: "I am sure it will miseducate the American people, not educate."[6] Justice Sonia Sotomayor echoed that idea: "I don't think most viewers take the time to actually delve into either the briefs or the legal arguments to appreciate what the court is doing. They speculate about . . . the judge favors this point rather than that point. Very few of them understand what the process is, which is to play devil's advocate."[7] Justice Clarence Thomas was equally critical: "[Allowing cameras in the courtroom] runs the risk of undermining the manner in which we consider the cases. . . . Certainly, it will change our proceedings. And I don't think for the better."[8] And Justice Anthony Kennedy expressed his fears in that regard when testifying before a House Appropriations Subcommittee: "If you introduce cameras, it is human nature for me to suspect that one of my colleagues is saying something for a soundbite. Please don't introduce that insidious dynamic into what is now a collegial court."[9]

In more recent years, the Roberts Court has been just as adamant. When the Coalition for Court Transparency, an association of media and legal groups, petitioned the Court in March of 2014 to televise oral arguments, the Court's press office replied curtly: "There are no plans to change the Court's current practices."[10] Chief Justice John Roberts was diplomatic, but direct: "We [Justices] worry about the impact on lawyers. . . . I worry about the impact on judges. . . . We, unfortunately, fall into grandstanding with a couple of hundred people in the courtroom. . . . I'm a little concerned about what the impact would be."[11]

❧

Tellingly, many Justices steered a different course when they were Supreme Court *nominees* testifying at a Senate Judiciary Committee hearing. For example, "before they were confirmed, at least four members of the high court indicated that they favored or were open to TV cameras in the courtroom. Since then, however, Justices Clarence Thomas, Antonin Scalia, Sonia Sotomayor and Elena Kagan have changed their minds and now reject video coverage."[12] Thus, when Clarence Thomas testified, he was open to the idea: "I have no objection beyond a concern that the cameras in the court room be unobtrusive or as unobtrusive as possible. . . . It's good for the American public to see what's going on in there."[13] Despite her post-confirmation statements to the contrary, Sonia Sotomayor once embraced the prospect of cameras in the Court. "I have had positive experiences with cameras," she said. "When I have been asked to join experiments of using cameras in the courtroom, I have participated. I have volunteered."[14] Likewise, at her confirmation hearings, Elena Kagan declared "it would be a terrific thing to have cameras in the courtroom. I think it would be a great thing for the institution, and more important, I think it would be a great thing for the American people." [15] Predictably, certainty turned to uncertainty once she became a Justice[16]: "people might play to the camera," she worried.[17] Justice Scalia likewise experienced this change of heart and mind: "When I first came on the court," he stressed, "I was in favor of having cameras in the court. I am less and less so. . . . I don't want it to become show biz."[18] Then there was the case of Chief Justice Warren Burger: while on the Court, he opposed the idea of cameras; yet after he retired he said he had "changed his mind and now saw that there was an edifying possibility."[19]

Oh, the devious turns of hypocrisy! But the Justices do not mind. And why should they? After all, they are supreme; they are the masters of their realm. Hence, more than a half-century after Justice Harlan's prediction, cameras remain barred from the chamber of the High Court. The public can *hear* the Justices via audiofiles, though not in real time. *Seeing and hearing* them (real time or not), however, is forbidden. As ideologically divided as the Court has been over the past several decades, on this point they have remained virtually united: no cameras in our courtroom.[20] Not even a First Amendment challenge to this ban can prevail in this Court.[21]

ౚ

The trajectory is that it is inevitable that television will be in the Supreme Court.

-- Tom Goldstein (2011)[22]

Louis Brandeis saw the future. In his 1928 dissent in *Olmstead v. United States*,[23] he recognized that yesterday's legal norms must adapt to today's technologies and to those of tomorrow. Time proved him right, though it took nearly four decades.[24] Brandeis refused to be captured by orthodoxy; he preferred to align his views with the inevitable. That move, among other things, ensured his greatness.

An astute Justice would do well to follow the Brandeis example in the context of video recording the proceedings of the high Court. It is certain: One day, the Court's arguments will be technologically visible to all. Even before that day, however, the perceptive Justice can accrue a respectful measure of distinction by catering to the media's self-interests. He or she can become their darling simply by playing their court-access arguments back to them, though always with judicious decorum.

The plot might involve a distinguished lecture at Harvard or Yale Law School,†† which would be televised by CNN or C-SPAN and covered by the press corps. Justice X might preface her comments with a cautionary observation: "I am duly mindful of the objections of my

---

†. In this regard, recall Justice Potter Stewart's 1974 lecture ("Or of the Press") at Yale Law

colleagues, and do not lightly take exception to them. In the spirit of informed discussion, I would welcome any rebuttals to my comments. That said, it is hard for me to discount the compelling arguments in favor of allowing all Americans to see and hear how we administer justice in our Courtroom." Justice X might tender, for example, the following arguments:

- Cameras now broadcast the proceedings in the high courts of the United Kingdom and Canada.[25]
- Only three States and the District of Columbia bar video recording, while 34 States allow it and 13 only conditionally so.[26]
- Cameras are virtually nonintrusive and invisible due to modern technological advancements.[27]
- Cameras promote the goal of transparency in governance.[28]
- Cameras would better educate the public about the workings of the Supreme Court.[29]
- Cameras enhance the legitimacy of the high Court's decisionmaking.[30]
- Cameras are not foreign to the Justices, who appear comfortable when they promote their books or advance their ideas in televised interviews (and events posted on YouTube).[31]
- Cameras in the courtroom are consistent with the will of the vast majority of Americans.[32]

When nearing the conclusion of her lecture, Justice X would be wise to draw upon what her colleague, Elena Kagan, stated in 2009: "If cameras were in the courtroom, the American public would see an extraordinary event. This Court, I think, is so smart and so prepared and so engaged, and everybody who gets up there at the podium is [confronted with] the toughest questions, the most challenging questions. And there is a debate of really extraordinarily intellectual adeptness and richness.

School. Unsurprisingly, his advocacy of special constitutional protections for the press was well received by many media figures and their attorneys. See, e.g., Floyd Abrams, "The Press Is Different: Reflections on Justice Stewart and the Autonomous Press," *Hofstra Law Review* 7: 563 (1979).

When C-SPAN first came on, they put cameras in legislative chambers. And it was clear that nobody was there. I think if you put cameras in the Courtroom, people would say, 'wow.' They would see their government working at a really high level."[33] In closing, she might simply declare: "I concur."

Whether or not these arguments are demonstrably true[34] need not concern Justice X, so long as they are colorable. An appealing veneer will do. Whether or not these arguments are fully believed by Justice X should not impede her, so long as they serve her interests and persuade others. Given the inevitability of cameras in the high Court, all that matters is that Justice X is viewed as the prophet of progress. And to that end, she can always rely on the media for enthusiastic and ongoing support. Beyond her speeches to this effect, she might find an occasion to usher this gospel into a Supreme Court opinion (for example, a dissent in a case as monumental as *Bush v. Gore*,[35] in which the Court refused a request from major broadcasters to televise the oral arguments.[36]).

In all of a Justice's rhetorical maneuverings, care must be taken to perpetuate the mystique of the Court, but only to the extent that it is self-serving. It is best to remember that mystique is a key attribute of power. And what is mystique other than a type of hiding or lying? Today the Justices opt for the mystique of invisibility – the Wizard of Oz façade that hides the manipulator behind the curtain. Tomorrow the Machiavellian Justice opts for openness, but uses deception and hypocrisy to maintain mystique. The jurist who honors this lesson stands to become a modern Wizard of Oz unaffected by visibility. There is nothing like the lie of the eye.

Chapter 21

On Television

The Medium Is Not the Message

Television is not famous for reasoned discourse.

-- Walter Goodman[1]

Television is the medium of the masses. It provides a boundless surfeit of amusement. Frivolity is its coin, vacuity its currency. The medium is ideal for its messages – imagistic sound bites. It trades in the visuality of drama, action, and pseudo-reality programming. It is a communicative technology made for the likes of the 2016 Presidential candidate Donald Trump. This shock master realized TV's potential; he used it to transform politics into a game show. In the end, it all became a carnival culture[2] in which the evening news was dominated by the spectacle of the bizarre. That television might be tapped for such attention-grabbing purposes is, to be sure, a topic for students of Presidential power. But that is another book for another day.†+ For now, we must remain focused on the topic at hand: Judicial power.

In contrast to television, law's domain is staid, cerebral, and cabined in codes and cases. Appellate law does not titillate the way that the "Judge Judy" show does or the O.J. Simpson trial did. Hence, jurisprudence is not well suited for the entertainment fare of commercial television. Of course, and as we note in Chapter 20, there are certain tactical reasons why a Justice might applaud cameras in the Courtroom. That

---

†. This and related topics are examined in one of our earlier books, *The Death of Discourse* (Durham, NC: Carolina Academic Press, 2nd ed., 2008).

is another matter entirely, however, one quite different from a Justice's appearance on popular TV programs. To be sure, there will be times when a Justice may find it advantageous to do so, but those times must be few and carefully orchestrated. Nonetheless, a Justice must always bear in mind that, generally speaking, this medium is not meant for his or her message.

ॐ

Celebrity Justice is a double-edged sword.

-- *Richard Hasen*[3]

A Justice is a person of the law. He or she may also be a public intellectual. And for those purposes, a Justice may find it desirable to show a human and humane side. Beyond that, however, care should be taken to prevent TV from doing what it does best – dumbing down and tarting up.[4] Dry C-SPAN coverage of a commencement address should be preferred over a trifling appearance on a late-night talk show.

A Justice is not a jurist for the masses – his or her message can never resonate with the crowd that delights in flying saucer stories. Similarly, such a Justice is not the people's voice in Washington – his or her message can never appease the audiences that savor highly partisan politics. *En masse* is not on a Justice's calling card. Remember: a Justice is unelected and unaccountable. That alone is reason enough to be cautious about how, if at all, to engage with a populist medium.

Hooping it up on the airwaves may make for good television, but it does little, if anything, to help a Justice secure the kind of power and prestige needed to lay claim to greatness in the world of law. So why do Justices appear on TV (or YouTube)? The answer: vanity, money, or strategy. There may also be more noble reasons, such as educational or civic ones. Whatever the reason, the attentive Justice should avoid television's temptations unless his or her message can trump that of the medium and harness it to work to judicial advantage.

Years ago (in 1958), Justice William O. Douglas appeared on a CBS program for an interview with Mike Wallace.[5] Years later (in 2015),

Justice Stephen Breyer appeared on the *Late Show with Stephen Colbert*.[6] One was intellectual and educational; the other was awkwardly out-of-touch and uncomfortably funny. Television served the Justice well in the case of the former, whereas it did not in the case of the latter.

While a Justice may indeed be partisan, he or she should never appear so. Thus, it was ill advised for Justice Antonin Scalia to admonish Democrats to "get over it"[7] when he spoke about *Bush v. Gore*[8] on *Piers Morgan Tonight*. By the same measure, it was imprudent for Justice Ruth Bader Ginsberg to go TV-public with her views on same-sex marriage.[9] Similarly, televised appearances before partisan groups (e.g. the conservative Federalist Society or the liberal American Constitution Society) should be frowned upon.†+ In all of this, television may only stir up public sentiment, which soon enough could lead to calls for recusals,[10] if not more.

Today, if a Justice signs a big book contract, replete with a hefty advance, chances are the author will be required to undergo television and radio appearances. For that reason, Justice Clarence Thomas[11] appeared on *60 Minutes,* as did Justices Sonia Sotomayor[12] and Antonin Scalia.[13] These interviews certainly helped book sales, and to some extent they showed each Justice's more human side. But even in such a rarified TV context as these relatively tame CBS interviews, things can go south as evidenced by Justice Hugo Black's 1968 CBS interview with Eric Sevareid and Martin Agronsky.[14] Not surprisingly, the sensitive topic of Black's 1921 involvement with the Ku Klux Klan came up. Though that portion of the interview was deleted, other damaging segments (about the Vietnam War and protests) were not. While Justice Black did have his engaging populist moments, the interview, nonetheless, had its cutting edges.

Commencement day addresses[15] and testimonial appearances before Congress[16] typically make for good C-SPAN coverage and can prove to be of interest to its limited audience. Even so, and especially in these divisive times, a jurist should always anticipate the possibility of rowdy hecklers at a commencement address or hostile representatives

---

+. If a public forum is desired for some address, the National Constitution Center in Philadelphia might make for a suitable non-partisan venue.

at a congressional hearing. Much thought, therefore, should be given to the wisdom of participating in such events.

With the advent of SCOTUS Map[17] the Justices' public appearances are becoming ever more public. Perhaps that is because more of the Justices (such as Breyer and Sotomayor) are becoming ever more televisual.[18] Consequently, they become great fare for late-night comedians."fodder.[19] Whether such celebrity status actually helps a jurist is very doubtful; and it may even prove detrimental. Hence, the TV temptation should be resisted on more occasions than not.

The bottom line: For the Machiavellian Judge it is better to be an obscurantist than a celebrity. It is better to do one's crafted work on the printed page than on a televised screen. And it is often better to avoid the public eye rather than to seek it out. Or in the words of the great Florentine philosopher: "Nothing makes a [Justice] so esteemed as doing great enterprises and giving rare examples of himself."[20] Such rare examples might include television appearances. If so, one must be an expert manipulator of the medium.

Chapter 22

On Publishing Books

When and of What Kind

Some men are born posthumously.

– Friedrich Nietzsche[1]

We think of Niccolò Machiavelli in various ways – as an advisor to princes, a military strategist, an analyst of power, a hardheaded advocate of political realism, a clear-eyed reformer, and an unorthodox teacher of ethics.[2] But he was also a *writer* who turned the grammar of power into a science of politics.[3] One of the greatest Machiavellian moves, however, is routinely ignored, much as fish take for granted the water in which they swim. His ideas were committed to *writing*, first in manuscript form and then, five years after his death, in print form. When he was given the booklet in 1515, it is not at all clear that Lorenzo de' Medici "ever opened it and certainly didn't take time to study Machiavelli's carefully crafted reflections."[4] Whatever its immediate impact, it is well to remember that the author of *The Prince* intended[5] his work to be "useful to whoever understands it."[6] By that measure, it might be understood as a work "written for the future."[7] That is to say, the great Florentine philosopher sought not only to influence the politics of his day, but also, and perhaps more importantly, to influence the future of politics in ways associated with the name Niccolò Machiavelli. In other words, *legacy* mattered. For our purposes, our Machiavellian lessons stand to serve in this world *and* in the next – power seized and power perpetuated. The

Great John Marshall (see Chapter 2) understood that; hence, his legacy continues to shape our law.

There are three main reasons for a Justice to publish a book: There is the *influence*; there is the *remuneration*†; and there is the *history*. The first moves the law in one's preferred direction; the second makes one rich; and the third allows one (if *Fortuna* permits) to write history in one's own image and also to perpetuate one's preferences. The latter includes autobiographical works such as William O. Douglas' *The Court Years: 1939-1975* and Sandra Day O'Connor's *Lazy B – Growing Up on a Cattle Ranch in the American Southwest*. Of course, they are two very different kinds of autobiographical works, the former being potentially worthwhile to a Justice while the latter making for attention-grabbing biographical puffery, which is of little real and lasting value. Autobiographical works, if they are to be truly worthwhile, take considerable time, care, and planning, and must begin early in the judicial day and end late in one's career. Since most are not so wrought, most are of little value. But there are other ways to rewrite history, as when one comments on the law in a book dedicated to such an enterprise. We will say more about that in a moment.

There are, of course, other reasons ranging from intellectual curiosity to vanity. And to be sure, a jurist may have more than one reason for writing a book, as evidenced by the 354 books published during the lifetimes of the Supreme Court Justices, many of whom wrote no books.[8] More recently, five members of the Roberts Court – Justices Anthony Kennedy, Antonin Scalia, Stephen Breyer, Clarence Thomas, and Sonia Sotomayor – have published books while on the Court.[9] One of them proved influential and two proved profitable. Beyond that, there is curiosity and vanity, but those are not very good reasons for an extraordinary Justice to publish a book.

What is one's purpose? Who is the audience?[10] And what kind of book,[11] if any, might be best suited to serving that purpose and reaching

---

†. It is said that William O. Douglas, the most book-prolific of all the Justices, turned to publishing books in order to help pay off his multiple alimonies. See Noah Feldman, *Scorpions: The Battles & Triumphs of FDR's Great Supreme Court Justices* (New York, NY: Twelve, 2010), p. 322.

that audience? Those are the questions to be asked by any Justice venturing to maximize his or her influence and power. Some few books may serve such purposes, while the vast majority do not. Hence, in writing a book an extraordinary Justice must consider such matters, and should craft a work accordingly. If he does so, many will like what they see, even if they do not fully understand what they read.

✎

In December 1833, the *American Monthly Review* commented on a newly published book by Joseph Story. By that time, the fifty-four-year-old Supreme Court Justice had written or edited some twelve books. These works included a treatise on bills of exchange, a treatise on pleading, yet another on pleading and assumpsit, and commentaries on the law of bailments. In other words, early on in the new Republic, Story was making his mark on the law. To that end, he published a work with a long title: *Commentaries on the Constitution of the United States; With a Preliminary Review of the Constitutional History of the Colonies and States, Before the Adoption of the Constitution.*[12] Of this book an *American Monthly* reviewer wrote:

> [T]he work is a rare union of patience, brilliancy, and acuteness, and . . . [contains] all the learning on the Constitution brought down to the latest period, so as to be invaluable to the lawyer, statesman, politician, and in fine, to every citizen who aims to have a knowledge of the great Charter under which he lives.[13]

That review was among the first of many such laudatory notices of a treatise that went on to become canonical in the history of American constitutional law. Before he died in 1845, Joseph Story published another twenty-one books after his *Commentaries*. More shaping, more influence, and more works that made the law synonymous with the name Story. This is owing to the fact that commentaries provide the exceptional Justice exceptional opportunities to mold the law. Thus, Arthur Sutherland once noted, and with ample justification, that Sir William

Blackstone's *Commentaries on the Laws of England* "revolutionized the study of law."[14] To *revolutionize*: meaning to change something significantly or completely, to reorganize or reconstruct it in new or radical ways. Viewed from that perspective, when publishing his *Commentaries* Story cast the nature of the Constitution in a new light, described the role of the Supreme Court in a new way, and explained provisions of the Constitution and Bill of Rights in a new manner – and all of this while claiming to remain faithful to the Founders' original intent.

For all of the respect that the treatise has garnered over the generations, nonetheless it has been noted that Story's *Commentaries* were the product of a certain bias toward " 'Hamilton and Marshall supplemented by a host of decisions by Federalist Judges.' It was loaded with history, [and] 'crabbed and narrow legalism.' [It was] nothing but a 'new modeled Federalism, adapted to changing conditions.' "[15] As Story's biographer, R. Kent Newmeyer put it: "Story, it would seem, was as influential as he was partisan."[16] And yet, the good Justice continues to be praised for his fidelity to originalism and to the Founders' true intent.[17]

In *The Prince*, Machiavelli declared that in order "not to give up [one's] free will . . . it may be true that [fortune] decides half of what we do, but it leaves the other half, more or less, to us."[18] Part of that other half involves knowing when and what to write in a book. The lesson is: Be like Justice Story – appear objective, be subjective; invoke history, mold history. And if done well, the reward will be great and long-enduring. Indeed, Story's *Commentaries* continue to be invoked by the Supreme Court in recent cases, such as *Harmelin v. Michigan*[19] (Eight Amendment cruel and unusual punishment) and *District of Columbia v. Heller*,[20] (Second Amendment right to bear arms). Justice Antonin Scalia authored both opinions. In so doing, he followed in Justice Story's footsteps. Hence, Justice Scalia likewise laid claim to fortune's other half.

❧

[N]ot since Justice Story has a sitting Justice of the Supreme Court written about interpretation as comprehensively as [Justice Scalia].

— *Judge Frank Easterbrook*[21]

It is true: The power to interpret is the power to create . . . especially when invoking the former to advance the latter. It is the flip-side of commentary, of being a commentator. For example, to interpret or explain *The Talmud*, or *The Bible*, or *Plato's Laws*, or Rousseau's *First and Second Discourses*, or the *Federalist Papers*, or the Constitution of the United States, or any Supreme Court opinion, all afford the opportunity to be creative in ways conducive to one's wishes. Central to that task, properly understood, is the need to appear neutral, scholarly, and convincing. While one must seem faithful to his or her text, one must never take that charge seriously when contrary to one's objectives. In such instances, one must be prepared to abandon his or her textual creed.[22] Some label true and full fidelity admirable; it is the mark of a real judge. We label it irresponsible and the mark of a real fool. That is, it is foolish to believe in such objectivity (we live, after all, in post-modern times), and even more foolhardy to yield to it even if one believes in it. If you wish, believe in either Power or Principle. If you believe in the latter, the former will soon enough conquer you.

In light of this, let us tender a few words of praise for *Reading Law: The Interpretation of Legal Texts* (2012) by Justice Scalia and legal lexicographer Bryan Garner. It is a book to behold. Though it lacks the narrative flair of Justice Clarence Thomas's *My Grandfather's Son: A Memoir*, and did not draw the kind of advance ($1.2 million dollars[23]) that Justice Sonia Sotomayor's *My Beloved World* did, and does not have the same populist élan of Justice Breyer's *Making Our Democracy Work*, the Scalia-Garner book is, nevertheless, a work to be reckoned with – a book with a thousand tentacles reaching out and onto everything within their grasp.

In *Reading Law*, Scalia and Garner tapped into something fundamental in the human psyche – the need to *believe* in something and to believe in the possibility of life and law being *orderly*. Give people a reason to believe and then order based on that belief, and you will win their faith. Hugo Black (the old savvy textualist /originalist) understood that. It is all set out with great devotion in his 1968 book *A Constitutional Faith*. But that old-time legal gospel faded over the years as secularism and skepticism took root. And then came Scalia, the *pater* of "the new textualism"[24] who cast originalism in his own light[25] – and the word was made sacred again. Principles were restored, objectivity returned, and the will of the framers (of constitutions, statutes, contracts, and wills) resurrected back into the world of the law. It made for such a wondrous world, one so delightfully vulnerable to the will of the interpreter. But an interpreter needs canons of interpretation, which is just what Scalia and Garner so ingeniously provided.

"Our legal system must regain a mooring that it has lost: a generally agreed-upon approach to the interpretation of legal texts."[26] Scalia and Garner admonish us that we need to be anchored again. But how? The answer goes back to words, the words of legal texts. Much as Martin Luther called on the faithful to return to the text of the Bible (as he translated it), so, too, Scalia and Garner elevate the legal text over all other interpretive creeds, and to that end offer up 57 canons (aka "Fundamental Principles") of construction and expose 13 "falsities" used to counter their canons. It is all there in 567 pages of text – the permissible and impermissible, the general and the particular, the supreme and subordinate, and the significant or superfluous. The promise of such canons: the law will be predictable, judges will be constrained, results will be fair, and the textual will of the Framers will reign supreme. To follow their canons is *ipso facto* to follow the law. It is also a detailed map for others to follow in their direction.

Fate being what it is, some sophisticated scholars have criticized these canons.[27] So, too, has a learned appellate judge.[28] But so what? Let them carp! And while they do, judges who decide cases, lawyers who litigate cases, and students who peruse cases will heed the canons and take them as gospel.[29] Thus, for example, some 300-plus federal and state courts have already invoked *Reading Law: The Interpretation of Legal Texts* in order to resolve interpretive questions.[30] The figures are revealing: Judges in all the federal Circuit Courts (including the Federal Court, Tax Court, Bankruptcy Court, and the Court of Claims) have invoked it; Federal District Court judges in 25 states have referred to it; and appellate judges in 29 states have relied on this work. Moreover, the Supreme Court has itself applied these canons of construction in four cases:

1. *Lockhart v. United States* (2016, per Sotomayor, J.)[31]
2. *T-Mobile South, LLC v. City of Roswell, Ga.* (2015, per Sotomayor, J.)[32]
3. *Heien v. North Carolina* (2014, per Roberts, C.J.)[33]
4. *Maracich v. Spears* (2013, per Kennedy, J.)[34]

Even the liberal Justice Elena Kagan, writing in dissent, once turned to the Scalia-Garner canons to make an interpretive point.[35]

It is one thing to do one's own bidding in a majority opinion (if you can get it), but to have *others* do that bidding is magnificent.[†] And *that* is the kind of influence that is welcome, the kind that a Justice should aim for in any book he or she publishes. This example alone reveals how an astute jurist (who is otherwise too temperamental in his dealing with his colleagues) can have an enormous impact on the law. Thus to Justice Scalia: *Alziamo i nostri bicchieri in tuo onore* (We raise our glasses in your honor).

Unlike Justice Stephen Breyer, Justice Scalia never appeared on any of the comical late-night TV programs to "discuss" his latest book. Even so, Justice Breyer's "slow, measured tone," wrote the editors of *The Atlantic*, "didn't really gel with [Stephen] Colbert's bantering interviewing style. Breyer didn't get a chance to discuss his new book, which ponders the Supreme Court's evolving (and controversial) relationship with foreign legal thinking. Questions about jurisprudence or recent decisions were neither asked nor answered."[36] While Breyer turned to TV to hawk his *The Court and the World*, Scalia pitched his *Reading Law: The Interpretation of Legal Texts* to those who could change

---

[†]. The tallies we have presented above do not include the number of times the Scalia-Garner book is used by lawyers in their appellate briefs. And then there is the number of law schools that use the book in classes.

the world. Measured by the effect of realpolitik, one was the work of an Ivy-League jurist dabbling in popular culture (a curious mix), the other that of serious jurist busily reconfiguring the canons of the law (a transformative mix).

When all the pages were turned, Story and Scalia best exemplify the kind of book- author a Justice should strive to be – one who influences the law in his own times and sets the stage for future generations to do likewise. Story commented on the law and Scalia commented on how to interpret it. In the end, both engaged in a similar enterprise – reworking the law while appearing to do otherwise. So, too, both of them had the insight and foresight to realize the utility of espousing objectivity and order as values to be publicly espoused in their calculating approaches to jurisprudence. On them *Fortuna* smiles.

Chapter 23

The Threat of Impeachment and How to Avoid It

Fortune favors the bold but not the reckless. So it is said, and so it is. This maxim is important to consider when contemplating Article III, §1 of the Constitution, which declares that the Justices of the Supreme Court "shall hold their offices during good behaviour."[1] If they run afoul of that command, they may be impeached by the House of Representatives (Art. I, §2, cl. 5) and tried by the Senate (Art. I, §3, cls. 6 & 7).[2] Only one member of the Supreme Court, Justice Samuel Chase, has ever been impeached (circa 1804), but he was not convicted and removed.[3] That historical fact alone suggests that the threat of impeachment need not concern a Justice very much. Still, circumstances matter, and when they turn the wrong way one may soon enough find the wolf at his or her door.

The potential breadth of what constitutes an impeachable offense is reason for some concern. "An impeachable offense," said then-Congressman Gerald Ford, "is whatever a majority of the House of Representatives considers it to be at a given moment in history."[4] Precisely for that reason a Justice must proceed cautiously and never appear to be acting in a non-judicious or overtly political way. Since the impeachment process "is political rather than legal,"[5] runaway partisan emotions†‡ may trump whatever might be deemed to be the rule of law in such proceedings. To compound the problem for any jurist caught in the web of impeachment, the governing view is that there is no judicial review of congressional action taken in this regard.[6]

---

†. Congressman Ford and 109 other Representatives joined to impeach Justice William O. Douglas for everything from his alleged financial improprieties to his blatantly liberal judicial opinions. The attempt failed.

While the penalty is great, the risk is slight. This gives a calculating Justice immense behavioral latitude. Even so, Justice Samuel Chase foolishly confused that leeway with unbridled prerogative and thus invited impeachment. Justice Robert Grier never crossed the impeachment line, though he came close. Justice Abe Fortas dodged an impeachment bullet by resigning before it came his way. And Chief Justice Earl Warren tempted Fate, but he was never called to constitutional account.

Four jurists: Chase was bold in the interests of political partisanship; Grier was bold in the pursuit of provincial matters; Fortas was bold in the service of greed; and Warren was bold in the cause of judicial activism. Only Earl Warren's boldness justified the risks taken. In these four examples we can discern four models of behavior related to impeachment: (1) acts performed publicly and for purely political purposes; (2) acts, whether improper or illegal, designed to favor friends; (3) acts, whether unethical or unlawful, undertaken for monetary gain; and (4) acts, whether or not consistent with precedent and "neutral principles," performed to enhance the judiciary's institutional power. Measured by the perils of impeachment, the first is suicidal; the second is imprudent; the third is dangerous; and the fourth is admirable. Of course, circumstance is always a qualifier, and can affect the wisdom of any course of action. Context, after all, is the ultimate Judge.

The fatal flaw that invites impeachment is not partisan, political, or ideological judicial behavior; if it were, proceedings would have commenced against many a Supreme Court Justice. Because Justices are not above politics, they can hardly be held to constitutional account for being political or partisan. To hold otherwise would be to trade sober realism for intoxicated romanticism. Still, while Justices are not above the political fray, they must nonetheless be careful not to enter it too publicly and audaciously – particularly when the other branches of government are gunning for a fight. Samuel Chase did what John Marshall would not: He acted without nuance or stratagem; he thus made himself highly vulnerable to an incensed President (Thomas Jefferson). By this gauge, it is better for a Justice to be cunning rather than combative, better to be cautiously political than openly so, and better to be partisan in ways that appear non-partisan.

Impeachment is a remedy for an abuse of power. In that constitutional equation, *power* is the key word; it is that word that ought to drive the conduct of any extraordinary Justice. As for *abuse*, it is not a word that need restrain a Justice provided he or she is not inattentive to political realities, oblivious to the demands of caution, or unmindful of the need to appear judicious. In other words, be John-Marshall-like, not Samuel-Chase-like; be Earl-Warren-like, not Abe-Fortas-like; and never roll the impeachment dice the way Robert Grier did, cunning as he was. In these ways and others, which we will discuss next, a Justice can best avoid the threat of impeachment.

✎

Acts performed publicly and for purely political purposes: Samuel Chase served as an Associate Justice on the Supreme Court from 1796 to 1811. He had the markings of a great jurist and, it has been said, was "a more impressive figure than the great Chief Justice [John Marshall] himself."[7] But he wasted that potential and is thus "usually dismissed by most American historians as nothing but a rabid partisan."[8] He openly prejudiced a trial in ways that were "demonstrably unfair and oppressive"[9] in order to further his Federalist purposes. Moreover, he brazenly ventured into a political maelstrom: "The bluntness of Chase's attack on Jefferson," it has been said, was nothing short of "stunning."[10] In these ways and others, Chase tempted fate; he invited impeachment. True, and thanks to allies and the fine lawyering skills of Luther Martin[11] (who had been a delegate at the Constitutional Convention), Chase's political opponents failed to secure the necessary two-thirds majority of the Senate needed to convict him on any of the eight articles of impeachment leveled against him.[12] Even so, Justice Chase deserved to be impeached and convicted. Why? The answer is not so much that he failed to satisfy the "good behaviour" norm (which he did fail and grossly so). He should have been convicted in order to set an historical example of the kind of punishment[13] that ought be meted out to one so obtuse in taking political risks. Generally speaking, swimming in the waters of a political Leviathan is extremely dangerous, and it is especially so when one's protection is no more than a black judicial robe. In such circumstances, it is best to leave monsters alone and to swim elsewhere.

Acts designed to favor friends: Robert Cooper Grier served as an Associate Justice on the Supreme Court from 1846 to 1870. He is an unknown person, even to most constitutional scholars – this though he authored a few important opinions, such as his concurrence in *Dred Scott v. Sandford* (1857)[14] and his majority opinion in the *Prize Cases* (1863).[15] His importance, marginal though it is, revolves around the fact that he jeopardized his judicial power in a fight over a bridge. He wanted to please a few friends and favor his home state (Pennsylvania) in a legal dispute over the height of a bridge. To that end it seems that he violated the letter and spirit of the law, presiding over a case beyond his jurisdiction, ostensibly soliciting a bribe, leaking the results of a Supreme Court decision to the advantage of one of the parties, and intentionally disregarding an act of Congress.[16]

When all of this came before the House Judiciary Committee in 1854, the clever Grier benefitted from the favor of a congressman he knew, the same congressman who prepared a report on his alleged misconduct. Predictably, the report found the Justice to be "an upright and honest man" who is "entirely and absolutely exonerated."[17] Grier also benefitted from the fact that this report was presented to Congress late on the last day of its 1855 session, with the result that the report was tabled and never revived.[18] There is more, but it is all dusty detail. Our point: Justice Grier spent too much judicial capital to please friends and help his home state, and he did so in ways too blatant to give him the sort of cover he needed. As for his money matters, we turn to that next in our discussion of Justice Fortas.

Acts undertaken for monetary gain: Abe Fortas served as an Associate Justice on the Supreme Court from 1965 to 1969, and was nominated by President Lyndon Johnson to be Chief Justice. Fortas was well connected (to Franklin Delano Roosevelt and Johnson, among others), well credentialed (a onetime Yale law professor and successful Supreme Court litigator), and somewhat well regarded (he authored the landmark ruling in *Tinker v. Des Moines Independent Community School District*[19]). But it was his desire to become wealthier that robbed him of fame and power. In other words, his greed destroyed his career, though he was never formally impeached by the House or convicted by the Senate. His fate was, nonetheless, sealed by a 45 to 43 vote for cloture in the Senate, which meant that his nomination to be Chief Justice never went anywhere (though it was a godsend for Nixon's nominee, Warren Burger).

So what brought Abe Fortas down? What caused his dramatic fall from power? What made him the first Justice in American history to resign in disgrace? And this without any formal filings of articles of impeachment.[†] His failings: avarice, pride, indiscretion, dishonesty, overconfidence, and imprudence, among other things. Just as he overestimated his political strength, he also underestimated the power of his political enemies who reveled in the news of his financial transgressions, ranging from a suspiciously funded and generous salary to teach a summer school seminar to a $20,000 honorarium (in 1967 dollars) he received from a charitable foundation headed by a former client who had been indicted twice.[20]

Add to the mix that Justice Fortas caught himself at the end of a dying political era – the demise of the Warren Court and the decline of the Johnson Administration.[21] Call it the Fortas Failure: The wrong man, the wrong temperament, the wrong indiscretions, in the wrong political stream, at the wrong time, with wrong responses to his legal and ethical troubles, and all of this fueled by a strong streak of arrogance. The result: At age 59, after a mere four years on the Court, Fortas stepped down. And with that, the Warren Court came to an end.

Abe Fortas combined the worst of follies. He was openly hostile to dangerous political opponents, and he dabbled in financial improprieties with neither caution nor foresight. In this sense he was somewhat like the reckless William O. Douglas. Fate saved the latter but ruined the former, and rightfully so. Similar to Samuel Chase, Abe Fortas deserved

---

†. "On May 11, [1968], Congressman H.R. Gross announced that he had prepared articles of impeachment [against Fortas], and the House Judiciary Committee Chairman . . . called for 'some further exploration.' By the twelfth, . . . rumors began flying around the Hill that Fortas was about to resign." Bruce Allen Murphy, *Fortas* (William Morrow & Co., 1988), p. 566.

to be impeached. His impeachable offence: Unchecked greed and foolish pride of the kind that ignited a political firestorm.

The moral: Money is always dangerous in judicial circles. It is the snake hiding in the garden of greed, waiting for someone like Robert Grier or Abe Fortas to enter. A seasoned Justice knows how to walk gingerly in that garden. There is everything from fat advances for book contracts to any variety of generous opportunities following retirement. Hence, it is rarely, if ever, advisable to risk impeachment (or forced resignation or criminal sanctions) in the name of avarice.

Acts done to enhance the judiciary's institutional power: Earl Warren served as Chief Justice of the United States from 1953 to 1969. Call him a judicial activist or label him a quasi-legislative reformer. Perhaps his constitutional opinions were not as rigorous as they might have been; maybe his rulings departed too far from long-established precedents; and perchance he moved ahead with little regard to those constraints. Conceivably, too, his opinions for the Court in *Brown v. Board of Education* (1954),[22] *Reynolds v. Sims* (1964),[23] *Miranda v. Arizona* (1966),[24] and *Powell v. McCormick* (1969),[25] among others, might have been better crafted. Maybe so. But all of them are routinely prefaced with the adjective "landmark." In other words, Earl Warren made his mark on American constitutional law, and it was a bold and largely lasting one. And he did so with enough personal finesse, collaborative care, and political savvy to prevail whenever it mattered most. If it is a bit overstated, it is nonetheless largely factual: This man with a mission was, more than all the rest, "the Judge who changed America."[26]

Judicial activism (be it liberal or conservative) has consequences, which can range from insignificant to calamitous. In the case of Chief Justice Warren, the consequences were nil insofar as any serious threat of impeachment was concerned. Yes, in 1961 the John Birch Society "launched a campaign to drive [Earl] Warren from the Court."[27] But it came to naught; the ever affable Chief Justice took it in stride – it was a ridiculous "public relations stunt"[28] he said. Earl Warren was right.

❧

Judged by impeachment standards, entering a political fray as Samuel Chase did is rife with peril; granting personal favors of the kind traded by Robert Grier is unwise; pursuing monetary gain as Abe Fortas did invites ruin; and seizing the activist moment when he did, and how he did, moved Earl Warren beyond the pale of impeachment and onto the glorious pages of history.

Chapter 24

When It Is Best to Retire

Time can rob us. All the planning in the world is of little moment if one ignores the demands of time. For this reason, a learned Justice must take care of his or her health and must strive not to yield easily to the Grim Reaper.[†] By the same token, such a jurist must give considerable thought to when to retire – neither too soon nor too late. Many a great opportunity has been lost and a legacy marred by inattentiveness to such matters. Plot, plot, plot – it is a campaign that must continue from one's first days on the Court to one's last. Any jurist who desires greatness and accrues power must not let time steal that bounty.

∾

What should a Machiavellian jurist take into consideration to perpetuate his legacy? What must he or she do to avoid an ill fate? At a minimum, the following criteria for retirement should be part of the Justice's mindset, whatever his or her particular ideological stripes:

- *Age and Health*: Any jurist who reaches 70 or thereabouts must begin to plot his or her plans for retirement. Obviously, if there are serious health issues prior to that time, it is rash to wait even that long. After all, high blood pressure or high cholesterol can alter the demographic profile of a judge at any age.
- *The President in Office and the Party in Control*: To the extent possible, a Justice should strive to retire when the sitting

---

†. Chief Justice Fred Vinson cared not about such matters. He was a heavy drinker, a chain smoker, and overweight. His health condition deprived him of a monumental moment – authorship of the Court's opinion in *Brown v. Board of Education* (1954). See Chapter 5.

President and the membership of the Senate are aligned with his or her ideology. This, naturally, involves some speculation and a measure of luck, which is all the more reason to be calculating. Thus, the decision to retire should be informed by the President's party, the number of years left in his or her term, and the political bent of the majority party in the Senate.

- *The Ideological Makeup of the Court:* To be sure, a large part of a jurist's calculation depends on the composition of the Court when retirement is planned. Will there be a dramatic ideological shift with one's retirement (e.g., the Roberts Court, circa 2016)? Or would the ideological alignment remain largely unaffected by one's retirement (e.g., the FDR Court, circa 1944)?

Unless such matters are considered, a Justice spins the roulette wheel at the price of everything he or she had worked for.

∻

Louis Brandeis was prudent. The progressive jurist appreciated the importance of retaining his seat beyond the terms of the Republican Presidents Calvin Coolidge and Herbert Hoover. Brandeis was 77 and in good health when President Franklin Delano Roosevelt assumed office in 1933. The progressive jurist had already served on the Court for 21 years when, in 1937, he first thought of retiring.[1] He relinquished his seat two years later when he was 83. At that point, FDR was midway into his second presidential term. Prior to the 1940 election, no president had ever served a third term, and Brandeis could not reasonably expect otherwise. Moreover, the Democrats securely controlled the Senate in the year of Brandeis's retirement. Hence, his seat went to the liberal William O. Douglas, who was confirmed by a vote of 62-4. Brandeis died two years later in 1941.

Hugo Black was imprudent. "I will stay on until my next to last breath," Justice Black told a friend in 1968.[2] His main concern at the time was with breaking "the longevity record" then held by Chief Justice John Marshall and Justice Stephen Field. Black was so obsessed with this goal that he "kept on his desk a small card noting the exact dates of the two justices . . . who had served longer than he thus far." To set a new record, he had to survive until March 2, 1972 – he failed, dying on September 25, 1971.[3] Had Black not been so carelessly vain, he might have retired in 1968 when Lyndon B. Johnson was President and the Democrats controlled the Senate. As it turned out, the advantage went to Nixon who nominated Lewis F. Powell.

Ruth Bader Ginsburg, who has had two long bouts with cancer, has been heedless. In March of 2014, Dean Erwin Chemerinksy, one of the nation's most prominent constitutionalists, wrote a provocative and insightful op-ed in the Los Angeles Times.[4] It concerned Justice Ginsburg. Here is how it began: "Ginsburg should retire from the Supreme Court after the completion of the current term in June. She turned 81 on Saturday and by all accounts she is healthy and physically and mentally able to continue." But why, then, should the Justice have stepped down? Here is Chemerinsky's response: "Only by resigning this summer can she ensure that a Democratic president will be able to choose a successor who shares her views and values." Turning to the merits of his argument, Chemerinsky added: "A great deal turns on who picks Ginsburg's successor. There are, for example, four likely votes to overturn Roe vs. Wade on the current Court. . . . If a Republican president selects Ginsburg's replacement, that justice easily could be the fifth vote needed to allow the government to prohibit all abortions." Other "hot-button" cases, of course, hung in the decisional balance.

Justice Ginsburg ignored Dean Chemerinsky's advice. Hers was a gamble, one that she need not have countenanced. Her defense: "Anybody who thinks that if I step down, Obama could appoint someone like me, they're misguided."[5] But that is beside the point. Had Ginsburg retired before or at the time of the Chemerinsky op-ed, the President may well have successfully replaced her with a liberal justice in the mold of Sonia Sotomayor or Elena Kagan, both Obama appointees. But that never happened, leaving the distinct possibility that her successor will be picked by President Donald Trump.

Hugo Black was unlucky. Ruth Bader Ginsberg has been lucky thus far. Either way, a Machiavellian Justice would follow neither example. That crafty jurist would cast his or her legacy lot with Louis Brandeis.

Chapter 25

Directing History

A Justice's Working Papers and What to Do with Them

The world of today is one that might be manipulated, but what of tomorrow? That is a question that any Justice must consider if his or her words are to live on after death has claimed its due. For how one is remembered depends in important part on how one writes history while alive. That is where one's working papers come into play. In actuality such papers may be neither entirely private[1] nor actually paper – today, they are largely digital. That said, as long as the Court's tradition continues to treat such working papers as private, and as long as the other branches of government continue to yield to such usurpation of power, the prudent Justice should plan accordingly, though always duly prepared for unexpected changes. Shortly, we will say more about how the digitalization phenomenon affects a Justice's calculations regarding what should or should not be conveyed in communications within the Court. For now, let us reiterate our key point: Controlling one's Court communications (in whatever format) is a way of controlling the future if done with caution and foresight.

Justices treat their working papers[2] in various ways, sometimes prudently so, sometimes not. Thurgood Marshall gave all his papers (replete with a wealth of insider information[3]) to the Library of Congress with the requirement that they be released upon his death. That upset Chief

Justice William Rehnquist, who urged the Library to block access, since some of the files contained information about recent cases and sitting Justices.[4] The Library declined to honor that request. [5] By contrast, Justice David Souter provided that his papers be stored in the New Hampshire Historical Society, but that they not become public until a half-century after his retirement.[6] Even so, Justice Harry Blackmun's papers (some 1,500 boxes of documents), which are now public, reveal various communications between Justices Blackmun and Souter,[7] among others. Taking another tack, Justice William Brennan entrusted his papers to his biographer, who even many years after Brennan's death revealed that Justice White had reservations as late as the mid-1980s[8] about continuing to honor the landmark ruling in *New York Times, Co., v. Sullivan.*[9] Thus, the Brennan account of the story – favorable to Brennan, unfavorable to White – trumped the White one, at least up to now.

As is apparent, "this ad hoc system . . . allows the preferences of individual judges . . . to determine the fate of judicial papers."[10] That has its downsides and upsides for the Justice attentive to such matters. On the one hand, if one is on the Court with a Marshall or Blackmun type, their revelations *while one is still sitting on the Court* can upset many a Machiavellian applecart. On the other hand, such revelations might be useful to one depending on the nature of the disclosure. Hence, special care must be taken with how one interacts with one's colleagues, especially when there is some paper trail and/or when one knows, or has reason to know, that a colleague shares the full-and-timely disclosure mindset of a Justice Marshall or Blackmun.

Speaking generally, an extraordinary Justice should consider the following counsel, mindful of the status quo: First and foremost, try to avoid creating a record of anything that might later reflect ill on you. Second, if there are Marshall/Blackmun types on the Court, be both careful and strategic in what is given or said to them. Communications might be directed to them if only to plant in their papers information useful to one's cause. Third, communications with law clerks ought to be largely oral or otherwise not committed to a record that is circulated among one's colleagues. Fourth, keep a daily diary or memorandum account of the workings of the Court, but written always in beneficial ways.†† Fifth, plan in advance on where one's papers are to be stored and the conditions under which they are to be made public. And finally, arrange early on for a suitable and trustworthy biographer who will have private access to one's working Court papers (much as what Justice Louis Brandeis did[11]).

Of course, one has no real control over what colleagues write in their own papers. Thus, all one can do is attempt to minimize any damage that might be done and maximize any potential that might be realized.

≪

By way of a preface to our discussion of the significance of the digitization of intra-Court communication, let us quote from an observation made by Professor Kathryn Watts:

> In the immediate aftermath of the Supreme Court's blockbuster June 2012 ruling on the constitutionality of the Affordable Care Act, something fairly remarkable occurred: Sources within the Court leaked behind-the-scenes details. Just days after the Court's ruling came down, a CBS News report – relying upon "two sources with specific knowledge" of the deliberations that took place among the Justices – confirmed widespread speculation among Court watchers that "Chief Justice John Roberts initially sided with the Supreme Court's four conservative justices to strike down the heart of President Obama's health care reform law . . . but later changed his position and formed an alliance with liberals to uphold the bulk of the law."[12]

Predictably, the purported move by the Chief Justice was not well received by his conservative colleagues:

---

† To be on the safe side, such a diary should be stored in one's own private laptop computer, just in case there is any attempt to make such work documents stored on government computers public in ways consistent with the application of the Presidential Records Act and/or any other relevant laws.

According to CBS's inside sources, Chief Justice Roberts's change in position provoked the ire of the four conservatives and pushed them to independently craft a highly unusual unsigned joint dissent. A different media outlet – quoting a "source within the court with direct knowledge of the drafting process" – also reported that Chief Justice Roberts had changed his vote in the case but countered the CBS account by reporting that "most of the material in the first three quarters of the joint dissent" was actually drafted in Chief Justice Roberts's chambers before Roberts changed his vote, not in the chambers of the four conservative dissenting Justices.[13]

For now, such claims are mere speculation, and perhaps even untrue. Who can tell for sure? The answer: Time will tell. And how? The final answer will come by way of the working papers of one or more of the Justices. And that time may come soon depending on when such papers might be released and under what conditions. For example, assume that Justice X retires and provides that his or her papers be stored at the Library of Congress and released one year following retirement. At that time the controversial details of *National Federation of Independent Business v. Sebelius*[14] could become public. And those details could be even more problematic to the concerns of the Chief Justice than current news reports. It is one thing to bargain and barter in secret; it is quite another to have such dealings made public, and this while one is still sitting.

The digitalization of information creates yet other problems. In the past, this or that Justice saved this or that portion of his or her Court papers. Our digital world stands to change everything today. A Justice might have a lifetime of papers – e-mails, draft opinions, and memoranda – all stored on a single hard drive. Think of it: every e-mail Justice X received from colleagues†† could be stored on that hard drive, along

---

†. What of a Justice's conference notes? In the past, those were sometimes recorded in long hand, and sometimes made public years later when a Justice left the Court or died. But what if today a Justice were to bring a laptop into the conference? Or what if the Justice took extensive penned notes and thereafter had them all transcribed immediately after the conference?

with every draft of every opinion, and every digital exchange with law clerks, all of them. Such a bounty of information might now be available as never before.

The digitalization phenomenon has its advantages and disadvantages. As far as the latter is concerned, it means that a Justice must now, more than ever, be very careful of what he or she does before hitting either the *send* key or the *save* button. Furthermore, a Justice (mindful of the experience of the Chief Justice in the Health Care Case) must be attentive to what colleagues might say of him or her in their own e-mails or internal digital documents. Of course, a Justice cannot control such matters, but can muddy the waters by planting his or her own side of the story into the digital pool (and even encouraging colleagues, albeit cautiously, to do likewise).

&

Professor Harold Koh has aptly noted: "Harry Blackmun fooled everyone."[15] Thus, credit must be given to the sly Justice Harry Blackmun. Recall, he turned over a tome of his work papers to the Library of Congress. Beyond that, and shortly after his retirement, he also engaged in 38 hours of video-recorded interviews with one of his former clerks,[16] which interviews are now available at the Library and some even online.[17] In these ways, Blackmun really defined the Court's history much as he viewed it. And let us not forget the importance of a Justice's *letters*, and how one drafts them, and to whom he directs them, and what steps he takes to preserve them. In this regard, the best exemplar is Justice Holmes, who cherry-picked those letters he saved – the collections were later published in several books.[18] Here, too, he was able to frame history on his own terms.

Chapter 26

How to Best Secure
an Enduring Legacy

*If he ranks with Marshall as a maker of the Constitution, [Holmes]
ranks with Kent and Story as a molder of the thinking of lawyers and
law teachers, and the combination is unique.*

– Roscoe Pound[1]

Ambition is the partner of power. One must have the will to greatness if
one is to be powerful. And the path to greatness is long, playing out in
real time and spanning well beyond a lifetime. Ambition, power, greatness, legacy – they are all parts of that rich mix that makes for the Judge
whom we have lauded throughout our book. That is why we focus in
our final lesson on Justice Oliver Wendell Holmes, a jurist who in many
important ways personifies The Judge.

Holmes always had his eyes on the clock, both the short and long
hands. Justice Holmes's life and legacy provide a fitting complement to
that of Chief Justice John Marshall (see Chapter 2). Both were bright;
both were acutely mindful of their circumstances; both were daring in
ways best to secure success; both wrote their own opinions attentive
to substance and style; both realized the importance of timing; both
manipulated the law while appearing to honor it; both seized as much
judicial power as practical; and both planted seeds for their enduring
legacies.

We know: Some vilify Holmes,[2] and others portray him as a monster;[3]
some see him as a bridge between Hobbes and Hitler,[4] whereas others
accuse him of heartless Darwinism or self-interested Malthusianism;[5]

some claim he secretly "espoused a kind of fascist ideology,"[6] and still others depict him as a nihilist,[7] a man without values.[8] When it came to Grand Gospels, he delighted "in exposing prejudices that masqueraded as timeless truths."[9] The man did, after all, have his dark side. Thus, it is easy to list his "repulsive aspects: his naïve attraction to pseudoscientific eugenics, his fatalism, his indifference to human suffering, his egotism and vanity, his near-worship of force and obedience."[10] All true. That said, the same renowned scholar who laid those condemnations at Holmes's biographical door quickly qualified his claims: "But even when all that is taken into account, I am drawn in by Holmes's charms of person and of style, charms enhanced for the interpretive suitor by the complexities that shroud his character and thought."[11] Much to the same effect, Judge Richard Posner, who edited a revealing book on Holmes, posited: Holmes "wasn't perfect" or moral, or humanitarian; "he was only great."[12] Indeed, very great.

Judge him as you might, but Holmes towers over every other jurist of his day and also over those who followed him. Even with all the numerous broadsides published against him, he remains a monumental figure in the history of our law — "the great oracle of American law"[13] is how he has been tagged. If a jurist aspires to power and greatness, such a judge would be well served by studying the career of Holmes, and how he first breathed his own life into the law, which in time breathed life into his lasting legacy.

⋘

Much has been said, and continues to be said, about Holmes's long service on the nation's high Court from 1902-1932. What is particularly important about his tenure is a handful of opinions that were artfully reasoned and even more artfully presented. Those in the law know them well. There is his 1905 dissent in *Lochner v. New York*[14] (all the more delicious coming from such an avowed capitalist); there is his 1918 dissent in *Hammer v. Dagenhart*[15] (revealing his "humanity" toward the plight of children); there is his 1919 majority opinion in *Schenck v. United States*[16] (masterfully sneaking the "clear and present danger" test into First Amendment law); there is his revered dissent in *Abrams v. United States*[17] (an opinion that became canonical); there is his 1920 opinion in

Silverthorne Lumber Co. v. United States[18] (a landmark case on criminal justice); there is his 1923 dissent in *Adkins v. Children's Hospital*[19] (showing his "solidarity" with working progressives); there is his 1925 dissent in *Gitlow v. New York*[20] (more frosting on his First Amendment cake); and there is his 1930 dissent in *Baldwin v. Missouri*[21] (a well-crafted liberal defense of states rights). There are more, but that is certainly enough to win him the fame that so readily came his way.

Holmes was a master of dissent. He skillfully pitched his ideas and words to the Court of tomorrow. As in his non-judicial writings, he tapped into a blend of ambiguous substance combined with metaphoric style. He appreciated pithiness; he valued elegant phraseology; and he never let a bad law stand in the way of what he believed to be good policy. No opinion reads as well in a casebook as a Holmes opinion. No metaphoric articulations of the law rival those of Holmes. And no judicial dissent waits to be embraced by future generations more than a Holmes opinion. The result: He made his opinions irresistible to judges, lawyers, law professors, and law students. While he did make some mistakes,†† they were more than balanced away by several striking opinions.

As we stressed throughout our lessons, a Justice needs to give great examples of himself or herself. On that score, Holmes was unlike most – he personified greatness both in his judicial and extra-judicial writings.

૭

Holmes' greatness was . . . the conscious product of a systematic campaign
    of publicity, a campaign in which Holmes participated.

                                        – G. Edward White[22]

Holmes saved everything – everything, that is, that reflected favorably on his life and life's work. He saved most of his Civil War letters and

---

†. Holmes did not always act in his own best reputational interest. For example, he let his dark Darwinian tendencies color his thinking in *Buck v. Bell*, 274 U.S. 200 (1927), a pitiful case in which he defended eugenic reform in an 8-1 majority opinion for the Court. With poor judgment as to his own legacy, Holmes wrote: "Three generations of imbeciles are enough." Incredibly, he let Justice Pierce Butler (a lackluster jurist governed by religious sentiments) get the better of him by way of a dissent issued *sans* any opinion.

diaries,[23] many of his personal letters to prominent people and others[24] (though not anything he wrote to his purported mistress[25]), the bulk of his public speeches, and more. Much of that, including some sample opinions, is presented in a magnificent three-volume, 1,400 page set entitled *The Collected Works of Justice Holmes*.[26] This comes on top of numerous other published collections and works spanning the time from 1891[27] to 2013.[28] More incredible still, there are six major biographies of Justice Holmes[29] (plus a fictional biography[30]), along with numerous book-length commentaries on his work[31] and scholarly articles too many to list. In sum, Holmes left a great biographical footprint for others to follow, and follow they did.

The word commonly used is "canonization," as in the canonization of Justice Holmes.[32] It is an ironic use of the word to describe a man who had little or no interest or belief in the Beatific Beyond, "the upward and onward"[33] as he labeled it. "In life, there was little heavenly about the irreverent agnostic, the twinkling skeptic, the down-to-the-ground judicial realist." It was once said that it took years "to elevate Mr. Justice Holmes from deity to mortality."[34] Since Holmes's life and legacy abound in irony, it is entirely understandable that such words have been used to describe the making of Holmesian memories and myths.

The canonization began when Holmes was alive, and with his approval and even encouragement. It all traced back to the time of the *New Republic* boys. In 1916, Holmes was introduced to Harold Laski, the noted British political theorist, economist, and author. It was one of those meetings that pointed to unlimited opportunities. Later, in July of 1919, Laski introduced Holmes to Harvard Law Professor Zechariah Chafee; this, too, was a propitious encounter, one that would serve Holmes well for decades. Professor Chafee invested in Holmes by both informing him and defending him. As things progressed, Holmes developed relationships with still others, including the young progressive crowd affiliated with *The New Republic*. Soon enough, these *TNR* liberals joined forces with Chafee to venerate Holmes in newspapers, magazines, books, scholarly articles,†† and at conferences. To that end, in the summer of 1919 Laski first proposed and then arranged to

---

†. Holmes's secretaries (or law clerks) alone "published at least thirty-one books, articles, and book reviews praising him." Albert Alschuler, *Law Without Values* (Chicago, IL: University of Chicago Press), p. 184.

have Holmes's collected legal papers published by a respected house, Harcourt, Brace and Howe. Predictably, there was a "generous review" (by Morris Cohen) in *The New Republic*.[35]

There was one other member in this Committee of Admiration. He was the most important figure of them all and the kind of publicist that Holmes depended upon to bolster his fame. "Holmes was fortunate to have as one of his principal boosters a person who was eminently suited to launch such a campaign and highly motivated to do so."[36] That person was Felix Frankfurter – the man who introduced Holmes to a bevy of young admirers, who secured favorable coverage in *The New Republic*, who organized tributes in the *Harvard Law Review*, and who arranged for laudatory books to be published by Harvard University Press. Once Frankfurter lowered the PR needle into the groove, it played on in perpetual admiration of the "great judge."

Thus, "the story of Holmes's rise to 'greatness' " is, to an important extent, the story of his friendship with Felix Frankfurter."[37] When it came to publicizing Holmes's virtues, or defending him, or helping to secure his enduring legacy, no one outshined Frankfurter. For almost four decades, he dedicated himself to glorifying his beloved judicial forebear. (Amazingly, what Frankfurter did for Holmes he was never able to do for himself once he became a Supreme Court Justice.) Frankfurter's pull-out-all-the-stops campaign (buttressed by the mystique of Holmes's life and the breadth, eloquence, and force of his diverse writing[38]) helped to secure for Holmes a reputation rivaling that of Chief Justice John Marshall, whom he once honored publicly.[39] To be sure, all of that situated Holmes in an Olympian place in the history of the law.

❧

No one, before him or since, has so prepared himself for greatness as Oliver Wendell Holmes, Jr. No one has dedicated himself so thoroughly and continuously to wisely amassing so much reputational power as Holmes. To cap it all off (and here, too, one will find Felix Frankfurter's fingerprints), two events lifted Holmes high into the realm of unprecedented greatness and admiration.

The first was Holmes's remarkable 1931 national radio address on the occasion of his 90th birthday. The second event came shortly after Holmes's death. He died on March 6, 1935, two days before his ninety-fourth birthday. His funeral service was held at All Souls' Unitarian Church on March 8, his birthday. His fellow Justices served as honorary pallbearers. A poem – "Mysterious Night," by Joseph Blanco White – was read at the service. During it, the reverend Ulysses Pierce quoted a passage from an 1899 memorial speech Holmes gave in which he closed by saying: "At the grave of a hero . . . we end not with sorrow at the inevitable loss, but with the contagion of his courage; and with a kind of desperate joy we go back to the fight." When the service at the church ended, the great jurist's casket was transported to Arlington National Cemetery. There President Franklin Roosevelt joined the procession.[40] "At Arlington National Cemetery the coffin was placed upon a caisson drawn by artillery horses and accompanied by a guard of honor. The Army Band played 'The Battle Hymn of the Republic,' and the riderless horse with the boots reversed in the stirrups walked in the procession."[41] At the gravesite, soldiers fired a three-volley salute as the casket was lowered into the grave. A single bugler played "Taps." Another memorable event, another Holmesian moment.

It all paid off. Incredibly, even in the popular culture Holmes's words inspired well-regarded novels,[42] well-attended movies,[43] and even marketing management articles.[44] His words once became the title for a cover of *Time* magazine.[45] There was also an entire Hollywood movie (a fawning film) on Holmes. Metro-Goldwyn-Mayer released it in 1950; it was titled *The Magnificent Yankee*, which was based on a Broadway play that derived from a book by Francis Biddle, who once clerked for Justice Holmes and who was also a friend of Felix Frankfurter.

There is also his fame in the law. Today, all law professors and law students know his name. His opinions in constitutional law set the agenda for a line of precedents that survive today. Little wonder, then, that they are in all the casebooks and shape much of the discussion. In the domain of free speech law, he is the *pater* par excellence of modern First Amendment law. There is more, but these examples are sufficient to drive home the point: The tall and distinguished jurist with a winged moustache stood on a mountain so high that those below could do little but look up to him.

There are many lessons to be learned from the life and legacy of Oliver Wendell Holmes. Among other things, they are lessons about genius in the service of a will to greatness, persistence in the service of shrewdness, boldness in the service of power, patience in the service of objectives, style in the service of substance, acumen in the service of strategy, and perceptiveness of the kind that realized the immense value of a sycophant such as Felix Frankfurter.

To be Holmesian – it all seems daunting, difficult, even impossible. Perhaps. Then again, it points to the kind of jurist it takes to appreciate and benefit from the 26 lessons *The Judge* offers.

EPILOGUE

What you have read may have disturbed you since we appeared to endorse so much that was so ruthless. You may feel that we have no respect for the rule of law, and that we are happy to side with the darker forces in human nature. Understandable. If you think that, however, we urge you to reconsider the six points we stressed in our Prologue. Otherwise, you will misjudge us.

We presented our narrative in the grammar of power in order that there might be some mind-opening frank talk about what the merger of judicial law and politics could mean if taken seriously. Our 26 lessons operate in the vortex of that world. While we realize that a certain amount of judicial decision-making occurs without apparent political bias,[1] we nonetheless maintain that enough of it goes on at the Supreme Court level and in a sufficient number of significant cases to justify our tactics. More importantly, there is the perception – in the press, among scholars, and within the general public – that much judicial law has become politicized. That alone justifies our provocative book.

But there is more. There is the reality of what has been happening in the nation's high Court in recent years – in cases involving abortion, capital punishment, gun control, campaign finance spending, affirmative action, gay rights, voting rights, religious rights, labor union rights, rights of the accused, presidential elections, national health care, separation of powers, the law of standing, and on and on. The polarization on the Court in such cases[2] feeds the law-is-politics perception, and with some real justification.

It has been said, and correctly so, that *The Prince* "is the most famous book on politics when politics is thought to be carried out for its own sake, unlimited by anything else."[3] The "for its own sake" qualification refers to one's personal sake – the advantage goes to the fox. That advantage includes the power that comes with shaping the law to one's liking and doing so in calculated ways that enhance one's reputation, both in the short and long runs. The "unlimited by anything else" qualification refers to such efforts done without the restraints of legal or moral norms. Of course, there is an important limitation one cannot always escape, that of Fate (or *Fortuna* as Machiavelli called it). One can, however, prepare for it, plan for it, and then try best to adapt to its circumstances as they arise.

The Judge operates in this Machiavellian world, in a world free of twinges of conscience, moral frowns, professional scruples, or any of the feelings that come with idealistic notions of steadfast fidelity to the rule of law. This is not to deny that there will be occasions when fidelity can be to one's advantage. In such cases, ethical motivation is of no moment, though attention to the desired end always will be.

The gospel of power is one of departure; it departs from tradition, precedent, legal ethics, and ineffectual notions of judicial modesty. It diverges from the orders of others and the norms that rule the weak. It is assertive, not subservient. It unmasks disadvantageous pretense for what it is, and employs that same pretense to its own calculated advantage. The gospel of power, then, is the gospel of worldly prudence, a gospel of "icy realism."[4]

Again, "he is prosperous who adapts his mode of proceeding to the qualities of the times."[5] That may well be the key lesson to be gleaned from *The Prince*. Building on that, the qualities of our times are neither those inspired by St. Augustine's *City of God* nor those suggested by John Roberts' baseball umpire metaphor.[6] But if you believe that judicial rules derive either from God or baseball, then our lessons will be of no value to you. If you believe otherwise, however, *The Judge* may teach you much.

ৎ

Circuit Court Judge Richard A. Posner holds that "to the extent the Court is a constitutional court, it is a political body."[7] The Supreme Court, "when it is deciding constitutional cases," he adds, "is political in the sense of having and exercising discretionary power as capacious as a legislature's."[8] Though exaggerated – the Court's discretionary power is hardly as vast as a legislature's – the claim is more than interesting given the source. Judge Posner is a widely known jurist who has devoted considerable attention to perfecting the art of judging and judicial reputation.[9] And the good Judge is, after all, the one who reminds us

- that "rhetorical power may be a more important attribute of judicial excellence than analytical power;"[10]
- that Justices who "are asked to resolve issues of great political significance . . . [and] [p]olitical issues . . . cannot be referred to as a neutral expert for resolution;"[11]
- that a "sponge is not constraining; nor in the Supreme Court is precedent;"[12]
- that the ruling in *Brown v. Board of Education* "is a classic legislative decision;"[13]
- that "the variety, generality, ambiguity – or in a word 'omnisignificance" – of a judge's work must not be discounted;"[14]
- that a well-crafted signed opinion "enables a judge to cultivate an admiring audience outside of, and even antagonistic to, his judicial colleagues."[15]
- and that "it is one of the marks of the great judge to recast the issues in cases in his own image rather than to assume a passive, 'umpireal' stance."[16]

There is, of course, more to the plot and practice of Judge Posner's judicial canon. Even so, there is no need to belabor the obvious other than to say that he is one of greatest jurists of our day, and this despite his curious character.[17] If you doubt our assertions, reread those of Judge Posner; if you disbelieve our claims, study those of Judge Posner; and if thereafter his sophisticated gradations bewilder you, then he will have done his job. To be sure, the Judge may feel it best to distance himself from *The Judge*. That is to be expected insofar as perception is paramount. Lest we be misread, however, we do not say that Judge Posner is out-and-out Machiavellian,[18] but rather that there is more than a spoonful of the Master's thinking in his writings and judicial craft.

႙

As long as law remains one of the most common means of formalizing public policy,
the judicial office in the United States will involve political, i.e. policy-making, power.

— Walter F. Murphy[19]

Because of the triumph of realism over moralism so evident in *The Prince*, Niccolò Machiavelli has rightfully come to be seen as the father of modern political science, the science of power politics. Today politics is so steeped in power that we tend to be oblivious to it, much as fish are to water, which is to say that though it is vital, it is not always publicly visible. Given Machiavelli's great contribution to the study of politics and his reformulation of that study, it was inevitable that a political scientist, a modern-day one, would discern the relevance of such lessons to the politics of American appellate judging. And so it came to pass. The professor was Walter F. Murphy; his inventive book was titled *Elements of Judicial Strategy*. Published more than a half-century ago, Murphy's work still stands as a monument to realism, a testament to how real judges sometimes act, and a learned refutation to those who demand that law can, or should, stand apart from a judge's personal preferences. We direct attention to the great work of the late Princeton Professor for a humble reason: We cannot take full credit for the drift of some of the ideas articulated in *The Judge*. While his book and ours do have their differences, what unites the two works is a common focus: "How can a Justice of the Supreme Court most efficiently utilize his resources, official and personal, to achieve a particular set of policy objectives?"[20]

Like Professor Murphy, who was schooled in the lessons of political philosophy, we set out to "explore the capabilities of the judicial branch of government to influence public policy formulations." Like him, we also tried to formulate "strategies oriented toward accomplishing the possible" rather than "the ideal." So, too, we ventured to identify "efficacious means," "devious stratagems," "tactical maneuvers," and "calculating outlooks" designed to complement a shrewd Justice's "priorities of action." Similarly, our maxims are crafted to help "minimize specific checks on a Justice's power," duly mindful of the respective uses of direct and circumspect judicial action. We also agree that ethical questions that arise in this power context are more "problems of prudence" than moral ones. Likewise, we see no benefit in countenancing illegal behavior such as bribery, fraud, commercial self-dealing, or threats of unlawful action, etcetera. And we wholeheartedly agree with the following advice: "No combination of strategy and tactics can substitute for the other qualities which go to make a good judge" – qualities such as "wisdom, skilled craftsmanship, energy, intellectual acumen, and that elusive capacity called statesmanship." Equally important, and as we stressed in our Prologue, "a Justice who would take fullest advantage of the strategies and tactics" we have identified "would have to possess or acquire a rare combination of characteristics." [21] Phrased differently, nothing is elementary, nothing simple, and nothing is so easy as to be accomplished without great foresight and good fortune.

While we could add more, it is safe to say what we have. We leave any further questions to be answered by those who would scrutinize the *Elements of Judicial Strategy*, among other works by Professor Murphy's successors[22] in judicial thinking. That said, there is one significant difference between our book and that of Professor Murphy. He cautioned that he did not intend his ideas "to be construed as advice to judges, present or future."[23] However earnest he was in that regard, we took his thinking seriously enough to tender precisely the kind of counsel he purported to shun. Armed with his thinking, and more, we ventured into the breach and onto the new frontiers where great jurists dare to journey.

ço

So we conclude. We end our philosophical expedition into the realm of judicial realism with the confidence that at least some of what we have said echoes the words and/or practices of certain renowned jurists, revered scholars, and respected professors of political science. Though our 26 lessons are now complete, we trust that the other lessons implicit in our work will become explicit in the minds of our more thoughtful readers. Like Machiavelli, there is more to the plan of the corpus of our thought than what is placed in plain view. That, however, is matter for another moment.

Our work done, we now return to the quiet of our own perch and behold the judicial world as it turns on the axis of power. We watch the wonder of it all from a safe distance.

ACKNOWLEDGEMENTS

Cultivate the habit of being grateful for every good thing that comes to you, and to give thanks continuously.

-- Ralph Waldo Emerson

We take Emerson's counsel seriously, and aim to give credit where credit is due.

First and foremost, we thank David McBride and Niko Pfund of *Oxford University Press* for long believing in this project, back to the day when it was little more than a conceptual seed. They remained believers despite our undue lag of time in bringing this work to fruition. Importantly, David and Niko were confident enough to invest in our ideas despite the unorthodox character of our venture. By our measure, they represent everything that is finest in publishing, and for that we are grateful.

This book, as with all of our previous ones, would have been impossible without the able assistance of our librarians – Mary Whisner and her colleagues at the Gallagher Law Library at the University of Washington School of Law, and Kelly Kunsch at the Seattle University

Law School Library. Additionally, we owe a debt to our dedicated Seattle University Law School student research assistants – Julie Pendleton, Jeremy Peterson, and David Rittenhouse.

An appreciative nod goes out, as well, to Professor David M. O'Brien of the University of Virginia for his invaluable advice regarding the Supreme Court, its members, and its history.

Alex Lubertozzi, our former publisher and friend, helped us sharpen the narrative and compile the book. Once again, we are happy to recognize his helpful support.

Several people, some of them judges, who assisted us have, quite understandably, asked not to be acknowledged. They know who they are, they understand how grateful we are, and they can rest assured that their identities will remain secret.

ᔐ

Ron Collins: Many of my thoughts in this book trace back to three of my college professors, who first introduced me to political philosophy – Professors Michael Ormond, Ronald Hathaway, and Thomas Schrock. Whatever insights this book may have are owed to their inspiration, while its shortcomings are my own.

And then there is Linda Hopkins, who returns to the scene time and again to help repair all the broken parts. Thanks to her my journey continues.

No acknowledgement can begin to express my gratitude to Susan Cohen, whose life example inspires me, and whose love saves me. Ah, to think that it all began at a Passover Seder followed by that crazy coke bottle that fell from on high.

David Skover: I had the good fortune to work under a truly honorable judge, Jon O. Newman of the U.S. Court of Appeals for the Second Circuit, with whom I never discussed the contents of this book. Though he may well take respectful exception to some of its lessons, I hope, nonetheless, that he appreciates parts of both the text and subtext of The Judge.

ABOUT THE AUTHORS

Ronald K.L. Collins is the Harold S. Shefelman Scholar at the University of Washington Law School. Before coming to the Law School, Collins served as a law clerk to Justice Hans A. Linde on the Oregon Supreme Court, a Supreme Court Fellow under Chief Justice Warren Burger, and a scholar at the Washington, D.C. office of the Newseum's First Amendment Center.

Collins has written constitutional briefs that were submitted to the Supreme Court and various other federal and state high courts. In addition to the books that he co-authored with David Skover, he is the editor of *Oliver Wendell Holmes: A Free Speech Reader* (Cambridge University Press, 2010) and co-author with Sam Chaltain of *We Must Not Be Afraid to Be Free* (Oxford University Press, 2011). His last solo book was *Nuanced Absolutism: Floyd Abrams and the First Amendment* (2013).

Collins is the book editor of *SCOTUSblog*, and writes a weekly blog (First Amendment News), which appears on the *Concurring Opinions* website.

❧

David M. Skover is the Fredric C. Tausend Professor of Law at Seattle University School of Law. He teaches, writes, and lectures in the fields of federal constitutional law, federal jurisdiction, and mass communications theory and the First Amendment.

Skover graduated from the Woodrow Wilson School of International and Domestic Affairs at Princeton University. He received his law degree from Yale Law School, where he was an editor of the *Yale Law Journal*. Thereafter, he served as a law clerk for Judge Jon O. Newman at the Federal District Court for the District of Connecticut and the U.S. Court of Appeals for the Second Circuit. In addition to the books that he co-authored with Ronald Collins, he is the co-author with Pierre Schlag of *Tactics of Legal Reasoning* (Carolina Academic Press, 1986).

&

Together, Collins and Skover have authored *The Death of Discourse* (1996 & 2005), *The Trials of Lenny Bruce: The Fall & Rise of an American Icon* (2002 & 2012), *Mania: The Outraged & Outrageous Lives that Launched a Cultural Revolution* (2013), *On Dissent: Its Meaning in America* (2013), and *When Money Speaks: The McCutcheon Decision, Campaign Finance Laws, and the First Amendment* (2014) They have also authored numerous scholarly articles in various journals including the *Harvard Law Review, Stanford Law Review, Michigan Law Review,* and the *Supreme Court Review*, among other publications. The *Trials of Lenny Bruce* (revised & expanded) and *Mania* are available in e-book form from Top Five Books. Their next book is *Robitica: Free Speech & the Discourse of Data* (Cambridge University Press, 2018).

NOTES

Prologue

1. Unless otherwise indicated, our references to judges and the law that they create are directed to American judges – specifically, appellate judges, and even more specifically to Justices of the U.S. Supreme Court. Furthermore, our references to law typically address constitutional law – that is, the supreme law of the United States as given meaning by jurists, typically Supreme Court Justices. Furthermore, certain controversial areas of existing law are far more likely than others to present the kind of circumstances described in this book. Those areas include "hot-button issues" such as abortion, affirmative action, campaign finance, capital punishment, Commerce Clause challenges to federal laws, certain areas of corporate law, criminal justice, disability discrimination, environmental regulation, election law, health care law, race discrimination, sex discrimination, and takings of private property without just compensation. Thus understood, the lessons set out in the text are offered primarily for the categories of cases in which the maxim of "law is politics" has strong resonance.

2. See, e.g., Ruth W. Grant, *Hypocrisy and Integrity: Machiavelli, Rousseau and the Ethics of Politics* (Chicago, IL: University of Chicago Press, 1997), pp. 18-19.

3. See Leo Paul de Alvarez, *The Machiavellian Enterprise: A Commentary on the Prince* (Dekalb, IL: Northern Illinois University Press, 2008), pp. 75-77.

4. Cass Sunstein, "If Judges Aren't Politicians, What Are They?," *Bloomberg Business*, 7 January 2013. Of course, the matter becomes more complex once one begins to look into voting patterns along a topical spectrum of cases

combined with the group dynamics of federal circuit judges and Supreme Court Justices. See Cass Sunstein, David Schkade, Lisa Michelle Ellman, and Andres Sawicki, *Are Judges Political?: An Empirical Analysis of the Federal Judiciary* (Washington, D.C.: Brookings Institute Press, 2006).

5. Burt Neuborne, SCOTUSblog on Camera, Part 1 (Winter 2015), at http://www.scotusblog.com/media/ scotusblog-on-camera-burt-neuborne-complete/.

6. Cass Sunstein, "Moneyball for Judges," *The New Republic*, 10 April 2013.

7. Richard Nelly, "The 9 Justices Are Legislators," *Newsday*, 15 July 1987, p. 73 (statement by a then-sitting Justice of the West Virginia high court).

8. Mark Tushnet, "Following the Rules Laid Down," *Harvard Law Review* 96: 781, 784 (1983).

9. Leslie Bender, "The Takings Clause: Principles or Politics?," *Buffalo Law Review* 34: 735, 811-12 (1986).

10. Erwin Chemerinsky, *The Case Against the Supreme Court* (New York, NY: Viking, 2014), p. 10.

11. Lincoln Caplan, "Why the Law Gets No Respect," *Washington Post*, 20 September 1987, sec. C, p. 2 (Sunday ed.).

12. Robert Barnes, "Round 2 for Obamacare Before the High Court," *Washington Post*, 4 March 2015, sec. A, p. 3 (quoting Elizabeth B. Wydra, chief counsel for the Constitutional Accountability Center).

13. Patricia Wald, "Some Thoughts on Judging as Gleaned from One Hundred Years of the *Harvard Law Review* and Other Great Books," *Harvard Law Review* 100: 887, 888 (1987).

14. Richard Posner, "Foreword: A Political Court," *Harvard Law Review* 119: 31, 34 (2005).

15. Richard Posner, ""The Supreme Court is a Political Court -- Republicans' actions are Proof," *Washington Post,* 10 March 2016.

16. Jessica Gresko, "Breyer: Court Isn't '9 Junior-Varsity Politicians,'" *Boston. com*, 13 September 2010 (Associated Press story quoting Justice Stephen Breyer).

17. Neal Devins and Lawrence Baum, "Split Definitive: How Party Polarization Turned the Supreme Court into a Partisan Court," *SSRN*, 2 May 2014, p. 3 ("Today's partisan split, while unprecedented, is likely enduring. The very political changes that underlie today's split suggest that, for the foreseeable future, a five-member Democratic Court will reach sets of decisions that are quite different from those of a five-member Republican Court. For this very reason, presidential elections matter more than ever before in defining Court decision-making.").

18. Though there are differences, in some important ways *The Judge* is situated on a branch of the same realist/philosophical perch as one of our earlier works – *The Death of Discourse* (Durham, NC: Carolina Academic Press, 2nd

ed., 2005), pp. xviii, xlix-lv, 201-210, 215-249. Here as there, careful reading helps to curb false impressions.

19. See, e.g., Devins and Baum, "Split Definitive."

20. See, e.g., *King v. Burwell*, 135 S. Ct. 2480 (2015) and *Burwell v. Hobby Lobby*, 134 S. Ct. 2751 (2014).

21. Consider Alan Ryan, *On Machiavelli: The Search for Glory* (New York, NY: Liveright, 201), pp. 76, 77, 78 ("[O]ne could be forgiven for thinking after a quick reading that being a Machiavellian hero is an exhausting and unprofitable activity . . . . Is the task hopeless? . . . . How well [one does] in a risky political enterprise . . . very much [depends on one's] style, temperament, [and] characteristic mode of operation [and how they all suit] the conditions [of the time] . . . [S]ometimes the schemes of a cautious man will come adrift because the situation demands boldness, [then again,] sometimes the cautious man will succeed where the bold one does not."). This is not to concede that the Machiavellian effort is a Sisyphean one, but rather to emphasize the need to readjust one's calculations from time to time, duly mindful of the role of chance.

22. See Ronald Collins, "The Principles of Power," in John Murley, Robert Stone, and William Braitwaite, eds., *Law and Philosophy: The Practice of Theory* (Athens, OH: Ohio University Press, 1992), Vol. II: 671-683.

23. The Borgia reference here, and the line of argument drawn from it, might be understood in non-conventional ways, much as Machiavelli's message was non-conventional. See Clifford Orwin, "The Riddle of Cesare Borgia & the Legacy of Machiavelli's *Prince*," in Timothy Fuller, editor, *Machiavelli's Legacy: The Prince After Five Hundred Years* (Philadelphia, PA: University of Pennsylvania Press, 2015), pp. 156, 157-158, 159, 162-163, 166, 170. See also Ryan, *On Machiavelli*, pp. 63-67.

24. Beyond the counsel contained in *The Prince*, we have also benefitted greatly from the parallel lessons set forth in Robert Greene, *The 48 Laws of Power* (New York, NY: Penguin, 1998).

25. Of course, Machiavelli wrote other works on ruling, most notably his *Discourses on the First Decade of Livy*. The relationship between *The Prince* and the *Discourses* has been the subject of much scholarly attention. See, e.g., de Alvarez, *The Machiavellian Enterprise*, pp. vii-ix; Niccolò Machiavelli, *The Discourses* (New York, NY: Penguin, 1974) (trans. Leslie Walker, with introduction by Bernard Crick), pp. 13-69; Alissa Ardito, *Machiavelli and the Modern State: The Prince, the Discourses on Livy, and the Extended Territorial Republic* (New York, NY: Cambridge University Press, 2015), pp. 12-28. See also Strauss, *Thoughts on Machiavelli*, pp. 54-173, 282-283. Since our enterprise is not a derivative one, such considerations, however important, need not constrain us.

26. Christopher S. Celenza, *Machiavelli: A Portrait* (Cambridge, MA: Harvard University Press, 2015), pp. 65-66.

27. See Felix Gilbert, *Machiavelli and Guicciardini: Politics and History in Sixteenth Century Florence* (New York, NY: W.W. Norton & Co., 1984), p. 168.

28. DeAlvarez, *The Machiavellian Enterprise*, p. 79.

29. Greene, *The 48 Laws of Power*, p. xvii.

30. See Sebastian de Grazia, *Machiavelli in Hell* (Princeton, NJ: Princeton University Press, 1989), p. 257. See also *ibid.*, p. 256 ("Men's desires and appetites are not only insatiable and wrongly directed, they are also deceptive. They distort vision, reason, and belief.").

31. Jacob E. Cooke, ed., *The Federalist* (Middletown, CN: Wesleyan University Press, 1961), p. 523 (Alexander Hamilton). See also David F. Epstein, *The Political Theory of The Federalist* (Chicago, IL: University of Chicago Press, 1984), p. 191 (commenting on the passage quoted in the text).

32. Ron Chernow, *Alexander Hamilton* (New York, NY: Penguin Books, 2004), p. 648.

33. See *Bush v. Gore*, 531 U.S. 98 (2000). For commentary, see Bruce Ackerman, ed., *Bush v. Gore: The Question of Legitimacy* (New Haven, CT: Yale University Press, 2002), pp. 129-228 (discussing political question aspect of ruling).

34. Alexander Bickel, *The Least Dangerous Branch: The Supreme Court at the Bar of Politics* (New York, NY: Bobbs-Merrill Co., 1962), p. 1

35. "Judges interpret words. And words do not bind the interpreters; rather the interpreters give meaning to the words. The meaning of words is not the same as the 'intent' of the writers. Often writers have no pertinent intent or have several intents. When they have an intent it does not control, because words are mere instruments for conveying thoughts to others. The critical people are the users, not the writers, of words." Frank Easterbrook, "Legal Interpretation and the Power of the Judiciary," *Harvard Journal of Law and Public Policy* 7: 87 (1984).

36. 347 U.S. 483 (1954).

37. See Raoul Berger, *Government by Judiciary: The Transformation of the Fourteenth Amendment* (Cambridge, MA: Harvard University Press, 1977), pp. 126-133, 243-245, 342, 348. See also Herbert Wechsler, "Toward Neutral Principles of Constitutional Law," *Harvard Law Review* 73: 1, 31-34 (1959) (arguing that *Brown* cannot be reconciled with principled adjudication).

38. See *Marbury v. Madison*, 5 U.S. (1 Cranch) 137 (1803) and *Cooper v. Aaron*, 358 U.S. 1 (1958).

39. Consider Gerald N. Rosenberg, *The Hollow Hope: Can Courts Bring About Social Change?* (Chicago, IL: University Of Chicago Press, 2nd ed., 2008) pp. 173-268 (re abortion politics, arguing that it is extremely difficult to generate significant reforms through litigation because, as the author maintains, American courts are ineffective and relatively weak). We will say more about this later in our book.

40. J.G.A. Pocock, *The Machiavellian Moment* (Princeton, NJ: Princeton University Press, 1975), p. 165.

41. In this regard, consider de Alvarez, *The Machiavellian Enterprise*, pp. 4-5 (discussing who is "the true addressee" of *The Prince*).

42. See Alexander Bickel, "Foreword: The Passive Virtues," *Harvard Law Review* 75: 40 (1961).

43. Miles J. Unger, *Machiavelli: A Biography* (New York, NY: Simon & Schuster, 2011), p. 238.

44. See de Alvarez, *The Machiavellian Enterprise*, pp. 78-79 (discussing why Machiavelli brings "indecent things to light").

45. Several political scientists (of whose ideas we will say more later) have been attentive to some of the concerns discussed in *The Judge*. See, e.g., Walter F. Murphy, *Elements of Judicial Strategy* (Chicago, IL: University of Chicago Press, 1964), and Laurence Baum, *Judges and Their Audiences* (Princeton, NJ: Princeton University Press, 2006).

46. For example, how a judge or justice votes may be influenced by such factors as the ideological makeup of his or her colleagues. See Cass R. Sunstein, Lisa Michelle Ellman, and David Schkade, "Ideological Voting on Federal Courts of Appeals: A Preliminary Investigation," *Virginia Law Review* 90: 301, 305 (2004).

47. Niccolò Machiavelli, *The Prince*, trans. Harvey C. Mansfield (Chicago, IL: University of Chicago Press, 2nd ed., 1998), pp. 37-38 (Ch. VIII).

48. Consider de Alvarez, *The Machiavellian Enterprise*, pp. 88-90 (discussing Machiavelli's "openness").

49. See James Miller, *Rousseau: Dreamer of Democracy* (New Haven, CT: Yale University Press, 1964), p. 68 (quoting Rousseau re Machiavelli: "While pretending to give lessons to Kings, [Machiavelli] gave great ones to the people.").

50. See Grant, *Hypocrisy and Integrity*, pp. 4-5.

51. See St. Augustine, "Against Lying," in Roy J. Deferrari, ed., *Saint Augustine: Treatises on Various Subjects* (New York, NY: Fathers of the Church, Inc., 1952), pp. 125-179.

52. See Quentin Skinner, *Machiavelli* (New York, NY: Hill & Wang, 1981).

53. See Pocock, *The Machiavellian Moment*.

54. See Leo Strauss, *Thoughts on Machiavelli* (Glencoe, Il: The Free Press, 1958) and Harvey C. Mansfield, "Strauss on *The Prince*," *Review of Politics*, 75: 659 (2013). See also Harvey C. Mansfield, Jr. and J.G.A. Pocock, "An Exchange on Strauss's Machiavelli," *Political Theory* (November, 1975) 3: 372-405.

55. See Philip Bobbitt, *The Garments of Court and Palace: Machiavelli and the World That He Made* (New York, NY: Atlantic Monthly Press, 2013).

56. See, e.g., Erica Benner, *Machiavelli's Prince: A New Reading* (New York, NY: Oxford University Press, 2013); Claude Lefort, *Machiavelli in the Making*, trans. Michael M. Smith (Evanston, Ill: Northwestern University

Press, 2012); and Fuller, *Machiavelli's Legacy*. In his essay "The Question of Machiavelli," Isaiah Berlin does a good job (circa 1971) of summarizing the many divergent views (no fewer than 20) concerning *The Prince* and Machiavelli's intentions. The relevant discussion in Berlin's essay appears in Machiavelli, *The Prince*, pp. 206-212, 235. See also Grant, *Hypocrisy and Integrity*, pp. 5-15 (discussing the views of *The Prince* as held by the likes of Rousseau, Spinoza, and Diderot and others). For Mr. Berlin's own perceptive comments on the Machiavellian mission and its more significant implications, see Machiavelli, *The Prince*, pp. 225-236.

57. For a thoughtful and informed critique of Machiavelli and his mission, see Unger, *Machiavelli: A Biography*, pp. 215-245. See also Ardito, *Machiavelli and the Modern State*.

58. See John Robertson, ed., *The Philosophical Works of Francis Bacon* (New York, NY: Routledge & Sons, 1905), p. 570 (re epigraph quote to this book).

59. Consider in this regard Robert M. Adams, "The Rise, Proliferation, and Degradation of Machiavellism: An Outline," in Machiavelli, *The Prince*, p. 273 ("The entire works of Machiavelli were placed on the Index of Prohibited Books, compiled by the Holy Inquisition of Rome. This act resulted from the decrees of the Council of Trent.").

Chapter 1

1. Robert Bork, "Tradition and Morality in Constitutional Law," reproduced in David M. O'Brien, editor, *Judges on Judging: Views From the Bench* (Chatham, NJ: Chatham House Publishers, Inc., 1997), p. 175.

2. For Bork's account of this, see his *Saving Justice: Watergate, the Saturday Night Massacre, and other Adventures of a Solicitor General* (New York, NY: Encounter Books, 2013), pp. 69-89.

3. Mark Gitenstein, *Matters of Principle: An Insider's Account of America's Rejection of Robert Bork's Nomination to the Supreme Court* (New York: Simon & Schuster, 1992), p. 203.

4. Robert Bork, *The Tempting of America: The Political Seduction of the Law* (New York: Touchstone, 1990), p. 292.

5. John Bolton quoted in Gitenstein, *Matters of Principle*, p. 206.

6. *Ibid.*

7. Ronald Dworkin, "The Bork Nomination," *New York Review of Books*, 13 August 1987, p. 3.

8. See Norman Vieira and Leonard Gross, *Supreme Court Appointments: Judge Bork and the Politicization of Senate* (Carbondale, IL: Southern Illinois University Press, 1988), pp. 11-52.

9. Quoted in Bork, *The Tempting of America*, p. 287.

10. Edward Kennedy quoted in Julie Novkov, *The Supreme Court and the Presidency: Struggles for Supremacy* (Thousand Oaks, CA: CQ Press, 2013), p. 106.

11. Lee Epstein and Jeffrey A. Segal, *Advice and Consent: The Politics of Judicial Appointments* (New York, NY: Oxford University Press, 2005), p. 97.

12. Richard Posner,"Why Didn't Robert Bork Reach the Supreme Court? -- Because of politics, of course—and that's fair enough," *Slate*, 19 December 2012.

13. Our visual portrays are taken from "Robert Bork Supreme Court Nomination Process Hearings Day 1 Part 2 (1987)" (the Bork Archive), *YouTube*, https://www.youtube.com/watch?v=RGNsZgI0MA0, 11 August 2015.

14. 316 U.S. 535 (1942).

15. 381 U.S. 479 (1965).

16. *Nomination of Robert H. Bork to be Associate Justice of the Supreme Court of the United States: Hearings before the Committee on the Judiciary, United States Senate* (One Hundredth Congress, first session, 15-30 September 1987), p. 115.

17. Much of the same informed Judge Bork's begrudging responses to Senator Dennis DeConcini when the hot topic of sex discrimination came up. "The Bork Hearings: Excepts from the Bork Hearing: Pinning Down His Positions," *New York Times*, 17 September 1987 ("You leave this Senator," DeConcini told Bork, "unsatisfied as to how [I] can conclude you are going to protect the citizens of this country in interpreting the Constitution on the Court as it relates to sex [discrimination].").

18. The text and quotes are from Linda Greenhouse, "Robert Bork's Tragedy," *New York Times*, 9 January 2013. In fairness to Judge Bork, his jurisprudence of original intent, however confusing, would probably have accommodated the judgment in *Brown*. See Ronald Dworkin, "The Bork Nomination," *Cardozo Law Review* 9:101, 105 (October 1987) ("Bork says that *Brown* was rightly decided . . . ."). That said, Judge Bork nonetheless took exception to the Court's holding in *Bolling v. Sharpe*, 347 U.S. 497 (1954) (companion case to *Brown* applying the equal protection doctrine to the District of Columbia). "I think," he said, "that constitutionally that is a troublesome case [and] I have not thought of a rationale for it." Quoted in *Nomination of Robert H. Bork*, pp. 262-264.

19. Consider, for example, Bork's exchange with Senator Patrick Leahy concerning his views on First Amendment law. See Gitenstein, *Matters of Principle*, pp. 232-233. See also Edward Walsh and Al Kamen, "Senators Question Bork's Consistency," *Washington Post*, 17 September 1987.

20. Epstein and Segal, *Advice and Consent*, p. 116.

21. Elena Kagan, "Confirmation Messes, Old and New," *University of Chicago Law Review* 62:919, 925.

22. *Ibid.,* p. 920. During during her confirmation hearing in 2009 to become Solicitor General, Kagan disavowed her prior positions. She told Senator Hatch, "I am not sure that sitting here today I would agree with that statement," lamenting that "I wrote that when I was in the position of sitting where the staff is now sitting and feeling a little bit frustrated that I really was not understanding completely what the judicial nominee in front of me meant and what she thought." See U.S. Congress, Senate Committee on the Judiciary, *Confirmation Hearings on the Nominations of Thomas Perrelli Nominee To Be Associate Attorney General of the United States and Elena Kagan Nominee To Be Solicitor General of the United States,* 111th Cong., 1st sess., February 10, 2009 (Washington, D.C.: GPO, 2009), p. 118, discussed in Randy E. Barnett and Josh Blackman, "Restoring the Lost Confirmation," 83 *University of Chicago Review Online* ___ (forthcoming 2016).

23. Nicollò Machiavelli, *The Prince* (Book XVIII), translated & edited by Robert A. Adams (New York, NY: Norton Critical editions, 2nd ed., 1992), p. 49.

24. *Confirmation Hearings on the Nominations of Thomas Perrelli, Nominee to be Associate Attorney General of the United States, and Elena Kagan, Nominee to be Solicitor General of the United States* (One Hundred Eleventh Congress, First Session, 10 February 2009), p. 329.

25. Bork, *The Tempting of America,* p. 348.

26. Notably, all Supreme Court nominees who have appeared before the Senate Judiciary Committee after Robert Bork have distanced themselves from his example . . . and have been confirmed. Among others, this was true of **Sandra Day O'Connor** (see Linda Hirshman, *Sisters in Law: How Sandra Day O'Connor and Ruth Bader Ginsburg Went to the Supreme Court and Changed the World* (New York, NY: Harper, 2015), p. 133), **Antonin Scalia** (see David E. Rosenbaum, "No-Comment is Common at Hearings for Nominees," *New York Times,* 12 July 2005), **Clarence Thomas** (see Jack Balkin, editor, *What Roe v. Wade Should Have Said* (New York, NY: New York University Press, 2005), p. 15), **Sonia Sotomayor** (see *Confirmation Hearing on the Nomination of Hon. Sonia Sotomayor, to be an Associate Justice of the Supreme Court of the United States, Committee on the Judiciary, United States Senate* (One Hundred Eleventh Congress, first session, 13-16 July 2009), p. 2.), and **John Roberts** (see "Roberts: 'My job is to call balls and strikes and not to pitch or bat,'" CNN.com, 12 September 2005 http://www.cnn.com/2005/POLITICS/09/12/roberts.statement/).

Chapter 2

1. Robert Greene, *The 33 Strategies of War* (New York, NY: Penguin, 2006), p. 147.

2. 5 U.S. 137 (1803).

3. Robert McCloskey, *The American Supreme Court* (Chicago, IL: University of Chicago Press, 1964), p. 40.

4. Leonard W. Levy, Kenneth L. Karst, and Dennis J. Mahoney, editors, *Encyclopedia of the American Constitution* (New York, NY: MacMillan, 1986), p. 1205 ("John Marshall" entry authored by Robert K. Faulkner).

5. Harlow G. Unger, *John Marshall: The Chief Justice Who Saved the Nation* (New York, NY: DaCapo, 2014).

6. Charles F. Hobson, *The Great Chief Justice: John Marshall and the Rule of Law* (Lawrence, KS: University Press of Kansas, 1996), p. 1.

7. Kermit L. Hall, James W. Ely Jr., and Joel B. Grossman, editors, *The Oxford Companion to The Supreme Court of the United States* (New York, NY: Oxford University Press, 2nd ed. 2005), p. 607 ("John Marshall" entry authored by R. Kent Newmyer).

8. William W. Van Alstyne, "A Critical Guide to *Marbury v. Madison*," *Duke Law Journal* 1969: 1, 2.

9. *Ibid.*, p. 1.

10. Harold H. Burton, "The Cornerstone of Constitutional Law: The Extraordinary Case of *Marbury v. Madison*," *American Bar Association Journal* 36: 805 (1950).

11. Thomas W. Merrill, "*Marbury v. Madison* as the First Great Administrative Law Decision," *John Marshall Law Review* 37: 481 (2004).

12. For the most widely recognized critique of *Marbury*, see Van Alstyne, "A Critical Guide," pp. 6-33. Of course, the Chief Justice's craftsmanship in *Marbury* has its defenders, although not from the realpolitik perspectives that we advance here. See, e.g., Robert Lowry Clinton, *Marbury v. Madison and Judicial Review* (Lawrence, KS: University Press of Kansas, 1989), pp. 81-127.

13. *Ibid.*, p. 127.

14. The bulleted points in the text derive from Van Alstyne, "A Critical Guide," pp. 5-6; Baker, *John Marshall*, pp. 363-364, 375-376, 394-397; Clinton, *Marbury v. Madison*, p. 85; Levy, Karst, and Mahoney, *Encyclopedia*, p. 1200 (*Marbury* entry authored by Leonard Levy).

15. *Ibid.*, p. 1202 (quoting Albert J. Beveridge).

16. Van Alstyne, *A Critical Guide*, p. 12 (referencing U.S. Const. Art. III).

17. Quoted in Levy, Karst, and Mahoney, *Encyclopedia*, p. 1201 (*Marbury* entry authored by Leonard Levy).

18. See, e.g., Van Alstyne, "A Critical Guide," pp. 14-33; Baker, *John Marshall*, pp. 406-412; Levy, Karst, and Mahoney, *Encyclopedia*, pp. 1201-1202 (*Marbury* entry authored by Leonard Levy).

19. David Forte, "Marbury's Travail: Federalist Politics and William Marbury's Appointment as Justice of the Peace," *Catholic University Law Review* 45: 349 (1996).

20. 358 U.S. 1 (1958).

21. 60 U.S. 393 (1857).

Chapter 3

1. Hadley Arkes, "Machiavelli in America," in Codevilla, editor, Nicolò Machiavelli, *The Prince*, pp. 124, 125.
2. Carnes Lord, "Machiavelli's Realism," in Angelo M. Codevilla, editor, Nicolò Machiavelli, *The Prince* (New Haven, CN: Yale University Press, 1997), pp. 114, 121.
3. See Leo Strauss, *Thoughts on Machiavelli* (Glencoe, IL: University of Chicago Press, 1958), p. 9 (We would not "shock" anyone if we "merely expose ourselves to good-natured or at any rate harmless ridicule, if we profess ourselves inclined to the old-fashioned and simple opinion according to which Machiavelli was a teacher of evil.").
4. Lincoln Caplan, "Does the Supreme Court Need a Code of Conduct?," *New Yorker*, 27 July 2015, http://www.newyorker.com/news/news-desk/does-the-supreme-court-need-a-code-of-conduct.
5. David M. O'Brien, *Storm Center: The Supreme Court in American Politics* (New York, NY: W. W. Norton & Co., 10th ed., 2014), p. 187 (emphasis added).
6. 28 U.S. Code §455(a) ("Any justice, judge, or magistrate judge of the United States shall disqualify himself in any proceeding in which his impartiality might reasonably be questioned."). See also 28 U.S.C. §144 ("Bias or prejudice of judge").
7. John G. Roberts, *2011 Year-End Report on the Federal Judiciary*, p. 8.
8. United States Courts, *Code of Conduct for United States Judges*, http://www.uscourts.gov/judges-judgeships/ code-conduct-united-states-judges.
9. Roberts, *2011 Year-End Report*, pp. 3-4.
10. 5 U.S. 137 (1803).
11. 325 U.S. 897 (1945).
12. Roger K. Newman, *Hugo Black: A Biography* (New York, NY: Pantheon Books, 1994), p. 334.
13. *Ibid.*
14. *Ibid.*, p. 335.
15. 325 U.S. 897 (1945) (Jackson, J. concurring, joined by Frankfurter, J.).
16. The internecine warfare notwithstanding, Justice Black's recusal would not have affected the ultimate outcome in the case, since a 4-4 judgment would have affirmed the lower court's ruling in favor of the union.
17. Newman, *Hugo Black*, p. 337.
18. 408 U.S. 1 (1972).
19. See Jeffrey W. Stempel, "Rehnquist, Recusal and Reform," *Brooklyn Law Journal* 53: 589, 593–94 (1987).
20. 409 U.S. 824 (1972).
21. Adam Liptak and Jonathan Glater, "Papers Offer Close-Up of Rehnquist and the Court," *New York Times*, 17 November 2008.

22. See, e.g., *Clapper v. Amnesty International USA*, 133 S. Ct. 1138 (2013) (invoking *Laird* approvingly).
23. See "Fix the Court Finds Chief Justice Roberts Missed a Stock Conflict," *Fix the Court*, 18 December 2015, http://fixthecourt.com/2015/12/recusalreport/ ("Chief Justice John Roberts overlooked a stock conflict when he and his colleagues were deciding whether to hear a Superfund cleanup case in October.").
24. *Ibid.*

Chapter 4

1. Quoted in Peter Irons, *A People's History of the Supreme Court* (New York, NY: Viking Penguin, 1999), p. 328.
2. Quoted in Michael Parrish, "Felix Frankfurter, the Progressive Tradition and the Warren Court," in Mark Tushnet, editor, *The Warren Court in Historical and Political Perspective* (Charlottesville, VA: University of Virginia Press, 1996), p. 52.
3. Quoted in David M. O'Brien, *Storm Center: The Supreme Court in American Politics* (New York, NY: W.W. Norton & Co., 10th ed., 2014), p. 59.
4. James Bradley Thayer, "The Origin & Scope of the American Doctrine of Constitutional Law," *Harvard Law Review*, 7: 129 (1893).
5. Leonard Baker, *Brandeis & Frankfurter: A Dual Biography* (New York, NY: Harper & Row, 1989), p. 417.
6. O'Brien, *Storm Center*, p. 254, referencing John P. Frank, *The Marble Palace* (New York, NY: Knopf, 1958), p. 105.
7. Quoted in Baker, *Brandeis & Frankfurter*, p. 418.
8. *Ibid.*, p. 419.
9. See, e.g., Bruce Allen Murphy, *Wild Bill: The Legend & Life of William O. Douglas* (New York, NY: Random House, 2003), pp. 185-188, 191-194, 204-207, 209-210, 235-236, 248-249, 300-301, 353-354, and James F. Simon, *Independent Journey: The Life of William O. Douglas* (New York, NY: Penguin Books, 1980), pp. 8-9, 11-13, 217-222, 245-246, 278.
10. See, e.g., Wallace Mendelson, *Justices Black & Frankfurter: Conflict in the Court* (Chicago, IL: University of Illinois Press, 1961), and Roger K. Newman, *Hugo Black: A Biography* (New York, NY: Pantheon, 1994), pp. 287-298, 485-486.
11. See H.N. Hirsch, *The Enigma of Felix Frankfurter* (New York, NY: Basic Books, 1981), pp. 210-212 (discussing Frankfurter's inability to deal with opposition, his difficulty with interpersonal relationships, his all-consuming desire to win, and his rationalization of his own behavior).
12. Baker, *Brandeis & Frankfurter*, p. 415.

13. Mark Silverstein, "Felix Frankfurter," in Roger K. Newman, editor, *The Yale Biographical Dictionary of American Law* (New Haven, CN: Yale University Press, 2009), pp. 204, 205.

14. Parrish, "Felix Frankfurter," p. 54.

15. Melvin Urofsky, *The Warren Court: Justices, Rulings, and Legacy* (Denver, CO: ABC-CLIO, 2001), p. 40.

16. See Bruce Allen Murphy, *The Brandeis-Frankfurter Connection* (New York, NY: Oxford University Press, 1982).

17. David Burner, "James Clark McReynolds," in Leon Friedman and Fred Israel, *Justices of the United States Supreme Court: Their Lives & Major Opinions* (New York, NY: Facts on File, 4th ed., 2013), vol. III, pp. 93, 95.

18. Quoted in *ibid.*, p. 85.

19. James Bond, "James Clark McReynolds," in Roger K. Newman, editor, *The Yale Biographical Dictionary of American Law* (New Haven, CN: Yale University Press, 2009), p. 375.

20. The statement is attributed to John Frush Knox, one of McReynolds' former law clerks. https://en.wikipedia.org/wiki/James_Clark_McReynolds -Attorney_General_and_Supreme_Court_tenure.

21. 163 U.S. 537 (1896) (Harlan, J., dissenting) (rejecting the doctrine of "separate but equal" in race civil rights cases).

22. 198 U.S. 45 (1905) (Holmes, J., dissenting) (rejecting the majority's endorsement of *laissez-faire* economic theory in constitutional cases).

23. 298 U.S. 238 (1936) (Cardozo, J., dissenting) (rejecting restraints on Congress's exercise of the commerce power in regulating the coal industry).

24. 478 U.S. 186 (1986) (Stevens, J., dissenting) (arguing against criminalization of same-sex sodomy).

25. Noah Feldman, *Scorpions: The Battles & Triumphs of FDR's Great Supreme Court Justices* (New York, NY: Twelve, 2010), p. 117.

26. Niccolò Machiavelli, *The Prince*, trans. Robert M. Adams (New York, NY: W.W. Norton, 2nd ed., 1977), p. 46 (Bk 17).

27. *Ibid.*

28. *Ibid.*

29. *Ibid.*

30. *Ibid.*, p. 47.

Chapter 5

1. William Shakespeare, *The Tragedy of King Lear*, Act II, scene 2.

2. Re the background of this turn of events, see Ronald K.L. Collins, editor, *The Fundamental Holmes: A Free Speech Chronicle & Reader* (New York, NY: Cambridge University Press, 2010), pp. 161-162, and G. Edward White,

Justice Oliver Wendell Holmes: Law and the Inner Self (New York, NY: Oxford University Press, 1993), pp. 299-307.

3. 268 US 652 (7-2 per Sanford, J., for the Court with Holmes & Brandeis dissenting) (First Amendment assumed to be applicable to the states but constitutional claim nonetheless denied).

4. 279 U.S. 644 (6-3, per Butler, J., for the Court, with Holmes, Brandeis & Sanford dissenting) (statutory free speech claim denied).

5. There was an occasional exception, such as *Stromberg v. California*, 283 U.S. 359 (1931) (7-2 with McReynolds & Butler dissenting) (First Amendment claim sustained).

6. 250 U.S. 616 (1919) (7-2 per Clark with Holmes & Brandeis dissenting).

7. Charles Evan Hughes, Memorial Remarks, 1 June 1931, quoted in Fred W. Friendly, *Minnesota Rag: The Dramatic Story of the Landmark Supreme Court Case That Gave New Meaning to Freedom of the Press* (New York, NY: Vintage Books, 1981), p. 148.

8. 283 U.S. 697 (1931) (5-4 per Hughes with Butler dissenting joined by Sutherland, Van Devanter and McReynolds).

9. See *ibid*, pp. 707 (application of press clause to the States), 713 (appropriate constitutional remedies), 716 (narrow qualifications), 718 (no prior restraints).

10. 283 U.S. at 723 (Butler, J., dissenting) ("The decision of the Court in this case declares Minnesota and every other state powerless to restrain by injunction the business of publishing and circulating among the people malicious, scandalous, and defamatory periodicals that in due course of judicial procedure have been adjudged to be a public nuisance. It gives to freedom of the press a meaning and a scope not heretofore recognized, and construes 'liberty' in the due process clause of the Fourteenth Amendment to put upon the states a federal restriction that is without precedent.").

11. Friendly, *Minnesota Rag*, p. 154.

12. Paul Murphy, *"Near v. Minnesota,"* in Kermit Hall, editor, *The Oxford Companion to the Supreme Court of the United States* (New York, NY: Oxford University Press 2005), p. 675.

13. *The Bee* (Danville, VA), 17 May 1954, p. 3.

14. See James St. Clair and Linda Gugin, *Chief Justice Fred M. Vinson of Kentucky: A Political Biography* (Lexington, KY: University Press of Kentucky, 2002), p. 336.

15. See, e.g., Michael Belknap *The Vinson Court: Justices, Rulings, and Legacy* (Santa Barbara, CA: ABC-CLIO, 2004), p. 164 (arguing that Fred Vinson could not have secured unanimity as Earl Warren did). See also Del Dickson, editor, *The Supreme Court in Conference (1940-1985): The Private Discussions Behind Nearly 300 Supreme Court Decisions* (New York, NY: Oxford University Press, 2001), p. 100 (accord).

16. The verdict on how Vinson would have voted is far from clear. See authorities cited in Carlton F.W. Larson, "What If Chief Justice Fred Vinson Had Not Died Of a Heart Attack in 1953?: Implications For *Brown* and Beyond," *Indiana Law Review*, 45: 131, 132-133, n. 15 (2011). See also Michael Belknap, "Fred Vinson," in David S. Tanenhaus, editor, *Encyclopedia of the Supreme Court of the United States* (Detroit, MI: Macmillan Reference, 2008), Vol. V, pp. 141, 143 ("He was clearly not enthusiastic about the idea of simply repudiating the separate but equal rule. Indeed, Vinson had dissented from a decision extending his own restrictive-covenant decision. On the one hand, he was attached to the idea of following precedent, and believed that whenever possible, change should be evolutionary rather than revolutionary. Justice Frankfurter believed Vinson was going to vote to retain the separate but equal rule. Vinson had spoken for a nearly united bench in past racial issues, and the pressure to maintain unanimity, along with his desire to write for the Court in such an important case, might have led him to join the majority in *Brown*. Because of his untimely death, we will never know for sure what Vinson would have done in *Brown v. Board of Education*.").

17. Just this scenario is played out, and credibly so, in Professor Larson's thoughtful and well-documented article, *ibid*. See also Mark Tushnet and Katya Lezin, "What Really Happened in *Brown v. Board of Education*," *Columbia Law Review*, 91:1903-1904 (1991) ("Nowhere in his [Conference] statement[s] did Vinson commit himself either to reaffirming the "separate but equal" doctrine or to overruling *Plessy*, but on balance the tone of his comments suggests that he would go along with a decision by a majority of the Court to hold segregation unconstitutional, as he had gone along in the university cases despite his initial inclination the other way.").

18. See, e.g., C. Herman Pritchett, *Civil Liberties and the Vinson Court* (Chicago, IL: University of Chicago Press, 1954).

19. Larson, "What If Chief Justice Fred Vinson Had Not Died Of a Heart Attack in 1953?," p. 134.

20. See *ibid*., pp. 134, 152-156 ("If Vinson had lived, there would have been no 'Warren Court,' or at least no such Court under Warren's leadership. Earl Warren would likely have been appointed to the open seat created by the death of Justice Robert Jackson in 1954, and subsequent appointments would most likely have created a majority of Justices devoted to the core principles of the 'Warren Court.' But the 'Warren Court' innovations would not have borne the imprimatur of the Chief Justice. Vinson's most likely successors were John Marshall Harlan, under President Eisenhower, or Byron White, under President Kennedy, both of whom were significantly less enthusiastic about 'Warren Court' decisions than was Earl Warren himself.").

21. Quoted in Richard Kluger, *Simple Justice: The History of Brown v. Board of Education and Black America* (New York, NY: Vintage Books, 2004), p. 681.

22. p. 283.

23. See *ibid.*, pp. 281-283.

24. Francis Biddle, *Justice Holmes, Natural Law, and the Supreme Court* (New York, NY: Macmillan Co., 1961), p. 20 (characterizing Holmes's beliefs re life and law).

25. Fate likewise played a critical role in the history of *Mapp v. Ohio*, 367 U.S. 643 (1961) (applying Fourth Amendment exclusionary rule to the States). See Ed Cray, *Chief Justice: A Biography of Earl Warren* (New York, NY: Simon & Schuster, 1997), pp. 374-375; Alex Wohl, *Father, Son, & Constitution: How Justice Tom Clark & Attorney General Ramsey Clark Shaped American Democracy* (Lawrence, KS: University Press of Kansas, 2013), p. 273; Seth Stern and Stephen Wermiel, *Justice Brennan: Liberal Champion* (Boston, MA: Houghton Mifflin Harcourt, 2010), p. 182.

26. Roger K. Newman, "Frederick Moore Vinson," in Roger Newman, editor, *The Yale Biographical Dictionary of American Law* (New Haven, CT: Yale University Press, 2009), pp. 561, 562.

Chapter 6

1. Richard Delgado, "*Naim v. Naim*," *Nevada Law Journal* 12: 525 (2012).

2. See Melvin Urofsky, *Felix Frankfurter: Judicial Restraint and Individual Liberties* (Woodbridge, CT: Twayne Publishers, 1991), pp. 137-142; Joseph P. Lash, *From the Diaries of Felix Frankfurter* (New York, NY: W.W. Norton & Co., 1975), p. 83; and Bernard Schwartz, *A History of the Supreme Court* (New York, NY: Oxford University Press, 1993), pp. 286-309. But cf. Del Dickson, ed., *The Supreme Court in Conference (1940-1985): The Private Discussions Behind Nearly 300 Supreme Court Decisions* (New York, NY: Oxford University Press, 2001), pp. 651-652, n. 53.

3. 347 U.S. 483 (1954).

4. 109 U.S. 3 (1883).

5. 163 U.S. 537 (1896).

6. Then Attorney General Tom Clark filed an amicus brief in *Shelley v. Kraemer*, 334 U.S. 1 (1948), successfully urging the Court not to enforce racial covenants. See Alexander Wohl, *Father, Son, and Constitution: How Justice Tom Clark and Attorney General Ramsey Clark Shaped American Democracy* (Lawrence, KS: University Press of Kansas, 2013), pp. 87-88, and Richard Kirkendall, "Tom C. Clark," in Leon Freidman and Fred Israel, editors, *Justices of the United States Supreme Court*, vol. III (New York, NY: Facts on File, 4th ed., 2013), p. 324.

7. His civil rights opinions included *Burton v. Wilmington Parking Authority*, 365 U.S. 715 (1961), *Heart of Atlanta Motel Inc. v. United States*, 379 U.S. 241 (1964), and *Katzenbach v. McClung*, 379 U.S. 294 (1964).

8. See generally Delgado, "*Naim,*" p. 531.

9. See the unanimous ruling in *Loving v. Virginia*, 388 U.S. 1 (1967).

10. *Jackson v. State*, 72 So.2d 114 (Ala. Ct. App.), cert. denied, 72 So.2d 116 (Ala. 1954), cert. denied, *Jackson v. Alabama*, 348 U.S. 888 (1954).

11. 87 S.E.2d 749 (Va. 1955), vacated and remanded, 350 U.S. 891 (1955), aff'd, 90 S.E.2d 849 (Va. 1955), motion to recall mandate denied and appeal dismissed, 350 U.S. 985 (1956).

12. Quoted in Gregory Michael Dorr, "Principled Expediency: Eugenics, *Naim v. Naim*, and the Supreme Court," *American Journal of Legal History*, 42: 119, 147, n. 121 (1988). For an expanded discussion, see Gregory Michael Dorr, *Segregation's Science: Eugenics and Society in Virginia* (Charlottesville, VA: University of Virginia Press, 2008).

13. 349 U.S. 294 (1955).

14. 106 U.S. 583 (1883). See David P. Currie, *The Constitution in the Supreme Court – the Supreme Court in the First Hundred Years, 1789-1888* (Chicago, IL: University of Chicago Press, 1985) pp. 387-90.

15. See PLD, "The Constitutionality of Miscegenation Statutes," *Howard Law Journal* 1: 87 (1955) ("The case . . . goes to the heart of the matter of racial segregation and poses a question which [in light of *Brown* and *Bolling v. Sharpe*] . . . demands a more searching inquiry into the legal grounds generally used to sustain these miscegenation statutes.").

16. See Paul Wallerstein, "Race, Marriage, and the Law of Freedom: Alabama and Virginia 1860s-1960 – Freedom: Personal Liberty and Private Law," *Chicago-Kent Law Review*, 70: 371, 415 (1994).

17. 348 U.S. 888 (1955).

18. Dorr, "Principled Expediency," p. 147.

19. "Chang M. Sohn details the NAACP's absence, and cites Thurgood Marshall's displeasure at the timing of the suit. The NAACP feared the effect *Naim* would have on *Brown's* implementation." Dorr, "Principled Expediency," p. 147, n. 121, citing Chang M. Sohn, "Principle and Expediency in Judicial Review," PhD Dissertation (Columbia University, 1970), pp. 77-83, 129, 133-134, 143-147.

20. Among other places, the matter is discussed in Peter Wallenstein's *Tell the Court I Love My Wife: Race, Marriage, and Law – An American History* (New York, NY: Palgrave Macmillan, 2002), pp. 175-185.

21. Quoted in Bernard Schwartz, *Super Chief: Earl Warren and His Supreme Court – A Judicial Biography* (New, York, NY: New York University Press, 1983), p. 159.

22. *Ibid.* See also Gerald Gunther, *Learned Hand: The Man and the Judge* (New York, N.Y.: Alfred A. Knopf, 1994), pp. 668-669 ("despite [Frankfurter's] general avowal of a restrained position on judicial review . . .

[he] was given to expediency, discretion, and manipulation in the interests of prudence and avoiding political attacks on the Court.").

23. Quoted in Dorr, "Principled Expediency," p. 151.

24. Schwartz, *Super Chief*, p. 159. See also Dorr, "Principled Expediency," p. 146 ("Justices Douglas, Black, and initially Warren, sought to rally the activists in a classic confrontation over the scope of judicial review and Supreme Court procedure.").

25. *Naim v. Naim*, 350 U.S. 891 (1955).

26. Schwartz, *Super Chief*, p. 160.

27. *Naim v. Naim*,197 Va. 734, 735 (1956).

28. Dorr, "Principled Expediency," p. 156.

29. *Richmond News Leader*,18 January 1956, p. 1.

30. Ed Cray, *Chief Justice: A Biography of Earl Warren* (New York, NY: Simon & Schuster, 1997), pp. 310, 451.

31. Dorr, "Principled Expediency," pp. 157-158.

32. *Ibid*, p. 158 and n. 170 ("'Since I regard the order of dismissal as completely impermissible in view of this Court's obligatory jurisdiction and its deeply rooted rules of decision, I am constrained to express my dissent.' He concluded, 'Wordsworth accurately called Duty the Stern Daughter of the voice of God. Here, sternness cannot make us shrink from her call. Congress has obliged this Court to decide the substantial constitutional questions [that] are properly and adequately presented in this appeal. I would NOTE PROBABLE JURISDICTION AND SET THE CASE DOWN FOR ARGUMENT.' [emphasis in original] Earl Warren Papers, box 369.").

33. *Naim v. Naim*, 350 U.S. 985 (1956).

34. Rachel F. Moran, *Interracial Intimacy: The Regulation of Race and Romance* (Chicago, IL: University of Chicago Press, 2001), pp. 90-91.

35. See Mark Graber, *A New Introduction to American Constitutionalism* (New York, NY: Oxford University Press, 2013), p. 135.

36. Lee Epstein & Jack Knight, *The Choices Justices Make* (Washington DC: CQ Press, 1998), p. 83.

37. See Walter F. Murphy, *Elements of Judicial Strategy* (Chicago, IL: University of Chicago Press, 1964), p. 193.

38. Dorr, "Principled Expediency," p. 120.

39. Alexander Bickel, *The Least Dangerous Branch: The Supreme Court at the Bar of Politics* (Indianapolis, IN: Bobbs-Merrill, Co., 1962), p. 174.

40. *Ibid*.

41. *Ibid*. For a response to Bickel, see Gerald Gunther, "The Subtle Vices of the 'Passive Virtues': A Comment on Principle & Expediency in Judicial Review," *Columbia Law Review*, 64: 1, 16-17 (1964).

42. Herbert Wechsler, "Neutral Principles of Constitutional Law," in *Principles, Politics, and Fundamental Law: Selected Essays* (Cambridge, MA: Harvard University Press, 1961) p. 47.

43. 388 U.S. 1 (1967).

Chapter 7

1. 539 US 654 (2003) (dismissing the writ of certiorari as improvidently granted).

2. 416 U.S. 312 (1974) (since the University of Washington Law School agreed to allow DeFunis to enroll and to earn a diploma, the case was moot).

3. 132 S.Ct. 1532 (2012).

4. Tejinder Singh, "Harmless error case dismissed as improvidently granted," *SCOTUSblog*, 2 April 2012, http://www.scotusblog.com/2012/04/opinion-analysis-harmless-error-case-dismissed-as-improvidently-granted/.

5. 135 S. Ct. 2584 (2015)

6. 409 U.S. 810 (1972) (the claim of a same-sex marriage right presents no substantial federal question).

7. 133 S.Ct. 2675 (2013) (federal government cannot deny benefits to legally married same-sex couples).

8. 133 S.Ct. 2652 (2013) (state initiative proponents have no standing to defend the constitutionality of California's Proposition 8 forbidding same-sex marriage).

9. The intervening Supreme Court cases considering gay rights claims other than marriage include *Bowers v. Hardwick*, 478 U.S. 186 (1986) (constitutional right of privacy does not extend to same-sex sodomy), *Romer v. Evans*, 517 U.S. 620 (1996) (invalidating state voter initiative that prohibited sexual orientation anti-discrimination laws), and *Lawrence v. Texas*, 539 U.S. 558 (2003) (overruling *Bowers* and recognizing a liberty to same-sex sodomy).

10. Formally, the *Obergefell* decision determined the unconstitutionality of the same-sex marriage bans of four States that were challenged in four separate cases consolidated for the Supreme Court's consideration: *Obergefell v. Hodges* (Ohio), *Tanco v. Haslam* (Tennessee), *DeBoer v. Snyder* (Michigan), and *Bourke v. Beshear* (Kentucky).

11. See Mark Sherman, "Gay Marriage: Supreme Court Sets Stage for Historic Ruling," *Associated Press*, 16 January 2015.

12. Adam Liptak, "Supreme Court to Decide Marriage Rights for Gay Couples Nationwide," *New York Times*, 16 January 2015.

13. "Legal Battle Over Gay Marriage Hits the Supreme Court Tuesday," *NPR*, 27 April 2015, www.npr.org/ sections/itsallpolitics/2015/04/27.402456198/legal-battle-over-gay-marriage-hits-the-supreme-court-tuesday.

14. 135 S.Ct. at pp. 2595-2596.
15. *Ibid.*, p. 2599.
16. *Ibid.*, p. 2605.
17. *Ibid.*, p. 2608.
18. Editorial, "A Profound Ruling Delivers Justice on Gay Marriage," *New York Times*, 26 June 2015.
19. Jess Bravin, "Supreme Court Rules Gay Marriage Is a Nationwide Right," *Wall Street Journal*, 26 June 2015.
20. Emily Bazelon, "Was This the Right Way to Legalize Gay Marriage?," *New York Times Magazine*, 26 June 2015.
21. See Jan Crawford Greenburg, *Supreme Conflict: The Inside Story of the Struggle for Control of the United States Supreme Court* (New York, NY: Penguin Press, 2007), p. 182.
22. Isaiah Berlin, *The Hedgehog & the Fox* (Princeton, NJ: Princeton University Press, 2nd ed., 2013).
23. Lawrence Tribe, "Equal Dignity: Speaking its Name," *Harvard Law Review Forum*, 129: 16 (2015) (endnote omitted) (describing the views of others).
24. *Ibid.*
25. 517 U.S. 620 (1996).
26. 539 U.S. 558 (2003).
27. 133 S.Ct. 2675 (2013).
28. 521 U.S. 702 (1997) (per Rehnquist, C.J.).
29. *Ibid.*, p. 721.
30. Tribe, "Equal Dignity," p. 21
31. *Ibid.*, p. 19.
32. *Ibid.*, p. 22 (endnote omitted).
33. Tribe, "Equal Dignity," p. 26.
34. *Ibid.*, p. 16.
35. See *ibid.*, pp. 23-28.
36. See *ibid.*, pp. 20-21.
37. 133 S.Ct. at p. 2659.
38. *Ibid.*, p. 2668.
39. Adam Liptak, "Supreme Court Bolsters Gay Marriage With Two Major Rulings, *New York Times*, 26 June 2013 (referring to the rulings in *Hollingsworth* and *United States v. Windsor*).
40. Lyle Denniston, "Marriage now open to same-sex couples," *SCOTUSblog*, 26 June, 2015, http://www.scotusblog.com/2015/06/opinion-analysis-marriage-now-open-to-same-sex-couples/.
41. 135 S.Ct. at p. 2611.
42. 60 U.S. 393 (1857).
43. 478 U.S. 186 (1986).

44. 133 S. Ct. at 2612 (Roberts, C.J., dissenting) (invoking traditional understandings of marriage as ascribed to Kalahari bushmen, the Carthaginians, and the Aztecs, among others).
45. See *Shelby County v. Holder*, 133 S. Ct. 2612 (2013) (5-4 per Roberts, C.J.).
46. Robert Barnes, "Supreme Court rules gay couples nationwide have a right to marry," *Washington Post*, 26 June 2015.

Chapter 8

1. Data Processing Service v. Camp, 397 U.S. 150, 151 (1970).
2. *Flast v. Cohen*, 392 U.S. 83, 129 (1968) (Harlan, J., dissenting) (footnote omitted).
3. See, e.g., *Flast v. Cohen*, 392 U.S. 83 (1968) (creating a First Amendment exception to the rule against taxpayer standing in *Frothingham v. Mellon*, 262 U.S. 447 (1923)).
4. See, e.g., *Sierra Club v. Morton*, 405 U.S. 727 (1972) (denying standing to an environmental group contesting legality of U.S. Forest Service permit to allow development near national park).
5. See, e.g., *United States v. Students Challenging Regulatory Agency Procedures*, 412 U.S. 669 (1973) (permitting "aesthetic and environmental" challenges brought by law students contesting nation railroad freight rate increases approved by the Interstate Commerce Commission).
6. See, e.g., *Valley Forge Christian College v. Americans United for Separation of Church and State*, 454 U.S. 464 (1982) (disallowed a challenge to an agency conveyance of government property to a church group and limited standing exception of *Flast v. Cohen* to challenges of congressional acts and not administrative agencies).
7. See, e.g., *Clapper v. Amnesty International USA*, 133 S. Ct 1138 (2013) (holding that various attorneys and human rights organizations lacked standing to challenge Foreign Intelligence Surveillance Act of 1978 absent any showing that future injury was "certainly impending" and that such injury was fairly traceable to application of the law challenged).
8. See Geoffrey R. Stone, Louis M. Seidman, Cass R. Sunstein, Mark V. Tushnet, and Pamela S. Karlan, *Constitutional Law* (Fredericks, MD: Wolters Kluwer Law & Business, 7th ed. 2013), p. 106.
9. 549 U.S. 497 (2007).
10. 549 U.S. at 526.
11. 549 U.S. at 520.
12. 549 U.S. at 536 (Roberts, C.J., dissenting).
13. 549 U.S. at 537 (Roberts, C.J., dissenting).
14. 549 U.S. at 539 (Roberts, C.J., dissenting).

15. 549 U.S. at 540 (Roberts, C.J., dissenting).
16. 549 U.S. at 541 (Roberts, C.J., dissenting).
17. *Ibid.*
18. 392 U.S. 83 (1968).
19. 454 U.S. 464 (1982).
20. 454 U.S. at 490 (Brennan, J., dissenting).
21. 563 U.S. 125 (2011) (per Kennedy, J., with Justices Kagan, Sotomayor, Ginsburg and Breyer dissenting).
22. 563 U.S. at 148 (Kagan, J., dissenting).

Chapter 9

1. John G. Roberts, Jr., "Oral Advocacy and the Re-Emergence of a Supreme Court Bar," *Journal of Supreme Court History*, 30: 68, 75, 70 (2005).
2. 17 U.S. 518 (1819).
3. Charles Fried, "Oral Arguments," in Kermit Hall, editor, *The Oxford Companion to the Supreme Court of the United States* (New York, NY: Oxford University Press, 2nd ed., 2005), p. 710. See also Leonard Baker, *John Marshall: A Life in Law* (New York, NY: Collier Books, 1974), pp. 656-663, and Timothy R. Johnson, *Oral Arguments and Decision Making on the United States Supreme Court* (Albany, NY: SUNY Press, 2011), pp. 1-2.
4. See, e.g., Jeffrey A. Segal and Harold J. Spaeth, *The Supreme Court & The Attitudinal Model Revisited* (New York, NY: Cambridge University Press, 2002), p. 280; Thomas G. Walker and Lee Epstein, *The Supreme Court of the United States: An Introduction* (New York, NY: St. Martin's Press, 1993), p. 106; Lawrence Wrightsman, *Oral Arguments Before the Supreme Court: An Empirical Approach* (New York, NY: Oxford University Press, 2008), pp. 3-24.
5. David M. O'Brien, *Storm Center: The Supreme Court in American Politics* (New York, NY: W.W. Norton & Co., 10th ed., 2014), pp. 253-257.
6. Quoted in Philippa Strum, "Change and Continuity on the Supreme Court: Conversations with Justice Harry A. Blackmun," *University of Richmond Law Review*, 34: 285, 298 (2000).
7. See Wrightsman, *Oral Arguments Before the Supreme Court*, pp. 28-38 (discussing various models re reasons for Justices' participating in oral arguments.). See also Johnson, *Oral Arguments*, pp. 125-126 ("justices use oral arguments to seek information about their policy options, other actors' preferences, and institutional rules that constrain their ability to make certain decisions. In the aggregate, justices devote over 40 percent of all their questions during oral arguments to policy considerations.").
8. See *ibid.*, p. 38 (Justice Thomas: Oral arguments may "make for a good show, but they are not altogether significant in the outcome.").

9. Timothy R. Johnson, James F. Spriggs II, and Paul J. Wahlbeck, "Oral Advocacy Before the United States Supreme Court: Does It Affect the Justices' Decisions?," *Washington University Law Review*, 85: 457, 459 (2007) (footnote omitted).

10. 384 U.S. 436 (1966).

11. 354 U.S. 476 (1957).

12. 491 U.S. 397 (1989).

13. 376 U.S. 254 (1964).

14. 369 US 186 (1962).

15. 367 US 643 (1961).

16. See David M. O'Brien, *Storm Center: The Supreme Court in American Politics* (New York, NY: W.W. Norton & Company, 2000), p. 254 (Justice Brennan: "often my idea of how a case shapes up is changed in oral argument. I have had too many occasions when my judgment on a decision has turned on what happened in oral argument."). Unfortunately, we do not have examples of such instances. Note: It is one thing for one's ideas about a case to change during arguments, it is still another for one's judgment to change.

17. See Jeffrey Toobin, "Did John Roberts Tip His Hand?," *The New Yorker*, 4 MRCH 2015.

18. 135 S.Ct. 2480 (2015).

19. Charles Lane, "Questions from the Bench Seen as Clues to Final Outcomes," *Washington Post*, 3 November 2003.

20. 132 S. Ct. 945 (2012) (9-0: majority opinion per Scalia, J.).

21. Transcript of oral arguments in *United States v. Jones*, November 8, 2011, *Oyez*, https://www.oyez.org/ cases/2011/10-1259, and *Alderson Reporting Company*, http://www.supremecourt.gov/oral_arguments/ argument_transcripts/10-1259.pdf, pp. 9-10.

22. Adam Liptak, "Justices Say GPS Tracker Violated Privacy Rights," *New York Times*, 23 January 2012.

23. Another example of an awe-inspiring question came in *Citizens United v. Federal Election Commission*, 558 U.S. 310 (2010), the election campaign finance case involving *Hillary: The Movie*. There, Justice Alito and Chief Justice Roberts posed questions about the applicability of the expenditure limitations to ban publication of a book, queries that proved to be eye-opening. See Adam Liptak, "Justices Seem Skeptical of Scope of Campaign Law," *New York Times*, 24 March 2009.

24. Art Lien, "Baseball Bats and Rotten Tomatoes," *Courtartist.com*, 25 February 2014, http://courtartist.com/ 2014/02/baseball-bats-rotten-tomatoes.html.

25. Mark Sherman, "Breyer, Court Master of the 'What If?'," *Washington Post*, 2 March 2008.

26. Nomination of Stephen G. Breyer to be an Associate Justice of the Supreme Court of the United States, Hearings Before the Committee on the Judiciary, United States Senate (103rd Congress, 2nd Session, July 12-15, 1994), p. 146.

27. Lyle Denniston, "For Want of a Good Hypothetical," *SCOTUSblog*, 11 December 2011.

28. 134 S. Ct. 1434 (2014).

29. See Scott Lemieux, "Who Cares About Clarence Thomas's Silence?," *The American Prospect*, 26 February 2014.

30. William H. Rehnquist, *The Supreme Court* (New York, NY: Random House, 2001), pp. 239-240 ("Several of my colleagues get what are called 'bench memos' from the law clerks on the cases. . . . I do not do this, simply because it does not fit my style of working.").

31. During oral arguments when Dollree Mapp's lawyer was pressed by Justices Frankfurter and Harlan if he were asking the Court to overrule *Wolf v. Colorado*, his response was simple: "No, I don't believe we are." Statement of K.L. Kearns, counsel for Petitioner, transcript of oral arguments in *Mapp v. Ohio*, 29 March 1961, https://www.oyez.org/cases/1960/236.

32. See Wrightsman, *Oral Arguments Before the Supreme Court*, pp. 71-77.

33. See O'Brien, *Storm Center* (2000), p. 261 (Justice Blackmun: Justice Scalia "asks far too many questions and he takes over the whole argument of counsel.").

34. 538 U.S. 343 (2003).

35. Transcript of oral arguments in *Virginia v. Black*, 11 December 2002, Alderson Reporting Company, pp. 23-24, http://www.supremecourt.gov/oral_arguments/argument_transcripts/01-1107.pdf.

36. Quoted in Wrightsman, *Oral Arguments Before the Supreme Court*, p. 117.

37. 403 U.S. 15 (1971).

38. Transcript of oral arguments in *Cohen v. California*, February 22, 1971, *Oyez* (Burger: "I might suggest to you that, as in most cases, the Court's thoroughly familiar with the factual setting of this case and it will not be necessary for you, I'm sure, to dwell on the facts."), https://www.oyez.org/cases/1970/299.

39. See *ibid*. (Mel Nimmer: "While walking through that corridor he was wearing a jacket upon which were inscribed the words 'Fuck the draft,' also were inscribed the words 'Stop war' and several peace symbols.").

Chapter 10

1. 371 U.S. 415 (1963) (associational rights protected against forced disclosure laws).

2. 378 U.S. 256 (1964) (press rights protected against defamation claims).

3. 380 U.S. 479 (1965) (federal injunctive relief to enjoin enforcement of state subversive advocacy laws).

4. 427 U.S. 539 (1976) (press rights protected against prior restraints).

5. 447 U.S. 455 (1980) (residential picketing protected against content discriminatory restrictions).

6. 491 U.S. 397 (1989) (flag-burning protected as political protest).

7. Roger Goldman with David Gallen, *Justice William J. Brennan, Jr.: Freedom First* (New York, NY: Carroll & Graf Publishers, Inc., 1994), p. 160.

8. 376 U.S. at 270.

9. Tom Wicker, "Speech: Uninhibited, Robust, and Wide-Open," in E. Joshua Rosenkranz and Bernard Schwartz, editors, *Reason and Passion: Justice Brennan's Enduring Influence* (New York, NY: W.W. Norton & Co., 1997), p. 46.

10. Niccolò Machiavelli, *The Prince*, translated by Harvey C. Mansfield (Chicago, IL: University of Chicago Press, 2nd edition 1998), pp. 68-69 (Chapter XVIII).

11. Quoted in Whitney Strub, *Obscenity Rules: Roth v. United States & The Long Struggle over Sexual Expression* (Lawrence, KS: University Press of Kansas, 2013), p. 159 (quoting Earl Warren during Court conference in *Roth*).

12. 315 U.S. 568 (1942) (obscenity among the categories of "unprotected speech" having slight social value).

13. *Ibid.*, p. 572.

14. Earlier the Court had decided *Butler v. Michigan*, 352 U.S. 380 (1957), in which it partially liberalized the law of sexual expression. Justice Felix Frankfurter's opinion for the Court "did not throw any light upon what kinds of material could or could not be outlawed under obscenity laws. But it did establish at the outset the basic proposition that the rights of the general population could not be curtailed in an effort to protect children, or any other limited segment of the population, against the evils of obscenity." Thomas I. Emerson, *The System of Freedom of Expression* (New York, NY: Vintage Books, 1970), p. 471 (footnote omitted).

15. 354 U.S. 476 (1957).

16. *Ibid.*, p. 479 n. 1.

17. See Kim Eisler, *A Justice for All* (New York, NY: Simon & Schuster, 1993), p. 142.

18. The oral arguments in *Roth* are found in Leon Friedman, editor, *Obscenity: The Complete Oral Arguments Before the Supreme Court in Major Obscenity Cases* (New York, NY: Chelsea House, 1970), pp., 15, 38-40, 54.

19. See Strub, *Obscenity Rules*, pp. 162-165.

20. Quoted in Bernard Schwartz, *Super Chief: Earl Warren & His Supreme Court – A Judicial Biography* (New York, NY: New York University Press, 1983), p. 219 (quoting from Frankfurter memo circulated after the Court's conference in *Roth*).

21. Quoted in *ibid.* (emphasis added) (Brennan re his sentiments concerning the Court's handling of *Butler v. Michigan*).
22. 354 U.S. at p. 481.
23. *Ibid.*, p. 484.
24. *Ibid.*, p. 485.
25. Strub, *Obscenity Rules*, p. 166.
26. 354 U.S. at p. 487.
27. *Ibid.*, p. 487 n. 20.
28. *Ibid.*, p. 484 (emphasis added).
29. *Regina v. Hicklin*, 3 Q.B. 360 (1868) (holding that all materials tending "to deprave and corrupt those whose minds are open to such immoral influences" were obscene, regardless of any artistic or literary merit).
30. 354 U.S. at p. 489.
31. Strub, *Obscenity Rules*, p. 167.
32. 354 U.S. at p. 496 (Warren, C.J., concurring in the result).
33. That same day, the Court handed down its ruling in another obscenity case, *Kingsley Books, Inc. v. Brown*, 354 US 436 (1957) (5-4 per Frankfurter with Warren, Douglas, Black and Brennan dissenting) (upholding over a First Amendment prior-restraint challenge a New York law that allowed local authorities to obtain a court order to enjoin the sale or distribution of obscene materials and to arrange for their destruction).
34. See Stern and Werniel, *Justice Brennan*, p. 124.
35. Strub, *Obscenity Rules*, p. 180 (quoting Joseph Rubenstein).
36. *Ibid.*, p. 166 (quoting Lucas Powe).
37. *Ibid.* (per Strub).
38. See *Paris Adult Theatre I. v. Slaton*, 413 U.S. 49, 73-74 (Brennan, J., dissenting) ("I am convinced that the approach initiated 16 years ago in Roth v. United States, 354 U.S. 476 (1957), and culminating in the Court's decision today, cannot bring stability to this area of the law without jeopardizing fundamental First Amendment values, and I have concluded that the time has come to make a significant departure from that approach."). See also Jeffrey Rosen, "We Hardly Know It When We See It: Obscenity and the Problem of Unprotected Speech," in Rosenkranz and Schwartz, *Reason & Passion*, pp. 64-65 (discussing evolution of Brenan's thought after *Roth*); Goldman and Gallen, *Justice William J. Brennan, Jr.*, pp. 165-168 (discussing evolution of Brennan's obscenity views).
39. See Strub, *Obscenity Rules*, p. 169 ("The most bitter irony of Brennan's opinion . . . was that it devised a test for obscenity under which Samuel Roth, had it been used at the trial court level, would almost surely have been exonerated.").
40. See Strub, *Obscenity Rules*, pp. 184-189. See also Ronald Collins and David Skover, *Mania: The Story of the Outraged & Outrageous Lives that Launched a*

Cultural Revolution (Oak Park, IL: Top Five Books, 2013), pp. 253-319 (discussing liberal application of *Roth* to prosecution of Allen Ginsberg's poem *HOWL*), and Ronald Collins and David Skover, *The Trials of Lenny Bruce: The Fall & Rise of an American Icon* (Naperville, IL: Sourcebooks, 2002), pp. 61-78 (discussing liberal application of *Roth* to prosecution of Lenny Bruce's comedy).

41. See *ibid.*, pp. 189-200.

Chapter 11

1. Chapter 11
   Thomas I. Emerson, "Justice Douglas and Lawyers with a Cause," *Yale Law Journal* 89: 616 (1979).
2. 381 U.S. 479 (1965).
3. *State v. Griswold*, 151 Conn. 544, 200 A. 2nd 479 (1964).
4. Substantive due process refers to the principle whereby courts protect "fundamental rights" from government abridgement under the authority of the Due Process clauses of the Fifth and Fourteenth Amendments. It is best exemplified by the Supreme Court's ruling and reasoning in *Lochner v. New York*, 198 U.S. 45 (1905) (striking down a state maximum hours law as a violation of individual rights of contract and property). The doctrine of economic substantive due process was abandoned in *Williamson v. Lee Optical of Oklahoma*, 348 U.S. 483 (1955).
5. *Poe v. Ullman*, 367 U.S. 497, 515-521 (1961) (Douglas, J., dissenting).
6. *Griswold v. Connecticut* oral arguments, 29 March 1965 (Oyez sound file & transcript), at http://www.oyez. org/cases/1960-1969/1964/1964_496.
7. 381 U.S. at p. 484.
8. *Ibid*, pp. 527-528 (Stewart, J., dissenting).
9. *Ibid*, pp. 485-486.
10. *Ibid*, p. 486.
11. Fred Graham, *New York Times*, 8 June 1964, p.1.
12. *Eisenstadt v. Baird*, 405 U.S. 438 (1972) and *Carey v. Population Services International*, 431 U.S. 678 (1977).
13. *Roe v. Wade*, 410 U.S. 113 (1973).
14. *Stanley v. Georgia*, 394 U.S. 557 (1969).
15. *Lawrence v. Texas*, 539 U.S. 558 (2003).
16. 478 U.S. 186 (1986).
17. 539 U.S. at 578.
18. 576 U.S. ____ (2015).

Chapter 12

1. 554 U.S. 570 (2008).
2. Harvey J. Wilkinson, "Of Guns, Abortions, and the Unraveling Rule of Law," *Virginia Law Review* 95: 253, 256 (2009).
3. Jeffrey Toobin, *The Oath: The Obama White House and the Supreme Court* (New York, NY: Doubleday, 2012), p. 111.
4. Antonin Scalia and Bryan A. Gardner, *Reading Law: The Interpretation of Legal Texts* (Egan, MN: Thompson/West, 2012). See also Antonin Scalia, *A Matter of Interpretation: Federal Courts and the Law* (Princeton, NJ: Princeton University Press, 1997), pp. 3-47.
5. Richard A. Posner, "In Defense of Looseness," *New Republic*, 27 August 2006, http://www. newrepublic.com/article/books/defense-looseness.
6. Richard A. Posner, "The Incoherence of Antonin Scalia," *The New Republic*, 24 August 2012, http://www. newrepublic.com/article/magazine/books-and-arts/106441/scalia-garner-reading-the-law-textual-originalism.
7. Posner, "In Defense of Looseness."
8. *Ibid.*
9. See *United States v. Cruikshank*, 92 U.S. 542 (1875), *Presser v. Illinois*, 116 U.S. 252 (1886), and *United States v. Miller*, 307 U.S. 174 (1939).
10. See, e.g., Wilkinson, "Of Guns," p. 2009 (footnote omitted); Posner, "The Incoherence of Antonin Scalia"; Toobin, *The Oath*, p. 115; Saul Cornell, "The Second Amendment and the Right to Bear Arms," *UCLA Law Review* 56: 1107-09 (2009); and Jack Rakove, "Thoughts on *Heller* from a 'Real Historian,'" Balkinization, 27 June 2008, http://balkin.blogspot.com/2008/06/thoughts-on-heller-from-real-historian.html.
11. Ed Whelan, "Richard A. Posner's Badly Confused Attack on Scalia/Garner," *National Review*, 7 September 2012, http://www.nationalreview.com/bench-memos/316221/richard-posners-badly-confused-attack-scaliagarner-part-5-ed-whelan;
12. *Brown v. Allen*, 344 U.S. 443, 540 (1953) (Jackson, J., concurring).
13. Bruce Allen Murphy, *Scalia: A Court of One* (New York, NY: Simon & Schuster, 2014), p. 390.
14. Quoted in *ibid.*

Chapter 13

1. 530 U.S. 428 (2000).
2. 384 U.S. 436 (1966).
3. William Rehnquist, Letter to Weakfish (Jim Rehnquist), 17 December 1986, in William H. Rehnquist Papers, Box 172/4, quoted in John A. Jenkins, *The*

Partisan: The Life of William Rehnquist (New York, NY: Public Affairs, 2012), p. 250.

4. Such moves and others are discussed more generally in Pierre Schlag & David Skover, *Tactics of Legal Reasoning* (Durham, NC: Carolina Academic Press, 1986), pp. 18-19, 29-30, 31-32, 45.

5. See, e.g., his majority opinion in *National League of Cities v. Usery*, 426 U.S. 833, 852-855 (1976).

6. See, e.g., Rehnquist's majority opinions in: *Illinois v. Gates*, 462 U.S. 213 (1983), which overruled *Aguilar v. Texas*, 378 U.S. 108 (1964) and *Spinelli v. United States*, 393 U.S. 410 (1969); *Seminole Tribe of Florida v. Florida*, 517 U.S. 44 (1996), which overruled *Pennsylvania v. Union Gas Co.*, 491 U.S. 1 (1989); and *Payne v. Tennessee*, 501 U.S. 808 (1991), which overruled *Booth v. Maryland*, 482 US 496 (1987) and *South Carolina v. Gathers*, 490 U.S. 805 (1989). For an insider's account of Rehnquist's purported maneuvering in the *Booth* and *Gathers* cases leading up to the *Payne* ruling, see Edward Lazarus, *Closed Chambers: The First Eye-Witness Account of Struggles Inside the Supreme Court* (New York, NY: Times Books, 1998), pp. 445-446.

7. See *Garcia v. San Antonio Metropolitan Transit Authority*, 469 U.S. 528 (1985), which overruled *Usery*, which was in turn functionally undermined by Rehnquist's opinion for the Court in *United States v. Lopez*, 514 U.S. 549 (1995).

8. 384 U.S. at 490 (emphasis added).

9. The constitutionality of §3501 is discussed at some length in Thomas Schrock, Robert Welsh, and Ronald Collins, "Interrogational Rights: Reflections on *Miranda v. Arizona*," *Southern California Law Review*, 52: 1-19, 56-60 (1978).

10. Memorandum from William Rehnquist to John Dean, III re "Constitutional Decisions Relating to Criminal Law," 1 April 1969, quoted in Yale Kamisar, "*Dickerson v. United States*: The Case that Disappointed *Miranda's* Critics – and then its Supporters," in Craig Bradley, *The Rehnquist Legacy* (New York, NY: Cambridge University Press, 2006), pp. 106, 109, 110. We greatly acknowledge our debt to Professor Kamisar insofar as we have relied on his informative article in drafting portions of this chapter.

11. See *ibid.*, pp. 109, 111.

12. 417 U.S. 433 (1974).

13. 417 U.S. at 439 (emphasis added).

14. 417 U.S. at 445-446 (emphasis added).

15. As evidenced by conference notes for *New York v. Quarles* and *Oregon v. Elstad*, Justices William Brennan and John Paul Stevens were quite aware of the importance of Rehnquist's handiwork. See Del Dickson, editor, *The Supreme Court in Conference (1940-1985) – The Private Papers Behind Nearly 300 Supreme Court Decisions* (New York, NY: Oxford University Press, 2001), p. 524 (Brennan: "I do not find it necessary to think of this case as one in

which *Miranda* would serve a merely 'prophylactic' purpose"), and p. 526 (Brennan: "as John Stevens noted during oral argument, the central question here is whether a *Miranda* violation is a *constitutional* violation.") (emphasis in original).

16. 467 U.S. 649 (1984).
17. 467 U.S. at 654 (emphasis added).
18. 470 U.S. 298 (1985).
19. 470 U.S. at 309 (emphasis added).
20. See, e.g., *United States v. Patane*, 542 U.S. 630, 638–41 (2004) (plurality opinion); *Chavez v. Martinez*, 538 U.S. 760, 770–73 (2003) (opinion of Thomas, J.); *Davis v. United States*, 512 U.S. 452, 457–58 (1994); *Withrow v. Williams*, 507 U.S. 680, 690–91 (1993); *Duckworth v. Eagan*, 492 U.S. 195, 203 (1989); *Arizona v. Roberson*, 486 U.S. 675, 680–81 (1988); *Connecticut v. Barrett*, 479 U.S. 523, 528 (1987); and *Edwards v. Arizona*, 451 U.S. 477, 491–92 (1981) (Powell, J., concurring in result). See also Lawrence Rosenthal, "Against Orthodoxy: *Miranda* is Not Prophylactic and the Constitution is Not Perfect," *Chapman Law Review*, 10: 579, 580 (2007).
21. See his majority opinion *New York v. Quarles*, 467 U.S. 649 (1984) (public safety exception to *Miranda*).
22. For a sampling of Fifth Amendment *post-Miranda* cases limiting its reach, see *Harris v. New York*, 401 U.S. 222 (1971) (impeachment exception), *Oregon v. Hass*, 420 U. S. 714 (1975) (impeachment exception), *Oregon v. Elstad*, 470 U. S. 298 (1985) (fruit of the poisonous tree doctrine not applicable to *Miranda*), *Oregon v. Mathiason*, 429 U.S. 492 (1977) (restricted interpretation of "custody" or "custodial interrogation"), *California v. Prysock*, 453 U.S. 355 (1981) (lax application of wording of warnings), *Duckworth v. Eagan*, 442 U.S. 195 (1989) (lax application of wording of warnings), *Rhode Island v. Innis*, 446 U.S. 291 (1980) (narrow interpretation of what constitutes interrogation under *Miranda*), *Brewer v. Williams*, 430 U.S. 387 (1977) (same), *Arizona v. Mauro*, 481 U.S. 520 (1987) (same), *Illinois v. Perkins*, 496 U.S. 292 (1990) (surreptitious interrogation upheld), *North Carolina v. Butler*, 441 U.S. 369 (1979) (implied waiver of *Miranda* rights upheld), *Connecticut v. Barrett*, 479 U.S. 523 (1987) (qualified waiver permitted), and *Fare v. Michael C.*, 442 U.S. 707 (1979) (rigid interpretation of when *Miranda* rights are invoked).
23. See Barry Friedman, "The Wages of Stealth Overruling (With Particular Attention to *Miranda v. Arizona*)," *Georgetown Law Journal*, 99:1 (2010).
24. Richard Posner, *How Judges Think* (Cambridge, MA: Harvard University Press, 2008), p. 277.
25. Brief of the United States in *Dickerson v. United States*, http://www.justice.gov/osg/brief/dickerson-v-united-states-response.
26. *United States v. Dickerson*, 166 F. 3rd 667 (4th Cir., 1999).

27. This issue is thoroughly and insightfully discussed in Erwin Chemerinsky, "The Court Should Have Remained Silent: Why the Court Erred in Deciding *Dickerson v. United States,*" *University of Pennsylvania Law Review,* 149: 287 (2000).
28. 530 U.S. at 441 n. 7.
29. Contrast *Hollingsworth v. Perry,* 133 S.Ct. 2652 (2013) (denying standing to outside third party).
30. See Donald A. Dripps, "Constitutional Theory for Criminal Procedure: *Dickerson, Miranda,* and the Continuing Quest for Broad-But-Shallow," *William & Mary Law Review,* 43: 1, 33 (2001) ("Once the Court granted certiorari in Dickerson, Court-watchers] knew the hour had come. At long last the Court would have to either repudiate *Miranda,* repudiate the prophylactic-rule cases, or offer some ingenious reconciliation of the two lines of precedent."), and Gary L. Stuart, Miranda: The Story of America's Right to Remain Silent (Tucson, AZ: University of Arizona Press, 2004) pp. 112-121.
31. 530 U.S. at 444, 445.
32. 530 U.S. at 432 (emphasis added).
33. 530 U.S. at 432 (emphasis added).
34. 530 U.S. at 429 (emphasis added).
35. 530 U.S. at 443 (emphasis added).
36. 530 U.S. at p. 430.
37. 530 U.S. at 465 (Scalia, J., dissenting).
38. Chemerinsky, "The Court Should Have Remained Silent," at p. 287 (2000) ("*Dickerson* . . . will be remembered, especially by students of constitutional law and the federal court system, for its importance in defining the relationship between Congress and the Supreme Court in the area of constitutional remedies.") This point is also discussed in Linda Greenhouse, "The Last Days of the Rehnquist Court: The Rewards of Patience and Power," *Arizona Law Review,* 45: 251, 256-258 (2003).
39. 542 US 630 (2004).
40. 542 US at 639.
41. 542 US at 640 (emphasis added).
42. Kamisar, "*Dickerson v. United States,*" p. 125.
43. Two years before *Patane,* Chief Justice Rehnquist joined Justice Thomas's plurality opinion in *Chavez v. Martinez,* 538 U.S. 760 (2002) (referring to *Miranda* as a "prophylactic rule," while reaffirming *Tucker* and *Elstad*).
44. Kamisar, "*Dickerson v. United States,*" p.127.
45. In the words of Linda Greenhouse, "Success over time on a collegial Court depends in no small measure on vision – the ability to keep the goal in mind while patiently filling in the blanks of a big picture that has yet to emerge. It depends on craft – the skill to frame issues in a manner that makes sense of messy facts and inchoate law, compelling attention even from those not

yet committed to the outcome. It depends on tenacity – the will to stick to the plan despite the distractions of a given day or month or term. William Rehnquist has enjoyed the gift of patience and the gift of power, and he has made the most of both." Greenhouse, "The Last Days of the Rehnquist Court," p. 267.

46. Suzanna Sherry, "The Unmaking of Precedent," *Supreme Court Review,* 2003:231.

47. *Payne v. Tennessee,* 501 U. S. 808, 828 (1991).

48. Given what has been said above in this Chapter, consider the following statement from Rehnquist's dissent in *Planned Parenthood v. Casey,* 504 U.S. 833, 955 (1992) (Rehnquist, C.J., dissenting): "We believe that *Roe* was wrongly decided, and that it can and should be overruled consistently with our traditional approach to stare decisis in constitutional cases."

Chapter 14

1. Niccolò Machiavelli, *Discourses on Livy,* Harvey Mansfield & Nathan Tarcov translation (Chicago, IL: University of Chicago Press, 1996), p. 265.

2. See Seth Stern and Stephen Wermiel, *Justice Brennan: Liberal Champion* (Lawrence KS: University Press of Kansas, 2010), pp. 29-33, 51, 117, 139, 153, 223, 228, 247, 468, 455, 545.

3. Chief Justice William Taft found McReynolds self-centered and prejudiced, "someone who seems to delight in making others uncomfortable . . . [H]e [is] a continual grouch, and is always offended because the Court is doing something that he regards as undignified." Letter from William Taft to Horace Taft, 26 December 1924, quoted in Henry F. Pringle, *The Life and Times of William Howard Taft. A Biography* (New York, NY: Farrack & Rinehart, Inc.,1939), p. 971.

4. See Mark Silverstein, "Felix Frankfurter," in Roger K. Newman, editor, *The Yale Biographical Dictionary of American Law* (New Haven, CT: Yale University Press, 2009), pp. 204, 205 ("His prickly personality and his habit of lecturing his colleagues in the manner of students quickly undercut his influence."). See also H.N. Hirsch, *The Enigma of Felix Frankfurter* (New York, NY: Basic Books, 1981), pp. 201-212 (discussing Frankfurter's "neurotic personality," his "insecurity," his compulsiveness, and his "arrogant-vindictive" qualities). Even so, and as we note in Chapter 26, Felix Frankfurter was a highly successful publicist for Oliver Wendell Holmes.

5. Nat Hentoff, "The Constitutionalist," *The New Yorker,* 12 March 1990 (quoting William Brennan).

6. 134 S. Ct. 2518 (2014).

7. 530 U. S. 703 (2000). A similar abortion-clinic protest case likewise divided the Court in *Madsen v. Women's Health Center, Inc.*, 512 U. S. 753 (1994).

8. 505 U.S. 833 (1992).

9. 550 U.S. 124 (2007).

10. Nina Totenberg, "Justices Appear Divided on Abortion Clinic Buffer Zones," *All Things Considered, NPR*, 15 January 2014.

11. Adam Liptak, "Justices Seem Split on Abortion Clinic Buffer Zones, but Crucial Voice Is Silent, *New York Times*, 16 January 2014.

12. Liptak, "Justices Seem Split on Abortion Clinic Buffer Zones."

13. Totenberg, "Justices Appear Divided on Abortion Clinic Buffer Zones."

14. Ken Jost, "Striking a Free-Speech Balance at Abortion Clinics," *Jost on Justice*, 19 January 2014, http://jostonjustice.blogspot.com/2014/01/striking-free-speech-balance-at.html.

15. Irin Carmon, "Ginsburg defends decision on abortion clinics' buffer zones," *MSNBC*, 1 August 2014.

16. Amicus brief of Planned Parenthood of Massachusetts and Planned Parenthood of America in support of Respondents in *McCullen v. Coakley* (Walter Dellinger, lead counsel), p. 6, http://sblog.s3.amazonaws.com/ wp-content/uploads/2013/12/12-1168-bsac-Planned-Parenthood-League-of-Massachusetts-et-al..pdf.

17. Amicus brief of the American Civil Liberties Union and the American Civil Liberties Union Foundation of Massachusetts in support of neither party in *McCullen v. Coakley* (Stephen R. Shapiro, lead counsel), pp. 12-22, http:// www.americanbar.org/content/dam/aba/publications/supreme_court_preview/briefs-v2/12-1168_np_amcu_aclu-aclu-fm.authcheckdam.pdf. As for the applied challenge, the ACLU urged the Court to remand that issue for further consideration and fact-finding. *Ibid*, pp. 22-31.

18. Brief of United States in support of Respondents in *McCullen v. Coakley* (Donald Verrilli, Jr., lead counsel), p. 10, http://www.americanbar.org/content/dam/aba/publications/supreme_court_preview/briefs-v3/12-1168_resp_amcu_usa.authcheckdam.pdf.

19. 134 S. Ct. at 2541 (Scalia, J., dissenting).

20. Quoted in Joan Biskupic, *American Original: The Life and Constitution of Supreme Court Justice Antonin Scalia* (New York, NY: Farrar, Straus & Giroux, 2009), p. 9 (Scalia commenting on opposition to *Bush v. Gore*).

21. See Kevin Russell, "What is Left of *Hill v. Colorado*?," SCOTUSblog, 26 June 2014 ("Did the Chief Justice effectively overrule *Hill* or its result as a practical matter, without saying so? The answer is unclear. Much of the decision . . . tracks *Hill's* reasoning."), http://www.scotusblog.com/2014/06/what-is-left-of-hill-v-colorado/, and Lyle Denniston, "Opinion Analysis: A Broader Right to Oppose Abortion," SCOTUSblog, 26 June 2014 ("The Chief Justice's approving remarks about the First Amendment right to engage in

counseling in public arenas appeared to contradict some of the reasoning of the 2000 decision."), http://www.scotusblog.com/2014/06/opinion-analysis-a-broader-right-to-oppose-abortion/.

22. *See* Case Note, "*McCullen v. Coakley*," *Harvard Law Review*, 128: 22 (2014) (criticizing majority's application of content-neutrality doctrine). Since the discussion of content-neutrality was not essential to the majority opinion, perhaps the liberals traded their votes and silence for this watered-down version of the doctrine. Contrast *Reed v. Town of Gilbert*, 135 S. Ct. 2218 (2015) (fortifying content-neutrality doctrine, with John Roberts joining the majority opinion).

23. See "Roberts: 'My job is to call balls and strikes and not to pitch or bat'," *CNN.com*, 12 September 2005 ("Judges are like umpires. Umpires don't make the rules; they apply them. The role of an umpire and a judge is critical. They make sure everybody plays by the rules. But it is a limited role. Nobody ever went to a ball game to see the umpire. . . . I will remember that it's my job to call balls and strikes and not to pitch or bat."), http://www.cnn.com/2005/POLITICS/09/12/roberts.statement/. For a critical evaluation of this baseball metaphor, see Richard Posner, *How Judges Think* (Cambridge, MA: Harvard University Press, 2010), pp. 78-79.

Chapter 15

1. Frank I. Michelman, "Machiavelli in Robes? The Court in the Election," in Arthur J. Jacobson and Michael Rosenfeld, editors, *The Longest Night: Polemics and Perspectives on Election 2000* (Berkeley, CA: University of California Press, 2002), p. 262.

2. Alexander Hamilton, Federalist No. 78, in Alexander Hamilton, James Madison, and John Jay *The Federalist Papers*, edited by Jim Miller (Mineola, NY: Dover Publications, 2014), p. 378.

3. Michelman, "Machiavelli in Robes?," p. 266.

4. *Bush v. Gore*, 531 U.S. 98 (2000).

5. Samuel Issachoff, Pamela Karlan, and Richard Pides, *When Elections Go Bad: The Law of Democracy and the Presidential Election of 2000* (New York, NY: Foundation Press, 2001), p. ii.

6. *Palm Beach County Canvassing Board v. Harris*, 772 So. 2d 1220 (Fla. S. Ct. November 21, 2000). Construing relevant state election statutes, the Florida Supreme Court held that "errors in the failure of the voting machinery to read a ballot" constituted grounds for a manual recount, and that the Secretary could reject a county canvassing board's results "only if the returns are submitted so late that their inclusion will preclude . . . Florida's voters from participating fully in the federal election process." Using its equitable powers,

the Court prevented Harris from "summarily disenfranchising innocent electors in an effort to punish dilatory Board members," and ordered her to accept amended certifications received by November 26th "in order to allow maximum time" for manual recounting to proceed.

7. *Bush v. Palm Beach County Canvassing Board (Bush I)*, 530 U.S. 70 (2000) (vacating the judgment of the Supreme Court of Florida and remanding the case for consideration of the conformity of its decision with the scope of the state legislature's authority under Art. II, §1, c. 2 and the state's interest in meeting the "safe harbor" provisions of 3 U.S.C. §5).

8. *Gore v. Harris*, 772 So. 2d 1243 (Fla. S. Ct. December 8, 2000).

9. *Bush v. Gore*, 531 U.S. 1046 (2000) (granting application for stay, treating the application as a petition for a writ of certiorari, granting the petition, and ordering that the Florida Supreme Court's mandate for a statewide manual recount is stayed).

10. *Palm Beach County Canvassing Board v. Harris*, 772 So. 2d 1273 (Fla. S. Ct. Dec. 11, 2000).

11. Linda Greenhouse, "Contesting the Vote: The Overview; Justices' Questions Underline Divide on Whether Hand Recount Can Be Fair," *New York Times*, 12 December 2000, sec. A, p. 1 ("The focus of the argument this time shifted from the constitutional theories that dominated the argument on Dec. 1 to the practicalities of what was actually happening in Florida during the few hours of manual recounts before the United States Supreme Court's 5-to-4 vote to grant Mr. Bush's request for an emergency stay.").

12. Howard J. Langer, editor, *America in Quotations: A Kaleidoscopic View of American History* (Greenwood Press, 2002), p. 402.

13. Arthur J. Jacobson and Michel Rosenfeld, editors, *The Longest Night: Polemics and Perspectives on Election 2000* (Berkeley, CA: University of California Press, 2002).

14. Professor John Yoo quoted in Charles Lane, "Court May Have Mapped New Territory, Bush v. Gore Could Be Entrée into State Election Disputes," *Washington Post*, 14 December 2000, sec. A, p. 24.

15. See, e.g., Charles L. Zelden, *Bush v. Gore: Exposing the Hidden Crisis in American Democracy* (Lawrence, KS: University Press of Kansas, 2010, abridged & updated edition), p. 170; Jeffrey Toobin, *The Nine: Inside the Secret World of the Supreme Court* (New York, NY: Doubleday, 2007), p. 173.

16. *Ibid.*, p. 175.

17. Zelden, *Bush v. Gore*, p. 170.

18. Despite the limiting language of the *per curiam* opinion, Professor Mark Tushnet tellingly observes that "the case is there to be used by progressives in the future." He specifies that "[t]he equal protection argument is at least available." Although he thinks it "quite unlikely that the Supreme Court would actually develop [the equal protection argument] in useful ways in the near

future," he suggests that "[l]ower courts may, however, and by the time the issues get to the Supreme Court, the Court's composition may have changed in ways that would lead that Court to find implications in *Bush v. Gore* that the present Court would not." Mark Tushnet, "Renormalizing *Bush v. Gore*: An Anticipatory Intellectual History," *Georgetown Law Review*, 90: 113, 125 & n. 67." Perhaps, but that would take a goodly measure of *Fortuna* that is "anticipatory," indeed. For an interesting argument that *Fortuna* may already be smiling on the judicial usage of *Bush v. Gore*, see Richard Hasen, "The 2012 Voting Wars, Judicial Backstops, and the Resurrection of *Bush v. Gore*," *George Washington Law Review*, 81: 1865 (2013).

19. For probing questions on this point, see, e.g., Issacharoff, Karlan, and Pildes, *When Elections Go Bad*, p. 89.
20. 531 U.S. at 109.
21. See, e.g., Zelden, *Bush v. Gore*, p. 170.
22. Quoted in Toobin, *The Nine*, p. 176.
23. Quoted in Patrick Martin, "Family Ties, Political Bias Linked US Supreme Court Justices to Bush Camp," *WSWS*, 22 December 2000 (referencing *Newsweek* article); Michael Isikoff, "The Truth Behind The Pillars," *Newsweek*, 24 December 2000. See also Neuman, "Conflicts of Interest in *Bush v. Gore*," pp. 375-378.
24. Quoted in Murphy, *Scalia*, p. 277. See also Jeffrey Toobin, "Justice O'Connor Regrets," *The New Yorker*, 6 May 2013.
25. 60 U.S. 393 (1857).
26. Mark A. Graber, *Dred Scott and the Problem of Constitutional Evil* (New York, NY: Cambridge University Press, 2006), pp. 20-90 (critiques and rebuttals regarding the legal soundness of *Dred Scott v. Sandford*).
27. 347 U.S. 483 (1954).
28. Herbert Wechsler, "Toward Neutral Principles of Constitutional Law," *Harvard Law Review* 73: 1 (1959) (criticizing the judicial reasoning in *Brown v. Board of Education*).
29. Cf. Hasen, "The 2012 Voting Wars, Judicial Backstops, and the Resurrection of *Bush v. Gore*," p. 1865 ("The results of this litigation were a mixed bag. For example, courts approved some voter identification laws, rejected others, and put Pennsylvania's and Wisconsin's laws on hold for the 2012 election. Overall, it appeared that in the most egregious cases of partisan overreach, courts were serving, often with surprising unanimity, as a judicial backstop. In Ohio, one of the twin epicenters (alongside Florida) of the 2012 voting wars, two important cases relied in part on *Bush v. Gore* to expand voting rights. The story of the 2012 voting wars is a story of Republican legislative, and to some extent administrative, overreach to contract voting rights, followed by a judicial and public backlash. The public backlash was somewhat expected – Democrats predictably made 'voter suppression'

a key talking point of the campaign. The judicial backlash and the resurrection of *Bush v. Gore* in the Sixth Circuit, however, were not. The judicial reaction from both liberal and conservative judges, often on a unanimous basis, suggests that courts may now be more willing to act as backstops to prevent egregious cutbacks in voting rights and perhaps to do even more to assure greater equality and fairness in voting. However, it is too early to know for certain.").

30. See, e.g., Zelden, *Bush v. Gore*, pp. 190-229 (listing and critiquing four possible reasons why the Justices might have wanted to hear *Bush v. Gore*).

31. See Neuman, "Conflicts of Interest in *Bush v. Gore*," pp. 410-411.

32. Murphy, *Scalia*, pp. 279-280.

33. 554 U.S. 570 (2008).

34. See Toobin, "Justice O'Connor Regrets" ("As for the Presidency of the younger Bush, O'Connor was disappointed, to put it mildly. The story of the last decade or so of her life is the story of her increasing alienation from the modern Republican Party. . . . In the past seven years, O'Connor has been increasingly clear about her disenchantment with the work of her successors, especially Chief Justice John G. Roberts and Samuel A. Alito, Jr., (who took her seat).").

35. See, e.g., *Lawrence v. Texas*, 539 U.S. 558 (2003).

36. See, e.g., *Citizens United v. Federal Election Commission*, 558 U.S. 310 (2010).

37. See Christopher P. Banks & David M. O'Brien, *The Judicial Process: Law, Courts, and Judicial Politics* (Thousand Oaks, CA: CQ Press, 2016), p. 278 (noting that Kennedy votes with Roberts 81.5% of the time).

38. Toobin, *The Nine*, p. 166.

39. See *ibid.*, p. 167-171.

40. *Ibid.*, p. 171.

41. John G. Roberts, Jr., "In Memoriam: William H. Rehnquist," *Harvard Law Review*, 119: 1 (2005); John G. Roberts, Jr., "A Tribute to William H. Rehnquist," *Columbia Law Review*, 106: 487 (2006).

42. Consider Adam Liptak, "Court Under Roberts Is Most Conservative in Decades," *New York Times*, 24 July 2010.

Chapter 16

1. Angelo Codevilla, "Words and Power," in Niccolò Machiavelli, *The Prince*, translated by Angelo Codevilla (New Haven, CN: Yale University Press, 1997), p. xxi.

2. Richard Posner, editor, *The Essential Holmes: Selections from the Letters, Speeches, Judicial Opinions, & Other Writings of Oliver Wendell Holmes, Jr.* (Chicago, IL: University of Chicago Press, 1992), p. xvii.

3. Oliver Wendell Holmes, Jr., *The Common Law*, introduction by Sheldon Novick (New York, NY: Dover Books, 1991), p. 1.

4. Richard Posner, *Cardozo: A Study in Reputation* (Chicago, IL: University of Chicago Press, 1990), p. 143.

5. *Baskin v. Bogan*, 766 F.3d 648, 662 (7th Cir., 2014) (per Posner, J.)

6. Louis J. Sirico Jr., "Failed Constitutional Metaphors: The Wall of Separation and the Penumbra," *University of Richmond Law Review*, 45: 459 (2011) ("Although courts use metaphors to explain the law, they also use metaphors for a more significant purpose: they use them to create the meaning of the law.") The passage quoted in the text derives from an abstract by the author and contained on an SSRN page, http://papers.ssrn.com/sol3/papers.cfm?abstract_id=2257926.

7. *Schenck v. United States*, 249 U.S. 47, 52 (1919).

8. *Abrams v. United States*, 250 U.S. 616, 630 (1919) (Holmes, J., dissenting).

9. 249 U.S. at 52 (Holmes, J., dissenting).

10. 250 U.S. at 627 (Holmes, J., dissenting).

11. For a sampling of such criticisms, see Ronald K.L. Collins, *The Fundamental Holmes: A Free Speech Reader & Chronicle* (New York, NY: Cambridge University Press, 2011), p. 232-235 (re *Schenck*) and pp. 283-289, 292-299 (re *Abrams*).

12. *Hyde v. United States*, 225 U.S. 347, 384 (1912) (Holmes, J., dissenting).

13. Felix Frankfurter, *Mr. Justice Holmes & the Supreme Court* (Cambridge, MA: Harvard University Press, 1938), pp. 54-55.

14. See Haig A. Bosmajian, *Metaphor and Reason in Judicial Opinions* (Carbondale, IL: Southern Illinois University Press, 1992), pp. 49-72, 186-198.

15. *Brown v. Board of Education*, 347 U.S. 483 (1954). See also *Brown v. Board of Education, II*, 349 U.S. 294 (1955).

16. We say "recast" to take into account the kind of objections leveled by Herbert Wechsler and Raoul Berger, among others.

17. There was considerable discussion back and forth as how exactly to fashion a remedy. See Del Dickson, editor, *The Supreme Court in Conference: 1940-1985* (New York, NY: Oxford University Press, 2001), pp. 663-669.

18. 349 U.S. at 301 ("The judgments below . . . are accordingly reversed and the cases are remanded to the District Courts to take such proceedings and enter such orders and decrees consistent with this opinion as are necessary and proper to admit to public schools on a racially nondiscriminatory basis with all deliberate speed the parties to these cases.").

19. See Mark Tushnet, *Making Civil Rights Law: Thurgood Marshall & the Supreme Court, 1936-1961* (New York, NY: Oxford University Press, 1994), p. 224.

20. *Ibid.*, p. 228.

21. Dennis Hutchinson, "*Brown v. Board of Education*," in Kermit L. Hall, editor, *The Oxford Companion to the Supreme Court of the United States* (New York, NY: Oxford University Press, 2005), p. 112.

22. See e.g., Hugo L. Black, *A Constitutional Faith* (New York, NY: Knopf, 1969), pp. 43-63.

23. *Dennis v. United States*, 341 U.S. 494, 581 (1951) (Black, J., dissenting).

24. *In re Anastaplo*, 366 U.S. 82, 116 (1961) (Black, J., dissenting).

25. Wallace Mendelson quoted in Roger K. Newman, *Hugo Black: A Biography* (New York, NY: Fordham University Press, 2nd ed., 1997), p. 571.

26. Stephen Barnett, one of Justice Brennan's law clerks, first drafted the phrase. See Ronald Collins, "Stephen Barnett: The Little-Known Man Behind the Well-Known Words," *Concurring Opinions*, 23 July 2014, http://concurringopinions.com/archives/2014/07/fan-24-first-amendment-news-stephen-barnett-the-little-known-man-behind-the-well-known-words.html. Rare though it is, this is one example when a Justice can actually receive a significant benefit from a law clerk. See also Seth Stern and Stephen Wermiel, *Justice Brennan: Liberal Champion* (New York, NY: Houghton Mifflin Harcourt, 2010), p. 224.

27. 376 U.S. 254, 270 (per Brennan, J., 1964).

28. See e.g., Richard A. Posner, *Reflections on Judging* (Cambridge, MA: 2013), pp. 255-260 ("Rules of Good Opinion Writing").

29. Consider, Leo Strauss, *What is Political Philosophy & Other Studies* (Chicago, IL: University of Chicago Press, 1959), pp. 134-154 and 155-169.

30. These and related points are discussed in Posner, *Reflections on Judging*, pp. 236-255.

31. See e.g. *State v. Robertson*, 293 Or. 402, 649 P.2d 569, 649 P.2d 569 (Or., 1982) (per Linde, J.).

32. This much is implicit in the most important chapter of *The Prince* where Machiavelli departs from the orders of others. See Niccolò Machiavelli, *The Prince*, translated by Harvey Mansfield (Chicago, IL: University of Chicago Press, 2nd ed., 1998), p. 61.

33. Codevilla, "Words and Power," in Niccolò Machiavelli, *The Prince*, p. xxiv. Professor Codevilla makes many telling points, including this one: "Machiavelli is the first philosopher to espouse the techniques, as well as some of the ends, we now associate with advertising." *Ibid.*, p. xxi. And what does advertising do? In that regard, consider Ronald Collins & David Skover, *The Death of Discourse* (Durham, NC: Carolina Academic Press, 2nd ed., 2005), pp, 83-97.

Chapter 17

1. Niccolò Machiavelli, *The Prince*, translated & edited by Harvey Mansfield (Chicago, IL: University of Chicago Press, 2nd ed., 1988), bk. 15, p. 61.

2. Antonin Scalia, "Dissenting Opinions," *Journal of Supreme Court History* (1994), pp. 33, 34.

3. *The Prince*, Mansfield trans., bk. 18, p. 69.

4. Harvey Mansfield, "Machiavelli's Enterprise," in Timothy Fuller, editor, *Machiavelli's Legacy: The Prince After 500 Years* (Philadelphia, PA: University of Pennsylvania Press, 2015), p. 15.

5. By way of a general analogy, consider the following statement: "Have we not seen in the twentieth century that atheist regimes can be as harmful to humanity, indeed far more harmful, than the religious ones that Machiavelli and Hobbes and all the other modern philosophers feared and despised and attempted to replace?" *Ibid.*, p. 32. That is to say that up to a point, at least, both religion and law have certain civilizing effects. Hence, if every American judge acted according to the dictates of *The Judge*, then we might face a Hobbesian dilemma. Thankfully, that will never occur if only because our lessons demand too much aptitude and willpower. All of this points back, of course, to what was set out in the five lessons we sketched in our Prologue.

6. *The Prince*, Mansfield trans., bk. 15, p. 61

7. Adam Liptak, "Justices Are Long on Words but Short on Guidance," *New York Times*, 17 November 2010.

8. Consider Leo Strauss, *Thoughts on Machiavelli* (Glencoe, NY: Free Press, 1958), p. 83 ("The new Moses will not be sad if he dies at the borders of the land of which he had promised, and if he will only see it from afar. For while it is fatal for a would-be conqueror not to conquer while he is alive, the discoverer of the all-important truth can conquer posthumously.").

9. See David M. O'Brien, *Storm Center: The Supreme Court in American Politics* (New York, NY: W.W. Norton, 10th ed., 2014), p. 305. Justice John Paul Stevens was in the same dissident camp; he authored 678 dissents between 1975 and 2010 (an average of 18.8 per term). *Ibid.*

10. 198 U.S. 45, 75 (1905) (Holmes, J., dissenting) ("This case is decided upon an economic theory which a large part of the country does not entertain. If it were a question whether I agreed with that theory, I should desire to study it further and long before making up my mind. But I do not conceive that to be my duty, because I strongly believe that my agreement or disagreement has nothing to do with the right of a majority to embody their opinions in law.")

11. 478 U.S. 186 (1986).

12. 478 U.S. at 197 (Burger, C.J., concurring).

13. See e.g., *Obergefell v. Hodges*, 576 US ____ (2015) (Scalia, J., dissenting) and Ryan Grim & Arthur Delaney, "Antonin Scalia Dissent In Marriage Equality Case Is Even More Unhinged Than You'd Think," *Huffington Post*, 26 June 2016; *King v. Burwell*, 576 U.S. ____, ____ (2015) (Scalia, J., dissenting), and "Justice Scalia wins for most snarky line in Supreme Court's Obamacare case," *Washington Post*, 25 June 2015. See generally, Erwin Chemerinsky, "Justice Scalia: Why he's a bad influence," *Los Angeles Times*, 14 July 2015 ("Scalia has long relied on ridicule. In past years he has dismissed his colleagues' decisions

as 'nothing short of ludicrous' and 'beyond absurd,' 'entirely irrational' and not 'pass[ing] the most gullible scrutiny.' He has called them 'preposterous' and 'so unsupported in reason and so absurd in application [as] unlikely to survive.' Scalia's opinions this term, however, were especially nasty, sarcastic and personal."). Cf. Carson Holloway, "Scalia's Derisive Dissents Have a Serious Purpose," *National Review*, 23 July 2015 ("although I am an admirer of Scalia — of both the substance of his legal thought and the style in which he expresses it — I must admit that I shared some of Chemerinsky's unease as I read Scalia's *Obergefell* dissent. After all, it is rather surprising — and somewhat painful — to find a dissenting justice telling you he would feel obliged to 'hide his head in a bag' if he had written the opening sentence of the Court's opinion. It's hard to imagine John Marshall saying something like this. As I pondered the question further, however, it occurred to me that Justice Scalia's bare-knuckled style might be justifiable in the right set of circumstances."). To be clear: our concern is not with the merits of Justice Scalia's dissents in these cases, but rather with the gratuitous *ad hominem* way he chose to make his points. In other words, why be openly combative when it serves no useful purpose?

14. Learned Hand, *The Bill of Rights* (Cambridge, MA: Harvard University Press, 1958), p. 54.

15. 347 U.S. 483 (1954).

16. Antonin Scalia, *A Matter of Interpretation: Federal Courts & the Law* (Princeton, NJ: Princeton University Press, 1997). See also what is set out in Chapter 24, *infra*.

17. O'Brien, *Storm Center*, p. 213.

18. 537 U.S. 968 (2002) (Stevens, J., dissenting from denial of *cert.*) (noting, among other things, that "in the last 13 years, a national consensus has developed that juvenile offenders should not be executed. No state has lowered the age of eligibility to either 16 or 17 since our decision in 1989.").

19. See Andrew Wolfson, "Governor Will Spare Jefferson Killer's Life," *The Courier-Journal*, 26 November 2003, sec. A, p. 6; J. Brumberg, "Separating the Killers From the Boys," *New York Times*, 18 December 2003, sec. A, p. 43.

20. 543 U.S. 551 (2005).

21. *Roper v. Simmons*, overruling *Stanford v. Kentucky*, 492 U.S. 361 (1989).

22. O'Brien, *Storm Center*, pp. 301-302.

23. 549 U.S. 346 (2007).

24. 408 U.S. 665, 710 (1972) (Powell, J., concurring).

25. See e.g., *McKevitt v. Pallasch*, 339 F.3d 530 (7th Cir. 2003) (per Posner, J.) (employing Powell test). *See also* Linda L. Berger, "Shielding the Unmedia: Using the Process of Journalism to Protect the Journalist's Privilege in an Infinite Universe of Publication," *Houston Law Review*, 39: 1371, 1390 (2003) ("In recognizing a qualified privilege, as Justice

Powell appeared to suggest, many lower courts also adopted the balancing test specifically advocated by Justice Stewart in his dissent."), and Donald Scarinci, "*Branzburg v. Hayes*: The Evolution of the Reporters' Privilege," *Constitutional Law Reporter*, 29 November 2012, http://scarinciattorney.com/branzburg-v-hayes-the-evolution-of-the-reporters-privilege/ ("Taking the majority and concurring opinions together, the federal courts, including the First, Second, Third, Fourth, Fifth, Ninth, Tenth, Eleventh, and D.C. Circuits, have all recognized the existence of a limited reporters' privilege. In addition, the majority of the states have enacted their own shield laws."). Ultimately, however, the reporters' privilege claim failed to carry the day. See *In re Grand Jury Subpoena, Judith Miller*, 397 F.3d 964, 975 (D.C. Cir. 2005), *cert. denied*, 125 S. Ct. 2977 (2005).

26. 436 U.S. 547, 568 (Powell, J., concurring).
27. Robert H. Jackson, *The Supreme Court & the American System of Government* (Cambridge, MA: Harvard University Ptess,1955), pp. 18-19.
28. Quoted in Melvin Urofsky, *Dissent and the Supreme Court: Its Role in the Court's History and the Nation's Constitutional Dialogue* (New York, NY: Pantheon, 2015), p. 4.
29. Oliver Wendell Holmes to Harold Laski, 16 August 1924, reproduced in Mark DeWolfe Howe, ed., *Holmes-Laski Letters: The Correspondence of Mr. Justice Holmes & Harold J. Laski, 1916-1935* (London: Geoffrey Cumberlege, Oxford University Press, 1953), vol. II, pp. 646-647.
30. See, e.g., *Lochner v. New York*, 198 U.S. 45, 75 (1905) (Holmes, J., dissenting), *Adair v. United States*, 208 U.S. 161, 190 (1908) (Holmes, J., dissenting), *Hammer v. Dagenhart*, 247 U.S. 251, 277 (1918) (Holmes, J., dissenting), *Abrams v. United States*, 250 U.S. 616, 624 (1919) (Holmes, J., dissenting), *Truax v. Corrigan*, 257 U.S. 312, 343 (1921) (Holmes, J., dissenting), *Adkins v. Children's Hospital*, 261 U.S. 525, 567 (1923) (Holmes, J., dissenting), *Gitlow v. New York*, 268 U.S. 652, 672 (1925) (Holmes, J., dissenting), *United States v. Schwimmer*, 279 U.S. 644, 653 (1928) (Holmes, J., dissenting), *Olmstead v. United States*, 277 U.S. 438, 469 (1928) (Holmes, J., dissenting), and *Baldwin v. Missouri*, 281 U.S. 586, 595 (1930) (Holmes, J., dissenting).
31. 2 U.S. 419 (1793) (Curtis, J., dissenting).
32. 274 U.S. 357, 372 (1927) (Brandeis, J., concurring).
33. 343 U.S. 579, 634 (1952) (Jackson, J., concurring).
34. Alexander Hamilton, Federalist Paper No. 81 in *The Federalist or the New Constitution: Papers by Alexander Hamilton, James Madison & John Jay* (Norwalk, CT: The Heritage Press, 1977), p. 547.
35. John P. Kaminski, Gaspare J. Saladino, Richard Leffler, and Charles H. Schoenleber, editors, *The Documentary History of the Ratification of the*

Constitution (Madison, WI: Wisconsin Historical Society Press, 1993), vol. X, p. 1414.

36. 2 U.S. (2 Dall.) 419 (1793).

37. *Whitney v. California*, 274 U.S. 357 (1927).

38. See Ronald K.L. Collins and David M. Skover, "Curious Concurrence: Justice Brandeis's Vote in *Whitney v. California*," *The Supreme Court Review* 2005: 333.

39. 274 U.S. at 375, 376 (Brandeis, J., concurring).

40. Vincent Blasi, "The First Amendment and the Ideal of Civic Courage: The Brandeis Opinion in *Whitney v. Calfornia*," *William & Mary Law Review* 29: 653, 668 (1988).

41. See Bradley C. Bobertz, "The Brandeis Gambit: The Making of America's 'First Freedom,' 1909-1931," *William & Mary Law Review* 40: 557, 645 (1999).

42. 343 U.S. 579 (1952). The *Youngstown* decision invalidated President Truman's executive order that directed the Secretary of Commerce to seize and operate most of the nation's steel mills in the face of a nationwide strike during the Korean War. Although six separate opinions agreed that President Truman's order violated his Article II powers, Justice Jackson's opinion has unquestionably been the most influential for future judicial analyses of presidential claims of inherent or emergency powers.

43. See, e.g., Curtis A. Bradley and Jack L. Goldsmith, *Foreign Relations Law* (New York, NY: Aspen Publishers, Inc., 2nd ed. 2006), p. 174; Louis Henkin, *Foreign Affairs & the U.S. Constitution* (Westbury, NY: Foundation Press, 2nd ed. 1996), p. 94; *Medellin v. Texas*, 552 U.S. 491, 524 (2008) ("Justice Jackson's familiar tripartite scheme provides the accepted framework for evaluating executive action in this area.").

44. William R. Casto, "Attorney General Robert Jackson's Brief Encounter with the Notion of Preclusive Presidential Power," *Pace Law Review* 30: 364 (2009) (footnotes omitted).

45. Urofsky, *Dissent and the Supreme Court*, p. S.

Chapter 18

1. Artemus Ward and David L. Weiden, *Sorcerers' Apprentices: 100 Years of Law Clerks at the United States Supreme Court* (New York, NY: New York University Press, 2006), p. 200.

2. *Ibid.*, p. 231.

3. *Ibid.*

4. See Todd C. Peppers, *Courtiers of the Marble Palace: The Rise & Influence of the Supreme Court Law Clerk* (Stanford, CA: Stanford University Press, 2006), pp. 203-205, and David M. O'Brien, *Storm Center: The Supreme*

Court in American Politics (New York, NY: W.W. Norton, 10th edition, 2014), pp. 122-123.

5. Melvin Urofsky, "William O. Douglas and His Clerks," *Western Legal History*, 3:1, 17 (1990) (quoting Justice Harry A. Blackmun's recollection of Justice Douglas).

6. 371 U.S. 415 (1963). See Ronald Collins, "Richard Posner & *NAACP v. Button* — A Short History," *Concurring Opinions*, 18 June 2014, http://concurringopinions.com/archives/2014/06/richard-posner-naacp-v-button-a-short-history.html.

7. *Korematsu v. United States*, 323 U.S. 214, 233 (1944) (Murphy, J., dissenting). See Ward and Weiden, *Sorcerers' Apprentices*, p. 204.

8. See generally Peppers, *Courtiers of the Marble Palace*, pp. 32-34.

9. Here, as elsewhere, vigilance is needed to guard against professors following the example of Felix Frankfurter, who in selecting "secretaries" for Justice Holmes and then law clerks for Justice Cardozo seemed at times to be more self-interested than concerned about finding the best fit for those two Justices.

10. In this regard, consider what one respected jurist rightfully observed in connection with a "tell all" book authored by a former law clerk to Justice Harry Blackmun. See Alex Kozinski, "Conduct Unbecoming," *Yale Law Journal*, 108: 835 (1999).

11. Edward Lazarus, *Closed Chambers: The First Eye-Witness Account of the Epic Struggles Inside the Supreme Court* (New York, NY: Times Books, 1998), p. 6.

12. Peppers, *Courtiers of the Marble Palace*, p. 143 (quoting John H. Mansfield re his selection as a Frankfurter law clerk).

13. *Ibid.*, pp. 38-70, 83-144, 145-205 (here we draw on Professor Peppers' classifications only in a very general sense). See also Ward and Weiden, *Sorcerers' Apprentices*, pp. 208 -236 (identifying three categories of law clerks: "delegation, retention, and collaboration").

14. See Peppers, *Courtiers of the Marble Palace*, pp. 151-152.

15. William O. Douglas, *The Court Years: 1939-1975* (New York, NY: Random House, 1980), p. 173.

16. Tony Mauro, "Afterword," in Todd Peppers and Artemus Ward, *In Chambers: Stories of Supreme Court Law Clerks & Their Justices* (Charlottesville, VA: University of Virginia Press, 2012), p. 405.

17. In this regard, for example, Kenneth Starr has noted: "Selecting 100 or so cases from the pool of 6,000 petitions is just too important to invest in very smart but brand-new lawyers." Quoted in Tony Mauro, "Justices Give Key Role to Novice Lawyers," *USA Today*, 5 June 5, 1998, sec. A, p. 1.

18. O'Brien, *Storm Center*, p. 140.

19. *Ibid.*, pp. 144-145 (footnote omitted).

20. *Ibid.*, p. 140.

21. *Ibid.* (footnote omitted).

22. Ward and Weiden, *Sorcerers' Apprentices*, p. 242. See also Peppers, *Courtiers of the Marble Palace*, p. 165 (noting tendency of some clerks in the cert. pool to misstate the facts), and Peppers & Ward, *In Chambers*, p. 329 (noting downside of "too much influence" by clerks drafting cert. memos).

23. See Bernard Schwartz, *Super Chief: Earl Warren & His Supreme Court – A Judicial Biography* (New York, NY: New York University Press, 1983), pp. 78-79, G. Edward White, *Earl Warren: A Public Life* (New York, NY: Oxford University Press, 1982), pp. 162-163, and David Adamany, "Alexander Bickel," in Kermit Hall, editor, *The Oxford Companion to the Supreme Court of the United States* (New York, NY: Oxford University Press, 2nd ed., 2005), p. 81.

24. 376 U.S. 254 (1964).

25. See Seth Stern and Stephen Wermiel, *Justice Brennan: Liberal Champion* (Lawrence, KS: University of Kansas Press, 2013) p. 224, and Ronald Collins, "Stephen Barnett: The Little-Known Man Behind the Well-Known Words," *Concurring Opinions*, 23 July 2014, http://concurringopinions.com/archives/2014/07/fan-24-first-amendment-news-stephen-barnett-the-little-known-man-behind-the-well-known-words.html.

26. 376 U.S. at 270.

27. Ward and Weiden, *Sorcerers' Apprentices*, p. 227.

28. Quoted in *ibid.*, p. 218.

29. See William Domnarski, "Judges Should Write Their Own Opinions," *New York Times*, 31 May 2012 ("An informal review of federal appellate court opinions over the past five years suggests that of the more than 150 active judges, only a tiny number almost always write their own opinions in full, among them Frank H. Easterbrook, Richard A. Posner and Diane P. Wood of the United States Court of Appeals for the Seventh Circuit, and Michael Boudin of the First Circuit.").

30. See Richard A. Posner, *How Judges Think* (Cambridge, MA: Harvard University Press, 2008), p. 286, and Posner, *Reflections on Judging*, p. 248-243.

31. Deborah L. Rhode, "Thurgood Marshall & His Clerks," in Peppers & Ward, *In Chambers*, pp. 314, 317 (emphasis added). See also Mark Tushnet, *Making Constitutional Law: Thurgood Marshall and the Supreme Court, 1961-1991* (New York, NY: Oxford University Press, 1997), p. 59 ("Marshall relied heavily on his law clerks for drafting once he decided what to do, and he probably edited their work less than most of his colleagues did.").

32. Quoted in Ward and Weiden, *Sorcerers' Apprentices*, p. 207 (endnote omitted).

33. See, e.g., Mark Tushnet, "Thurgood Marshall," in Roger K. Newman, editor, *The Yale Biographical Dictionary of American Law* (New Haven, CN: Yale University Press, 2009), p. 364 (quoting William Rehnquist: "Thurgood Marshall is unique because of his major contributions to constitutional law *before* becoming a member of the Court.") (emphasis in original); Bob

Woodward and Scott Armstrong, *The Brethren: Inside The Supreme Court* (New York, NY: Simon & Schuster, 1979), p. 197 ("Some of the clerks in the other chambers came to the conclusion that Marshall was unfit to sit on the Court. He was not willing to do his homework, not willing to prepare for his cases, not of the intellectual caliber of [some of his colleagues, and] not combative enough to take on the others in conference."); Seth Stern and Stephen Wermiel, *Justice Brennan: Liberal Champion* (Boston, MA: Houghton Mifflin Harcourt, 2010), p.431 (Few understood just how much Marshall's performance on the Court came to disappoint Brennan. . . . Brennan privately wondered what had come of the skilled lawyer who so dazzled him at oral arguments. 'What the hell happened when he came on the Court, I'm not sure, but he doesn't seem to have the same interest,' Brennan said."); Bernard Schwartz with Stephen Lesher, *Inside the Warren Court: 1953-1969* (New York, NY: Doubleday, 1983), pp. 255-256 ("There was serious questions about Marshall's judicial capabilities . . ." and Henry Friendly to Felix Frankfurter: "'I continue to be alarmed at Marshall's willingness to arrive at quick decisions on issues he does not understand.'").

34. 410 U.S. 113.

35. 411 U.S. 1, 70 (Marshall, J., dissenting). The *Rodriguez* dissent may be one of Marshall's finest judicial moments. See also Mark Tushnet, "A Clerk's-Eye View of *Keyes v. School District No. 1*," *Denver University Law Review*, 90: 1139 (2012).

36. Mark Tushnet, *Making Civil Rights Law: Thurgood Marshall and the Supreme Court, 1936-1961* (New York, NY: Oxford University Press, 1996), and Tushnet, *Making Constitutional Law.*

37. Mark Tushnet, editor, *Thurgood Marshall: His Speeches, Writings, Arguments, Opinions, and Reminiscences* (Chicago, IL: Chicago Review Press, 2001).

38. Mark Tushnet, *The NAACP's Legal Strategy Against Segregated Education: 1925-1950* (Chapel Hill, NC: University of North Carolina Press, 2005).

39. See, e.g., Mark Tushnet, "The Meritocratic Egalitarianism of Thurgood Marshall," *Howard Law Journal*, 52: 691 (2008); Mark Tushnet, "The Jurisprudence of Thurgood Marshall," *University of Illinois Law Review*, 1996: 1129; Mark Tushnet, "The Supreme Court and Race Discrimination, 1967-1991: The View from the Marshall Papers," *William & Mary Law Review*, 36: 473 (1994); Mark Tushnet, "Lawyer Thurgood Marshall," *Stanford Law Review*, 44: 1277 (1992); Mark Tushnet, "*Brown v. Board of Education* and Its Legacy: A Tribute to Justice Thurgood Marshall, Public Law Litigation and the Ambiguities of *Brown*," *Fordham Law Review* 61:23 (1992); Mark Tushnet, "Thurgood Marshall and the Brethren," *Georgetown Law Journal*, 80: 2109 (1991); Mark Tushnet, "Change and Continuity in the Concept of Civil Rights: Thurgood Marshall and Affirmative Action," *Social Philosophy*

& Policy, 8: 150 (1991); Mark Tushnet, "Thurgood Marshall and the Rule of Law," *Howard Law Journal*, 35: 7 (1991); Mark Tushnet, "In Honor of Justice Thurgood Marshall: The Inner-Directed Personality," *Valparaiso University Law Review*, 26: 1 (1991); Mark Tushnet and Katya Lezin, "What Really Happened in *Brown v. Board of Education*," *Columbia Law Review*, 91: 1867 (1991); Mark Tushnet, "The Legitimation of the Administrative State: Some Aspects of the Work of Thurgood Marshall," *Studies in American Political Development*, 5: 94 (1991); Mark Tushnet, "The Principled Dissenter," *American Bar Association Journal*, 72: 29 (1986); Mark Tushnet, "Thurgood Marshall as a Lawyer: The Campaign against School Segregation 1945-1950," *Maryland Law Review*, 40: 411 (1981); and Mark Tushnet, "Mr. Justice Marshall: A Tribute," *Black Law Journal*, 6: 142 (1978).

Chapter 19

1. One of the authors (RKLC) worked for the Chief Justice in 1982 as a Supreme Court Fellow. Nothing in this chapter or in this book reveals any confidential information learned during his tenure there other than any such information that has otherwise become public. Moreover, the depictions of Chief Justice Burger as set out in this chapter have been cast so as to comport with the demands of our undertaking and should not therefore be understood as suggesting any personal animus towards the Chief Justice, who was always kindly towards him.

2. See David M. O'Brien, *Storm Center: The Supreme Court in American Politics* (New York, NY: W.W. Norton & Co., 10ᵗʰ ed., 2014), p. 68 ("Burger came to the Court with the agenda of reversing the 'liberal jurisprudence' of the Warren Court and restoring 'law and order.'").

3. Fred Graham Interview, *New York Times*, 4 July 1971, quoted in Bernard Schwartz, *Packing the Courts: The Conservative Campaign to Rewrite the Constitution* (New York, NY: Charles Scribner's Sons, 1988), p. 15.

4. Quoted in Joseph Foote, "Mr. Justice Blackmun," *Harvard Law School Bulletin* 21: 18, 19 (June 1970).

5. Laura Kelman, Book Review, "'Becoming Justice Blackmun': Deconstructing Harry," *New York Times*, 8 May 2006 (Linda "Greenhouse maintains that it was *Roe* and its reception that forced Blackmun to begin the rest of his life and become Justice Blackmun."); Laurence Baum, *Judges & Their Audiences: A Perspective on Judicial Behavior* (Princeton, NJ: Princeton University Press, 2006), pp. 152-153.

6. 478 U.S. 186 (1986).

7. Thomas Sowell, "Blackmun Plays to the Crowd," *St Louis Post-Dispatch*, 4 March 1994, Sect. B, p. 7.

8. See, e.g., Note, "The Changing Social Vision of Justice Blackmun," *Harvard Law Review* 96: 717 (1983) and Theodore W. Ruger, "Justice Harry Blackmun and the Phenomenon of Judicial Preference Change," *Missouri Law Review*, 70: 1209, 1213 (2005).

9. 410 U.S. 113 (1973).

10. Bob Woodward and Scott Armstrong, *The Brethren: Inside the Supreme Court* (New York, NY: Simon & Schuster, 1979), p. 169 (quoting conference notes of one of the Justices). But see Greenhouse, *Becoming Justice Blackmun*, p. 81 (quoting Burger as saying: "I have trouble not finding the Texas statute unconstitutional.").

11. Though not without its problems, *The Brethren's* overall portrayals have fared relatively well. See Garrow, "The Supreme Court & *The Brethren*," p. 318 ("Over time, *The Brethren* has won a far more respectful reception from scholars than it did from its immediate reviewers. Former Marshall clerk Mark Tushnet has acknowledged that 'on most particulars and in its general depiction of the Supreme Court under Chief Justice Burger, its accuracy has not been impugned' and has often been confirmed."), quoting Mark Tushnet, "Thurgood Marshall and the Brethren," *Georgetown Law Journal* 80: 2109, 2109 n.2 (1992). Contrast Anthony Lewis, "Supreme Court Confidential," *The New York Review of Books*, 7 Feb. 1980 (critically reviewing *The Brethren*) and "The Evidence of 'The Brethren': An Exchange," *The New York Review of Books* (re Anthony Lewis's rejoinder to Woodward & Armstrong's reply).

12. *Roe* was first argued on December 12, 1971, then reargued on October 11, 1972, and finally decided on January 22, 1973.

13. See Woodward and Armstrong, *The Brethren*, pp. 169-178, 181-189, 229-240.

14. Greenhouse, *Becoming Justice Blackmun*, p. 82.

15. See, e.g., Jack Balkin, editor, *What Roe v. Wade Should Have Said: The Nation's Top Legal Experts Rewrite America's Most Controversial Decision* (New York, NY: New York University Press, 2007), pp. 31-62 (Balkin), pp. 63- 85 (Segal), pp. 86-91 (Tushnet), pp. 121-147 (West), and pp.148-151 (Sunstein).

16. See *Thornburgh v. American College of Obstetricians & Gynecologists*, 476 U.S. 747 (1986) (Burger, C.J., dissenting), and *Planned Parenthood of Central Missouri v. Danforth*, 428 U.S. 52 (1976) (Burger, C.J., concurring & dissenting in part).

17. 505 U.S. 883 (1992).

18. 550 U.S. 124 (2007).

19. 136 S. Ct. ___ (2016).

20. See Erwin Chemerinsky, *The Conservative Assault on the Constitution* (New York, NY: Simon & Schuster, 2010), pp. 180-181 (noting stark differences between the reasoning and rhetoric of Kennedy's joint opinion in *Casey* and his majority opinion in *Gonzales*).

21. Baum, *Judges & Their Audiences*, p. 138.

22. Cf. Carl Maltz, *The Chief Justiceship of Warren Burger, 1969-1986* (Columbia, SC: University of South Carolina Press, 2000).

23. The following cases illustrate the issues discussed in the text: *United States v. Nixon*, 418 U.S. 683 (1974); *Bowsher v. Synar*, 478 U.S. 714 (1986) and *Immigration and Naturalization Service v. Chadha*, 462 U.S. 919 (1983); *Miller v. California*, 413 U.S. 15 (1973) and *Wooley v. Maynard*, 430 US 705 (1977); *Richmond Newspapers Inc. v. Virginia*, 448 U.S. 555 (1980) and *Landmark Communications, Inc. v. Virginia*, 435 U.S. 829 (1978); *Marsh v. Chambers*, 463 U.S. 783 (1983); *United States v. U.S. District Court*, 407 U.S. 297 (1972); *Swann v. Charlotte-Mecklenburg Board of Education*, 402 U.S. 1 (1971).

24. He was also the driving force in the creation of the National Center for State Courts.

25. See Vincent Blasi, editor, *The Burger Court: The Counter-Revolution that Wasn't* (New Haven, CT: Yale University Press, 1983). Cf Leon Friedman, "Warren Burger," in Leon Friedman & Fred Israel, editors, *Justices of the United States Supreme Court*, vol. IV (New York, NY: Facts on File, 4th ed. 2013), pp. 157, 162-163 (contrasting Burger Court's civil liberties record with that of the Warren Court) and Keith Whittington, "The Burger Court," in Christopher Tomlins, editor, *The United States Supreme Court: The Pursuit of Justice* (Boston, MA: Houghton Miffline Co., 2005), pp. 320-321 (noting failures, but success in the area of criminal justice).

26. See Charles M. Lamb, "Chief Justice Warren E. Burger: A Conservative Chief for Conservative Times," in Charles L. Lamb & Stephen C. Halpern, *The Burger Court: Political and Judicial Profiles* (Urbana, IL: University of Illinois Press, 1991), pp. 129, 132-133, 159.

27. See, e.g., *Richmond Newspapers Inc. v. Virginia*, 448 U.S. 555 (1980) and *Landmark Communications, Inc. v. Virginia*, 435 U.S. 829 (1978). For a more detailed account, see Lyle Denniston, "The Burger Court & the Press," in Herman Schwartz, editor, *The Burger Years: Rights & Wrongs in the Supreme Court: 1969-1986* (New York, NY: Viking, 1987), pp. 23-44, and Sidney Zion, "Freedom of the Press: A Tale of Two Libel Theories," in Schwartz, *The Burger Years*, pp. 45-49.

28. The interviews were conducted by one of Blackmun's former law clerks, former Yale Law School dean Harold Koh.

29. Kelman, Book Review, "'Becoming Justice Blackmun'."

30. See Kelman, Book Review, "Becoming Justice Blackmun" ("The Blackmun whom Greenhouse paints in this page turner [of a biography] is a modest Minnesotan, who carries the weight of the world on his shoulders. He drives his Volkswagen to the court daily for breakfast with his clerks. A man of civility and compassion, he has a twinkle in his eye. He is kind to almost everyone, which makes his lack of sympathy for Burger as their friendship fades

startling. Greenhouse's Blackmun is endearingly quirky, the justice from Lake Wobegon. Garrison Keillor himself called Blackmun 'the shy person's justice.'").

31. Tinsley Yarbrough, *Harry A. Blackmun: The Outsider Justice* (New York, NY: Oxford University Press, 2008).

32. Book blurb by Bruce Allen Murphy, author of *Wild Bill: The Legend and Life of William O. Douglas* (New York, NY: Random House, 2003).

33. See Michael D. Shear, "Ruth Bader Ginsberg Apologizes for Criticizing Trump," *New York Times*, 14 July 2016 (conceding that her remarks were "ill advised.").

Chapter 20

1. *Estes v. Texas*, 381 U.S. 532, 595 (1965) (Harlan, J., concurring). Here, as elsewhere in this chapter, the authors acknowledge their reliance on Sonja R. West's article, "The Monster in the Courtroom," *Brigham Young University Law Review* 2012: 1953.

2. Warren E. Burger, Foreword to Mark Cannon and David M. O'Brien, editors, *Views from the Bench: The Judiciary and Constitutional Politics* (Chatham, NJ: Chatham House, 1985).

3. David M. O'Brien, *Storm Center: The Supreme Court in American Politics* (New York, NY: W.W. Norton & Co., 10ᵗʰ ed., 2014), p. ___, quoting letter from Chief Justice Rehnquist, 27 October 1989, *Thurgood Marshall Papers*, Library of Congress.

4. O'Brien, *Storm Center*, p. 125, referencing letters from Justice Steven, 11 February 1988 & 30 August 1990, *Thurgood Marshall Papers*, boxes 435 & 494, Library of Congress.

5. "On Cameras in Supreme Court, Souter Says, 'Over My Dead Body,'" *New York Times*, 30 March 1996, sec. A, p. 24.

6. Stephanie Condon, "Scalia: Cameras in the Court will 'Miseducate' People," *CBS News*, 26 July 2012, http://www.cbsnews.com/8301-503544_162-57480640-503544/scalia-cameras-in-the-court-will-miseducate-people/.

7. "Supreme Court Stubbornly Rejects Video Coverage," *All Gov*, 22 February 2013, http://www.allgov.com/news/controversies/supreme-court-stubbornly-rejects-video-coverage-130222?news =847149 (the remark was made to Charlie Rose).

8. Gina Holland, "Two Justices Criticize Cameras in High Court," *Boston Globe*, 5 April 2006.

9. Greg Beato, "Cameras in the Court," *Reason* 47.2: 70 (2015).

10. Jamie Schuman, "Holding Out against Cameras at the High Court," *Reporters Committee for Freedom of the Press*, Spring 2014, at http://www.rcfp.org/

browse-media-law-resources/news-media-law/news-media-and-law-spring-2014/holding-out-against-cameras.

11. Ariane de Vogue, "What Do the Supreme Court Justices Think of Cameras in Court?," *ABC News*, 1 December 2011, http://abcnews.go.com/blogs/politics/2011/12/what-do-the-   supreme-court-justices-think-of-cameras-in-court/.

12. "Supreme Court Stubbornly Rejects Video Coverage."

13. *Nomination of Judge Clarence Thomas to be Associate Justice of the Supreme Court of the United States: Hearing Before the Senate Committee on the Judiciary,* 102nd Cong. (1991), p. 385.

14. Adam Liptak, "Bucking a Trend, Supreme Court Justices Reject Video Coverage," *New York Times*, 18 February 2013.

15. *The Nomination of Elena Kagan to be an Associate Justice of the Supreme Court of the United States: Hearing Before the Senate Committee on the Judiciary,* 11th Cong. (2010), pp. 83-84.

16. See Debra Cassens Weiss, "Kagan Has Second Thoughts on Televised Arguments," *ABA Journal*, 10 September 2012, http://www.abajounal.com/news/article/kaganhas_second_thoughtsontelevisedarguments

17. "Supreme Court Stubbornly Rejects Video Coverage."

18. *Ibid.*

19. *Allowing Cameras and Electronic Media in the Courtroom: Hearing Before the Subcommittee on Administrative Oversight and the Courts, Senate Committee on the Judiciary,* 106th Cong. (2000), p. 56.

20. See, e.g., Liptak, "Bucking a Trend" (noting Justices' new or ongoing opposition to cameras in the Supreme Court).

21. See Alicia M. Cohn, "Justice Scalia: Cameras in Supreme Court Would 'Miseducate' Americans," *The Hill*, 26 July 2012, http://www.thehill.com/video/in- the-news/240519-justice-scalia-cameras-in-supreme-court-would-miseducate-americans/ (quoting Justice Scalia's view that "[t]he First Amendment has nothing to do with whether we have to televise our proceedings"); Michael Dorf, "Cameras in Courtrooms," *Dorf on Law*, 19 February 2013, http://www.dorfonlaw.org/2013/02/cameras-in- courtrooms.html (noting unlikelihood of First Amendment claim prevailing); and Cristina Carmody Tilley, "I am a Camera: Scrutinizing the Assumption that Cameras in the Courtroom Furnish Public Value by Operating as a Proxy for the Public," *University of Pennsylvania Journal of Constitutional Law* 16: 697, 699 n. 5, 709-710 (2014).

22. *Access to the Court: Televising the Supreme Court: Hearing before the Subcommittee on Administrative Oversight and the Courts of the Senate Committee on the Judiciary,* 112th Congress (2011), p. 9.

23. 277 U.S. 438, 471 (1928) (Brandeis, J., dissenting) (arguing for the extension of constitutional privacy protections to government wiretapping of telephone conversations).

24. *Olmstead* was overturned by *Katz v. United States*, 389 U.S. 347 (1967).

25. See, e.g., Liptak, "Bucking a Trend;" Tony Mauro, "In Canada's Supreme Court, Cameras Are No Big Deal, *BLT: The Blog of the Legal Times*, 31 August 2010, http://legaltimes.typepad.com/blt/2010/08/in-canadas-supreme-court-cameras-are-no-big-deal.html.

26. We are indebted to Professor Youm Kyu Ho of the University of Oregon School of Journalism for this tabulation.

27. See, e.g, M. Ray Doubles, "A Camera in the Courtroom," *Washington & Lee Law Review* 22: 1, 3 (1965). This persuasive argument, made over a half-century ago, is even more convincing today given the astonishing improvements in electronic technology.

28. See, e.g., Tony Mauro, "Let the Cameras Roll: Cameras in the Court and the Myth of Supreme Court Exceptionalism," *Reynolds Courts and Media Law Journal* 1: 259, 260-261 (2011); Erwin Chemerinksy, *The Case Against the Supreme Court* (New York, NY: Penguin Books, 2014), p. 317.

29. See, e.g., Alex Kozinski and Robert Johnson, "Cameras and Courtrooms," *Fordham Intellectual Property, Media and Entertainment Law Journal* 20: 1107, 1112 (2010); Judith Resnik, "Courts in and out of Sight, Site, and Cite," *Villanova Law Review* 53: 771, 802-809 (2008); Chemerinsky, *The Case Against the Supreme Court*, pp. 317-318.

30. See, e.g., *Access to the Court: Televising the Supreme Court*, pp. 8-9 (statement of Tom Goldstein); Chemerinsky, *The Case Against the Supreme Court*, pp. 318-320; Press Release, "Supreme Court of Ohio and the Ohio Judicial System, Chief Justice O'Connor Touts Openness and Access to Courts in Speech," 29 February 2012, http://www.supremecourt.ohio.gov/SCO/ justices/oconnor/news/2012/heathRotary.asp

31. In past years, the following Justices have appeared on television to discuss judicial decisionmaking or a newly published book: John Roberts, Clarence Thomas, Sonia Sotomayor, Stephen Breyer, Ruth Bader Ginsburg, Sandra Day O'Connor, Anthony Kennedy, William O. Douglas, and Hugo Black, among others. See, e.g., Mauro, "Let the Cameras Roll," p. 269.

32. See "Three-Fourths of Americans Want Cameras in the Supreme Court; Overwhelming Majorities Support Additional SCOTUS Transparency Measures," http://openscotus.com/SCOTUS poll release.pdf (summarizing 2014 report by Coalition for Court Transparency).

33. Elena Kagan, Appearance at a Ninth Circuit Judicial Conference, 23 July 2009, quoted in C-SPAN, "Cameras in the Court," http://www.c-span.org/ The-Courts/Cameras-in-The-Court/.

34. See, e.g., Jonathan R. Bruno, "The Weakness of the Case for Cameras in the United States Supreme Court," *Creighton Law Review* 48: 167 (2014).

35. 531 U.S. 98 (2000). See also *Bush v. Palm Beach County Canvassing Board*, 531 U.S. 70 (2000) (in which the Court also declined televising oral arguments).
36. Mauro, "Let the Cameras Roll," p. 266.

Chapter 20

1. Walter Goodman, "And Now, Heeeeeeer's a Referendum," *New York Times*, 23 June 1992, sec. H, p. 25.
2. See James Twitchell, *Carnival Culture: The Trashing of Taste in America* (New York, NY: Columbia University Press, 1992).
3. Richard Hasen, "Celebrity Justice: Supreme Court Edition," *Green Bag*, 19: 157, 169 (2015). The authors acknowledge their reliance on Professor Hasen's article in writing a portion of this chapter.
4. See Allan Bloom, *The Closing of the American Mind* (New York, NY: Simon & Schuster, 1987), p. 79 (re: show business glitz and Mick Jagger).
5. See *ibid.*, at pp. 160, 168.
6. See "Breyer v. Colbert," *The Atlantic*, 15 September 2015, http://www.theatlantic.com/politics/ archive/2015/09/breyer-colbert/405346/.
7. See Scott Lemieux, "Sorry, Still not over *Bush v. Gore*," *The American Prospect*, 19 July 2012.
8. 531 U.S. 98 (2000).
9. See Greg Stohr and Matthew Winkler, "Ruth Bader Ginsburg Thinks Americans Are Ready for Gay Marriage," *Bloomberg News*, 5 February 2015, http://www.bloomberg.com/news/articles/2015-02-12/ginsburg-says-u-s-ready-to-accept-ruling-approving-gay-marriage-i61z6gq2.
10. See Hasen, "Celebrity Justice," p. 158, n. 7.
11. "Clarence Thomas on *60 Minutes*," YouTube, 12 October 2002, https://vimeo.com/88519214.
12. "Sonia Sotomayor opens up on *60 Minutes*," CBS News, 14 January 2013, http://www.cbsnews.com/videos/ sonia-sotomayor-opens-up-on-60-minutes/.
13. "Justice Scalia On Life, Part 1," *YouTube*, 14 September 2008, https://www.youtube.com/ watch?v=FrFj7JAyutg, "Justice Scalia on Life, Part 2," *YouTube*, 14 September 2008, https:// www.youtube.com/watch?v=bU1n7RRUy84.
14. Discussed in Roger K. Newman, *Hugo Black: A Biography* (New York, NY: Pantheon, 1994), pp. 584-587.
15. See e.g. Antonin Scalia, "William and Mary Law School Commencement Address," *C-SPAN*, 11 May 2014, http://www.c-span.org/video/?319383-1/william-mary-law-school-commencement-address.
16. See e.g. Nicole Flatow, "Supreme Court Justices Blast The Corrections System," *Think Progress*, 24 March 2015 (testimony by Justices Kennedy and

Breyer), http://thinkprogress.org/justice/2015/03/24/3637885/ supreme-court-justices-implore-congress-reform-criminal-justice-system-not-humane/.
17. http://www.scotusmap.com (hosted by SCOTUS Blog, the map reveals where Justices will appear or have appeared in some public forum, either in the United States or abroad).
18. See Hasen, "Celebrity Justice," p. 164.
19. Robert Barnes, "Supreme Court Justices Are Being Served Up on Late-Night Television," *Washington Post*, 12 February 2012.
20. Niccolò Machiavelli, *The Prince*, Angelo Codevilla translation (New Haven, CN: Yale University Press, 1997), p. 81 (bk, 21).

Chapter 21

1. Friedrich Wilhelm Nietzsche, *The Antichrist*, trans. H. L. Mencken (New York, NY: Knopf, 1920), p. 37. It is noteworthy that Nietzsche's writings and their method of presentation resemble, if only in some ways, those of Machiavelli as displayed in *The Prince*. That is, they revel in "flair, shock, personality [and] temptation. Nietzsche's writings announce that they are the works of the devil." Laurence Lampert, *Leo Strauss & Nietzsche* (Chicago, IL: University of Chicago Press, 1996), p. 2. In other words, Nietzsche appears to favor "a new candor [and a willingness] to run the risk of openness," the peril of "public probity." *Ibid.*, pp. 20, 23.
2. See Niccolò Machiavelli, *The Prince & The Discourses*, introduction by Max Lerner (New York, NY: Random House, 1950), pp. xxvi, xxxi, xxxii, xxxv.
3. Of course, *The Prince* was not simply a "scientific" treatise. See Leo Strauss, *Thoughts on Machiavelli* (Glencoe, IL: The Free Press, 1958), p. 55 (re "treatise" and "tract").
4. Niccolò Machiavelli, *The Prince*, trans. Tim Parks (New York, NY: Penguin Books, 2009), p. xxi (translator's introduction). See also Niccolò Machiavelli, *The Prince*, trans. James B. Atkinson (New York, NY: Macmillan Publishing Co., 1985), p. 23 ("We have no evidence . . . that Lorenzo was ever officially presented with a copy of *The Prince*; but we do know that he did not repay Machiavelli in any way for his 'gift.' ").
5. See Strauss, *Thoughts on Machiavelli*, pp. 34-35, 54-84 (re Machiavelli's intentions and *The Prince*).
6. Niccolò Machiavelli, *The Prince*, trans. Harvey C. Mansfield (Chicago IL: University of Chicago Press, 2nd ed., 1998), p. 61 (Ch. 15). See also Strauss, *Thoughts on Machiavelli*, p. 23 (discussing intended audience of *The Prince*).
7. Machiavelli, *The Prince*, trans. Harvey C. Mansfield, p. xxvi (translator's comment).

8. See Ronald Collins, "Books by Supreme Court Justices," *Journal of Supreme Court History*, 38: 94, 95 (2013) (listing 353 books, which was the tally at the time of publication – since then Justice Breyer has published another book, which brings the tally to 354).

9. See *ibid*.

10. See, e.g., Anne Norton, *Leo Strauss & the Politics of American Empire* (New Haven, CN: Yale University Press, 2004), pp. 96, 97-99 (describing different audiences).

11. Such questions suggest a sociology of knowledge, a way of looking at a book as presented in a given context.

12. See Collins, "Books by Supreme Court Justices," pp. 103-105.

13. Book Review, *American Monthly Review*, 4: 499, 513 (December 1833).

14. Arthur Sutherland, *The Law at Harvard: A History of Ideas & Men, 1817-1967* (Cambridge, MA: Harvard University Press, 1967), p. 24.

15. R. Kent Newmyer, *Supreme Court Justice Joseph Story: Statesman of the Old Republic* (Chapel Hill, NC: University of North Carolina Press, 1985), pp. 181-182 (quoting Vernon Parrington).

16. *Ibid.*, p. 182.

17. See Ronald Rotunda and John Nowak, "Introduction" to Joseph Story, *Commentaries on the Constitution of the United States* (Durham, NC: Carolina Academic Press, 1987), pp. xviii-xx.

18. Machiavelli, *The Prince*, trans. Tim Parks (Ch. XXV).

19. 501 U.S. 957 (1991).

20. 554 U.S. 570 (2008).

21. Frank Easterbrook, "Foreword" to Antonin Scalia and Bryan Garner, *Reading Law: The Interpretation of Legal Texts* (St. Paul, MN: Thompson/West, 2012), p. xxv.

22. Consider *Johnson v. United States*, 135 S. Ct. 2551, 2577 (2015) (Alito, J., dissenting from majority opinion by Scalia, J.) ("When a statute's constitutionality is in doubt, we have an obligation to interpret the law, if possible, to avoid the constitutional problem. [Citation omitted] As one treatise puts it, '[a] statute should be interpreted in a way that avoids placing its constitutionality in doubt.'" A. Scalia & B. Garner, *Reading Law: The Interpretation of Legal Texts* §38, p. 247 (2012). This canon applies fully when considering vagueness challenges.").

23. See Associated Press, "Justice Sotomayor gets over $1 million for memoir," *SF Gate*, 30 May 2011.

24. William N. Eskridge, Jr., "The New Textualism," *UCLA Law Review*, 37: 621, 624 (1990).

25. See Antonin Scalia, *A Matter of Interpretation* (Princeton, NJ: Princeton University Press 1998).

26. Scalia and Garner, *Reading Law*, p. xxvii.

27. See, e.g., William N. Eskridge, Jr., "The New Textualism & Normative Canons," *Columbia Law Review*, 113: 531 (2013) (Scalia and Garner's canons "would not solve the problems of unpredictability or judicial policymaking"), and Margaret H. Lemos, "The Politics of Statutory Interpretation," *Notre Dame Law Review* 89: 849 (2013) ("To understand the relationship between textualism and conservatism is to appreciate the political potential of all methodological argument").

28. See, e.g., Richard Posner, "The Incoherence of Antonin Scalia," *The New Republic*, 24 August 2012, https://newrepublic.com/article/106441/scalia-garner-reading-the-law-textual-originalism.

29. The Federalist Society and the American Enterprise Institute held a major conference in Washington, D.C. in October of 2012 with Justice Scalia as the featured guest, speaking on *Reading Law*, which was available for sale, http://www.fed-soc.org/events/detail/justice-scalia-the-right-and-wrong-ways-to-interpret-legal-texts. Local chapters of the Federalist Society also held events on the book. See "At Federalist Society, Scalia Says He Doesn't 'Live or Die' for Bill of Rights Cases," *BLT*, 19 November 212 ("Scalia spoke November 17 at The Federalist Society's annual convention in downtown Washington. He was there to promote his new book, *Reading Law: The Interpretation of Legal Texts*").

30. This is based on a Westlaw search of November 22, 2015.

31. 577 U.S.___, __ S. Ct. ___ (2016) ("A leading treatise puts the point as follows: 'When there is a straightforward, parallel construction that involves all nouns or verbs in a series,' a modifier at the end of the list 'normally applies to the entire series.' A. Scalia & B. Garner, *Reading Law: The Interpretation of Legal Texts* 147 (2012).").

32. 135 S. Ct. 808, 817 (2015) ("By relying on other parts of Title 47 of the U. S. Code — some enacted in the Communications Act of 1934 decades before the enactment of the Telecommunications Act of 1996 at issue here — the Chamber stretches to invoke this canon of construction beyond its most forceful application. See A. Scalia & B. Garner, *Reading Law: The Interpretation of Legal Texts* 172–173 (2012).").

33. 135 S. Ct. 530, 539 (2014) ("But Heien's point does not consider the reality that an officer may 'suddenly confront' a situation in the field as to which the application of a statute is unclear — however clear it may later become. A law prohibiting 'vehicles' in the park either covers Segways or not, see A. Scalia & B. Garner, *Reading Law: The Interpretation of Legal Texts* 36–38 (2012), but an officer will nevertheless have to make a quick decision on the law the first time one whizzes by.").

34. 133 S. Ct. 2191, 2205 (2013) ("This would create significant tension in the DPPA between the litigation and solicitation exceptions. That inconsistency and the concomitant undermining of the statutory design are avoided

by interpreting (b)(4) so it does not authorize the use of personal information for the purpose of soliciting clients. See A. Scalia & B. Garner, *Reading Law: The Interpretation of Legal Texts* 180 (2012) ('The provisions of a text should be interpreted in a way that renders them compatible, not contradictory.... [T]here can be no justification for needlessly rendering provisions in conflict if they can be interpreted harmoniously').")

35. See *Yates v. United States*, 135 S. Ct. 1074, 1101 (2015) (Kagan, J., dissenting) ("And typically 'only the most compelling evidence' will persuade this Court that Congress intended 'nearly identical language' in provisions dealing with related subjects to bear different meanings. [Citation omitted]); see A. Scalia & B. Garner, *Reading Law: The Interpretation of Legal Texts* 252 (2012).”). See also *Scialabba v. Cuellar de Osorio*, 134 S. Ct. 2191, 2220 (2014) (Sotomayor, dissenting) ("In rushing to find a conflict within the statute, the plurality neglects a fundamental tenet of statutory interpretation: We do not lightly presume that Congress has legislated in self-contradicting terms. See A. Scalia & B. Garner, *Reading Law: The Interpretation of Legal Texts* 180 (2012) ('The provisions of a text should be interpreted in a way that renders them compatible, not contradictory. . . . [T]here can be no justification for needlessly rendering provisions in conflict if they can be interpreted harmoniously').").

36. "Breyer v. Colbert," *The Atlantic*, 15 September 2015.

Chapter 22

1. See Raoul Berger, *Impeachment: The Constitutional Problems* (Cambridge, MA: Harvard University Press, 1999), pp. 127-187 (defining "good behaviour"). See also Michael Gerhardt, *The Federal Impeachment Process: A Constitutional and Historical Analysis* (Chicago, IL: University of Chicago Press, 2nd ed., 2000), pp. 83-86 (discussing relationship between Good Behavior Clause and impeachment process).

2. Article II, §4 also provides: "The President, Vice President and all Civil Officers of the United States, shall be removed from Office on Impeachment for, and Conviction of, Treason, Bribery, or other high Crimes and Misdemeanors."

3. See William H. Rehnquist, *Grand Inquests: The Historic Impeachments of Justice Samuel Chase and President Andrew Johnson* (New York, NY: William Morrow & Co., 1992); Berger, *Impeachment*, pp. 234-262; Richard Ellis, "The Impeachment of Samuel Chase," in Michael R. Belknap, editor, *American Political Trials* (Westport, CT: 1994), pp. 57–76; Richard Lillich, "The Chase Impeachment," *American Journal of Legal History*, 4: 49–72 (1960); and Keith E. Whittington, "Reconstructing the Federal Judiciary: The

Chase Impeachment and the Constitution," *Studies in American Political Development*, 9: 55–116 (1995).

4. *Congressional Record*, House, 116: 3113-3114 (daily ed., 15 April 1970) (re proposed impeachment of Justice William O. Douglas).

5. Albert Broderick, "The Politics of Impeachment," *American Bar Association Journal*, 60: 554 (May 1974).

6. See Gerhardt, *The Federal Impeachment Process*, pp. 133-144, and Berger, *Impeachment*, pp. 108-126 (Professor Berger favored judicial review and pointed to the need for due process to be honored in such proceedings). See also Office of Legal Counsel, Department of Justice, *Legal Aspects of Impeachment: An Overview* (Washington, D.C., February 1974, on file at University of Washington School of Law Library), pp. 47-51 (discussing pro-and-cons of judicial review arguments).

7. Stephen B. Presser, "Samuel Chase," in Kermit L. Hall, editor, *The Oxford Companion to the Supreme Court of the United States* (New York, NY: Oxford University Press, 2005), p. 160.

8. *Ibid.*

9. See Berger, *Impeachment*, p. 235.

10. Mel Laracey, "The Impeachment of Supreme Court Justice Samuel Chase: New Perspectives from Thomas Jefferson's Presidential Newspaper," *Journal of Supreme Court History*, 40: 231, 245 (2015).

11. Berger, *Impeachment*, pp. 242, 356-358, and Rehnquist, *Grand Inquests*, pp. 23-25, 100-102.

12. See Rehnquist, *Grand Inquests*, pp. 103-105 (noting votes on each of the 8 counts).

13. See Berger, *Impeachment*, p. 234 (Chase's "removal would have served as a standing reminder that there is no room on our bench for an implacably prejudiced judge, and that his factional acquittal was a miscarriage of justice.").

14. 60 U.S. 393 (1857) (Grier, J., concurring opinion).

15. 67 U.S. 635 (1863) (5-4 with Grier, J., for the majority).

16. See Daniel J. Wisniewski, "Heating up a Case Gone Cold: Revisiting the Charges of Bribery and Official Misconduct Made Against Supreme Court Justice Robert Cooper Grier in 1854-1855," *Journal of Supreme Court History*, 38: 1, 5 (2013). The charges were leveled by the Wheeling and Bridge Company, one of the parties to the dispute in *Pennsylvania v. Wheeling & Belmont Bridge Company*, 54 U.S. 518 (1851).

17. Wisniewski, "Heating up a Case Gone Cold," pp. 5, 6-8.

18. *Ibid.*, pp. 12-13.

19. 393 U.S. 503 (1969).

20. See Laura Kelman, *Abe Fortas: A Biography* (New Haven, CT: Yale University Press, 1990), pp. 326-327, 351-352, 355 (re American University seminar), 360-365 (re $20,000 honorarium).

21. See Bruce Allen Murphy, *Fortas: The Rise and Ruin of a Supreme Court Justice* (New York, NY: William Morrow & Co., 1988), pp. 591-596.
22. 347 U.S. 483 (civil rights).
23. 377 U.S. 533 (legislative reapportionment).
24. 384 U.S. 436 (criminal justice).
25. 395 U.S. 486 (political question, separation of powers, and speech and debate clause).
26. See Jackson Harrison Pollack, *Earl Warren: The Judge Who Changed America* (Englewood Cliffs, NJ: Prentice-Hall, 1979).
27. Jim Newton, *Justice for All: Earl Warren & the Nation He Made* (New York, NY: Riverhead Books, 2006), p. 385. See also John D. Weaver, *Warren: The Man, the Court, the Era* (Boston, MA: Little, Brown & Co., 1967), pp. 284-285 (discussing John Birch Society campaign and 75-page memo attacking Earl Warren).
28. Earl Warren, *The Memoirs of Chief Justice Earl Warren* (New York, NY: Doubleday, 1977), p. 303.

Chapter 23

1. Melvin Urofsky, *Louis D. Brandeis: A Life* (New York, NY: Schocken Books, 2009), p. 748.
2. Quoted in Roger K. Newman, *Hugo Black: A Biography* (New York, NY: Pantheon Books, 1994), p. 619.
3. *Ibid.*, pp. 619 ("the longevity record"), 620 ("small card"), 623 (date of death).
4. Chemerinsky, "Much Depends on Ginsburg."
5. Jessica Weisberg, "Supreme Court Justice Ruth Bader Ginsburg: I'm Not Going Anywhere," *Elle*, 23 September 2014.

Chapter 24

1. See Kathryn Watts, "Judges and Their Private Papers," *New York University Law Review*, 88: 1665, 1694 (2013) ("Upon the thirty-fifth anniversary of the enactment of the Presidential Records Act, this Article argues that judges' working papers should be treated as governmental property – just as presidential papers are. Although there are important differences between the roles of president and judge, none of the differences suggest that judicial papers should be treated as a species of private property. Rather than counseling in favor of private ownership, the unique position of federal judges, including the judiciary's independence in our constitutional design, suggests the advisability of crafting rules that speak to reasonable access to and disposition of

judicial papers. Ultimately, this Article – giving renewed attention to a long-forgotten 1977 governmental study commissioned by Congress – argues that Congress should declare judicial papers public property and should empower the judiciary to promulgate rules implementing the shift to public ownership. These would include, for example, rules governing the timing of public release of judicial papers. . . . The bottom line is that because judges' papers are created by federal officials on government time relating to official governmental duties, there is no principled reason – other than historical happenstance – to continue treating judicial working papers as a species of private property."). But see Federal Judicial Center, *A Guide to the Preservation of Federal Judges' Papers* (Washington, D.C., 2nd ed., 2009), p. 1 ("The chambers papers of a federal judge remain the private property of that judge or the judge's heirs, and it is the prerogative of the judge or the judge's heirs to determine the disposition of those papers.").

2. See Alexandra K. Wigdor, *The Personal Papers of Supreme Court Justices: A Descriptive Guide* (New York, NY: Garland Publishing, 1986). The locations of the Justices' papers are listed in Lee Epstein, Jeffrey A. Segal, Harold J. Spaeth, and Thomas G. Walker, *The Supreme Court Compendium: Data, Decisions, and Developments* (Los Angeles, CA: Sage Publications, 6th ed., 2015), pp. 482- 490 (Table 5-11).

3. See Tony Mauro, "Marshall's Papers Cause Supreme Stir: Justice Tilted at Court's Windmills," *USA Today*, 27 May 1993; Benjamin Weiser and Joan Biskupic, "Secrets of the High Court: Papers Afford a Rare Glimpse of Justices' Deliberations," *Washington Post*, 23 May 1993.

4. See Don Williamson, Editorial, "Thanks, Thurgood: We Needed That," *Seattle Times*, 28 May 1993.

5. See "The Marshall Files: The Complaints and the Library's Response," *Washington Post*, 27 May 1993.

6. See Linda Greenhouse, "Down the Memory Hole," *New York Times*, 2 October 2009; Tony Mauro, "Don't Hold Your Breath For Souter's Papers," *Legal Times*, 22 April 2015.

7. See Tinsley Yarbrough, *David Hackett Souter: Traditional Republican on the Rehnquist Court* (New York, NY: Oxford University Press, 2005), p. 278 (listing various documents with communications between the two Justices)

8. See Lee Levine and Stephen Wermiel, "The Landmark That Wasn't: A First Amendment Play in Five Acts," *Washington Law Review*, 88:1 (2013); Lee Levine and Stephen Wermiel, *The Progeny: Justice William J. Brennan's Fight to Preserve the Legacy of New York Times v. Sullivan* (Chicago, IL: American Bar Association, 2014).

9. 376 U. S. 254 (1964) (per Brennan, J.).

10. Watts, "Judges and Their Private Papers," p. 1672.

11. See Sax, *Playing Darts with a Rembrandt*, p. 103.

12. Watts, "Judges and Their Private Papers," p. 1667 (footnotes omitted).

13. *Ibid.* (footnotes omitted).

14. 132 S. Ct 2566 (2012).

15. Harold Hongju Koh, "Justice Blackmun and the 'World Out There,'" *Yale Law Journal*, 104:23 (1994) ("Harry Blackmun fooled everyone. When Richard Nixon appointed him to the Supreme Court at age sixty-one, who would have predicted that this 'safe' conservative would retire twenty-four years later – the year Nixon died – as the Court's last liberal? Would anyone have guessed how sharply he would break from his "Minnesota Twin,' Warren Burger, or brake the Burger Court's retreat from the Warren Court? Did any foresee that a member of so many majorities would someday emerge as the *Carolene Products'* Justice of the Rehnquist Court: the spokesman for the have-nots, the excluded, the discrete and insular minorities?").

16. See Koh, "Justice Blackmun and the 'World Out There,'" p. 23 (1994).

17. See "Former Supreme Court Justice Harry Blackmun -- Oral History Videotapes," C-SPAN, 4 March 2004, http://www.c-span.org/video/ ?180846-1/justice-blackmuns-oral-history-interviews.

18. See Mark de Wolfe Howe, editor, *Holmes-Laski Letters: The Correspondence of Mr. Justice Holmes and Harold J. Laski* (Cambridge, MA: Harvard University Press, 1953) (2 vols.); James Bishop Peabody, editor, *The Holmes-Einstein Letters: Correspondence of Mr. Justice Holmes and Lewis Einstein 1903-1935* (New York, NY: Macmillan Co., 1964), and *Holmes-Pollock Letters; The Correspondence of Mr. Justice Holmes and Sir Frederick Pollock, 1874-1932* (Cambridge, MA, Harvard University Press, 1941) (2 vols.); David Burton, editor, *Holmes-Sheehan correspondence: The letters of Justice Oliver Wendell Holmes and Canon Patrick Augustine Sheehan* (New York, NY: Fordham University Press, 1993) (originally published 1976).

Chapter 25

1. Roscoe Pound as quoted in "Simplicity to Mark Last Rites Tomorrow on Holmes' Birthday," *Washington Post*, 7 March 1935, pp. 1, 4.

2. See e.g., H.L. Mencken, Book Review, "The Great Holmes Mystery," *American Mercury*, 26: 123 (May 1932) and Mortimer Adler, Book Review, "Legal Certainty," *Columbia Law Review*, 31: 91 (1931).

3. This was in response to his majority opinion in *Buck v. Bell*, 274 U.S. 200 (1927). See Paul A. Lombardo, *Three Generations, No Imbeciles: Eugenics, The Supreme Court & Buck v. Bell* (Baltimore, MD: Johns Hopkins University Press, 2008), p. 163 ("Holmes had embraced the most radical ideas for social improvement when the formal eugenics movement was only in its infancy.").

4. See Ben W. Palmer, "Hobbes, Holmes & Hitler," *American Bar Association Journal*, 31: 569 (1945).

5. See Ronald K.L. Collins, editor, *The Fundamental Holmes: A Free Speech Chronicle and Reader* (New York, NY: Cambridge University Press, 2010), p. 58.

6. Sheldon Novick, *Honorable Justice: The Life of Oliver Wendell Holmes* (New York, NY: Little Brown, 1989), p. xvii.

7. See e.g. Jeffrey Rosen, "Free to Develop Their Faculties," in Greil Marcus and Werner Sollors, *A New Literary History of America* (Cambridge, MA: Harvard University Press, 2009), pp. 612, 613.

8. See e.g. Albert Alschuler, *Law Without Values* (Chicago, IL: University of Chicago Press, 2000).

9. Louis Menand, *The Metaphysical Club: A Story of Ideas in America* (New York, NY: Farrar, Straus & Giroux, 2001), p. 67.

10. Thomas Grey, "Holmes and Legal Pragmatism," *Stanford Law Review* 41: 787, 792 (1988).

11. *Ibid.*

12. Richard A. Posner, editor, *The Essential Holmes* (Chicago: University of Chicago Press, 1992), p. xxx. In many ways, Judge Posner was the ideal jurist to publish a book about Holmes and his life's work, if only because of several significant similarities between the two jurists.

13. Alschuler, *Law Without Values*, p. 181.

14. 198 U.S. 45 (1905).

15. 247 U.S. 251 (1918).

16. 249 U.S. 47 (1919).

17. 250 U.S. 616 (1919).

18. 251 U.S. 385 (1920).

19. 261 U.S. 525 (1923).

20. 268 U.S. 652 (1925).

21. 281 U.S. 586 (1930).

22. G. Edward White, *Justice Oliver Wendell Holmes: Law and the Inner Self* (New York, NY: Oxford University Press, 1993), pp. 355-356.

23. See Mark DeWolfe Howe, editor, *Touched With Fire: Civil War Letters and Diary of Oliver Wendell Holmes Jr. 1861-1864* (Cambridge, MA: Harvard University Press, 1946).

24. See e.g., Robert Mennel and Christine Compston, *Holmes & Frankfurter: Their Correspondence* (Hannover, NH: University of New Hampshire Press, 1996); James Bishop Peabody, editor, *The Holmes-Einstein Letters: Correspondence of Mr. Justice Holmes & Lewis Einstein, 1903-1935* (New York, NY: St. Martin's Press, 1964); Mark DeWolfe Howe, editor, *Holmes-Pollock Letters: The Correspondence of Mr. Justice Holmes & Sir Frederick Pollok, 1874-1932* (Cambridge, MA: Harvard University Press, 1942) (2 vols.); Mark DeWolfe

Howe, editor, *Holmes-Laski Letters: The Correspondence of Justice Holmes & Harold J. Laski, 1916-1935* (Cambridge, MA: Harvard University Press, 1953) (2 vols.).

25. See White, *Justice Oliver Wendell Holmes*, pp. 230-250, 358-359, 601-606 (re Lady Clare Castletown).

26. Sheldon Novick, editor, *The Collected Works of Justice Holmes: Complete Public Writings & Selected Judicial Opinions of Oliver Wendell Holmes* (Chicago, IL: University of Chicago Press, 1995).

27. See Oliver Wendell Holmes, Jr., *Speeches* (Boston, MA: Little, Brown & Co., 1891).

28. See Thomas Healy, *The Great Dissenter: How Oliver Wendell Holmes Changed His Mind – and Changed the History of Free Speech in America* (New York, NY: Henry Holt & Company, 2013), p. 2013.

29. See White, *Justice Oliver Wendell Holmes*; Liva Baker, *The Justice from Beacon Hill: The Life and Times of Oliver Wendell Holmes* (New York, NY: HarperCollins, 1991); Sheldon Novick, *Honorable Justice: The Life of Oliver Wendell Holmes* (Boston, MA: Little, Brown & Company, 1989); Mark DeWolfe Howe, *Justice Oliver Wendell Holmes: The Proving Years, 1870-1882* (Cambridge, MA: Harvard University Press, 1957 & 1963) (2 vols.); Francis Biddle, *Mr. Justice Holmes* (New York, NY: Charles Scribner's Sons, 1943); and Silas Bent, *Justice Oliver Wendell Holmes: A Biography* (New York, NY: The Vanguard Press, 1932).

30. See Catherine Drinker Bowen, *Yankee From Olympus* (Boston, MA: Houghton Mifflin Co., 1943).

31. See e.g., Francis Biddle, *Justice Holmes, Natural Law and the Supreme Court* (New York, NY: Macmillan, 1960); Thomas Healy, *The Great Dissent: How Oliver Wendell Holmes Changed His Mind -- and Changed the History of Free Speech in America* (New York, NY: Metropolitan Books, 2013); Alschuler, *Law Without Values*; H.L. Pohlman, *Justice Oliver Wendell Holmes: Free Speech & The Living Constitution* (New York, NY: New York University Press, 1991); H.L. Pohlman, *Justice Oliver Wendell Holmes & The Unitarian Jurisprudence* (Cambridge, MA: Harvard University Press, 1984); James Willard Hurst, *Justice Holmes on Legal History* (New York, NY: Macmillan Co. 1964); Steven Burton, editor, *The Path of the Law & Its Influence: The Legacy of Oliver Wendell Holmes, Jr.* (New York, NY: Cambridge University Press, 2000); Robert W. Gordon, editor, *The Legacy of Oliver Wendell Holmes, Jr.* (Stanford, CA: Stanford University Press, 1992); Frederic Kellogg, *Oliver Wendell Holmes, Jr., Legal Theory, and Judicial Restraint* (New York, NY: Cambridge University Press 2007); and Max Lerner, editor, *The Mind and Faith of Justice Holmes* (Boston, MA: Little, Brown & Co., 1945).

32. See, e.g., G. Edward White, "The Canonization of Holmes and Brandeis: Epistemology and Judicial Reputations," *New York University Law*

Review 70: 576 (1995). See also Alschuler, *Law Without Values*, pp. 181-816 ("the Beatification of Oliver Wendell Holmes").

33. Letter from Oliver Wendell Holmes to Frederick Pollock, 26 May 1919, reproduced in Howe, *Holmes-Pollock Letters*, vol. II, p. 13.

34. Fred Rodell, *Nine Men: A Political History of the Supreme Court from 1790 to 1955* (New York, NY: Random House, 1955), pp. 179-180 (quoting, in part, Walton Hamilton).

35. See White, *Justice Oliver Wendell Holmes*, pp. 365-366.

36. *Ibid.*, pp. 355-356.

37. *Ibid.*, p. 356.

38. See Richard A. Posner, *Cardozo: A Study in Reputation* (Chicago, IL: University of Chicago Press, 1990), pp. 61-62.

39. "John Marshall," 4 February 1904, reproduced in Mark De Wolfe Howe, editor, *The Occasional Speeches of Justice Oliver Wendell Holmes* (Cambridge, MA: Harvard University Press, 1962), pp. 131-135.

40. White, *Justice Oliver Wendell Holmes*, p. 129.

41. John S. Morgan, *The Grand Panjandrum: Mellow Years of Justice Holmes* (Lanham, MD: University Press of America, 1988), p. 146.

42. See Tom Clancy, *Clear and Present Danger* (New York, NY: G.P. Putnam's Sons, 1989).

43. See Harrison Ford in *Clear and Present Danger* (Paramount Pictures, 1994).

44. See R. Jelinek and M. Ahearne, "The ABC's of ACB: Unveiling a Clear and Present Danger in the Sales Force," *Industrial Marketing Management*, 1 May 2006.

45. See Michael Elliott, "A Clear and Present Danger," *Time*, 8 October 2001.

Epilogue

1. See e.g., Cass Sunstein, "If Judges Aren't Politicians, What Are They?," *Bloomberg Business*, 7 January 2013 ("Armed with actual data, the researchers are finding that much of the conventional wisdom is wrong, or at least way off. Judges are far from mere politicians; we don't see anything like the kind of polarization found in Congress. At the same time, judicial predispositions matter, and they help explain why judges are divided on some of the great issues of the day. We also have reason to think that no fewer than three of the current justices are among the most conservative since the 1930s – and that none of the current justices ranks among the most liberal.").

2. See e.g., Joe Forward, "9-0 Decisions Down, 5-4 Decisions Up in U.S. Supreme Court's 2014-15 Term," *InsideTrack*, 19 April 2015, and David Paul Kuhn, "The Incredible Polarization and Politicization of the Supreme Court," *The Atlantic*, 29 June 2012. Cf., "Supreme Court had highest percentage of

unanimous decisions this session," CBS6 (CNN wire), 1 July 2014 ("There's no doubt this is a closely divided Supreme Court. That's been true for decades, and it's no less true now," said Thomas Goldstein, publisher of SCOTUSblog.com. "You have five sold conservative votes in the majority, but Justice [Anthony] Kennedy, who is the least conservative among them, does on occasion switch sides and join his more liberal colleagues. There's a constant battle going on in these ideological fights.").

3. Harvey C. Mansfield, "Introduction" in Niccolò Machiavelli, *The Prince*, translated by Harvey Mansfield (Chicago, IL: University of Chicago Press, 1985), p. vii.

4. Thomas C. Cronin, "Machiavelli's *Prince:* An American Perspective," in Timothy Fuller, editor, *Machiavelli's Legacy: The Prince After Five Hundred Years* (Philadelphia, PA: University of Pennsylvania Press, 2016), p. 127.

5. Mansfield, "Introduction" in Niccolò Machiavelli, *The Prince*, p. 99 (ch. 25).

6. See Bruce Weber, "Umpires vs Judges," *New York Times*, 11 July 2009 ("'Judges are like umpires,' Judge Roberts declared in the opening remarks to his own confirmation hearings. 'Umpires don't make the rules; they apply them. The role of an umpire and a judge is critical. They make sure everybody plays by the rules. But it is a limited role.'").

7. Richard A. Posner, "Foreword: A Political Court," *Harvard Law Review* 119: 32, 34 (2005).

8. *Ibid.*, p. 40.

9. See e.g., Richard A. Posner, *Cardozo: A Study in Reputation* (Chicago, IL: University of Chicago Press, 1990); Richard A. Posner, *How Judges Think* (Cambridge, MA: Harvard University Press, 2008); Richard A. Posner, *Reflections on Judging* (Cambridge, MA: Harvard University Press, 2013). See also Ronald Collins, "On Judicial Reputation: More Questions for Judge Posner," *Concurring Opinions*, 17 December, 2014, http:// concurringopin-ions.com/archives/2014/12/on-judicial-reputation-more-questions-for-judge-posner.html and Ronald Collins, "The Maverick – A Biographical Sketch of Judge Richard Posner: Part I," *Concurring Opinions*, 24 November 2014, http://concurringopinions.com/archives/2014/11/the-maverick-a-biographical-sketch-of-judge-richard-posner-part-i.html, Ronald Collins, "The Maverick – A Biographical Sketch of Judge Richard Posner: Part II," *Concurring Opinions*, 26 November 2014, http:// concurringopinions. com/archives/2014/11/the-maverick-a-biographical-sketch-of-judge-richard-posner-part-ii-the-will-to-greatness.html, and Ronald Collins, "Afterword: Posner at 75 – 'It's My Job,'" *Concurring Opinions*, 5 January 2015, http://concurringopinions.com/archives/2015/01/afterword-posner-at-75-its-my-job.html.

10. Posner, *Cardozo*, p. x.

11. Posner, *How Judges Think*, p. 272.

12. *Ibid*, p. 275.
13. *Ibid*, p. 281.
14. Posner, *Cardozo*, p. 73.
15. *Ibid*, p. 148.
16. *Ibid*, p. 144.
17. *See* Larissa MacFarquhar, "The Bench Burner," *The New Yorker*, 10 December 2001, http:// www.newyorker.com/magazine/2001/12/10/ the-bench-burner.
18. Posner's public concessions concerning the irrelevance of the Constitution's text for purposes of judicial decision-making is not very Machiavelllian. See Josh Blackmun, "Judge Posner on Judging, Birthright Citizenship, and Precedent," *Josh Blackmun's Blog* (6 November 2015), http://joshblackman. com/blog /2015/11/06/judge-posner-on-judging-birthright-citizenship-and-precedent/ (quoting Judge Posner: "I'm not particularly interested in the 18th century, nor am I particularly interested in the text of the Constitution. I don't believe that any document drafted in the 18th Century can guide our behavior today. Because the people in the 18th century could not foresee any of the problems of the 21st century.").
19. Walter F. Murphy, *Elements of Judicial Strategy* (Chicago, IL: University of Chicago Press, 1974), p. 1. *See* Alan Westin, Book Review, *The Annals of the American Academy*, 359: 191 (1965) ("Machiavelli wrote for Princes, Richard Neustadt for Presidents, and now, Walter Murphy of Princeton has written a power-maximizing manual for Supreme Court Justices."), and Martin Shapiro, Book Review, *Stanford Law Review*, 18: 544-547 (1966) (reviewing *Elements of Judicial Strategy*): "This book, written by a political scientist, is likely to annoy a good many lawyers. Indeed, judging from certain of the early reviews it already has annoyed a few. Conflict between lawyers and political scientists often arises over the subject of courts and judges. To a political scientist the judge is just another governmental official whose behavior must be studied and described. Whether that description contributes to the prestige of judicial office and the public reputation of courts is a matter of indifference to the political scientist qua political scientist . . . .").
20. Murphy, *Elements*, p. 3.
21. The quotations in this paragraph of the text derive consecutively from *ibid*, pp. 2, 176, 2, 209, 202, 207, 5, 202, 203-205, 179, 187, 192, 196, 5, 208 (quote abridged), and 4.
22. See e.g., Lee Epstein & Jack Knight, *The Choices Justices Make* (Washington, DC: CQ Press, 1997).
23. Murphy, *Elements*, p. 9.